D1541272

❧ Praise for *Struggling with Serendipity* ❧

"*Struggling with Serendipity* is a fantastic story of achievement and success in the midst of seemingly insurmountable challenges. Cindy and Beth Kolbe detail the incredible life they've lived, the sacrifices made along the way, and the joy they've shared in Beth's successes. I'm honored to know Cindy and Beth personally, and to have shared in some small part of Beth's swimming career. I can't recommend this book enough!" ~ **Julie Dussliere, Chief of Paralympic Sport, United States Olympic Committee**

"Christopher Reeve once said, 'A hero is an ordinary individual who finds the strength to persevere and endure in spite of overwhelming obstacles.' Cindy's fierce dedication to her daughter Beth is nothing short of heroic and her story, *Struggling with Serendipity*, captures the honesty and reality of having a loved one face a possible lifetime of paralysis. There is no greater power than a mother's love for her daughter. It is truly unbreakable. And, it is with love that Cindy and Beth find the joy inside the hardship and seize a new future full of hope and possibilities. Cindy's daily selfless acts, which benefit our entire community, reminds us that it is possible to persist and thrive no matter the circumstances." ~ **Peter Wilderotter, President and CEO of the Christopher & Dana Reeve Foundation**

"This is a remarkably honest and important book. Cindy Kolbe's teenage daughter Beth was left with quadriplegia after Cindy fell asleep at the wheel of her car. Cindy doesn't sugarcoat or maximize her daughter's struggle with disability or her own battles with guilt and depression. Cindy is not a 'victim;' her daughter is not a 'super-heroine.' This is an honest and meticulous account of how they both move forward to create successful lives not defined by tragedy or disability. It's an ultimate true story that's a privilege to read." ~ **Thea Flaum, President of the Hill Foundation and Founder of Facing Disability**

"As a mother, I imagine there's nothing stronger than a mother's love, except, perhaps, a mother's guilt. In *Struggling with Serendipity,* Cindy so beautifully illustrates her family's trauma. What I think I love most about her story is that it is, in fact, *her* story. She did not hijack her daughter Beth's story, but instead provides the important perspective of a caregiver and how truly intertwined our stories really are. This story is the epitome of transforming pain into passion." ~ **Danni Starr, Author of** *Empathy and Eyebrows: A Survivalist's Stories on Reviving Your Spirit After Soul-Crushing Sh*tstorms*

"*Struggling with Serendipity* shares Cindy's unique experience as a mom after a tragedy. The relationship between Cindy and her daughter Beth is a celebration of motherhood and the healing power of love. Their incredible challenges and adventures inspire readers to be the best they can be. You'll be glad you read this book!" ~ **April Perry, Founder of Power of Moms**

"In the wake of any tragedy, it's tempting to ask *Why?* But Cindy and Beth Kolbe chose instead to ask *How? How* could they move forward? *How* could they heal? *How* could they find meaning and purpose in their agony? With unflinching honesty, Cindy Kolbe offers readers both an intimate look at the answers that she and Beth found AND a universal roadmap for navigating adversity. This is a beautifully written book, and one that the world very much needs right now!" ~ **Jeff Bell, Author of *When in Doubt, Make Belief* and Founder of the Adversity 2 Advocacy Alliance**

"Want a grand perspective on life? Befriend someone with a disability. I've learned more about life and what it takes to be successful from Beth Kolbe than she ever learned from me, her swimming coach. Beth's story is one of tragedy and misfortune, but her potential and upward trajectory never wavered. I found her tenacity, her resourcefulness, and her bond with her family stronger than anyone before. Cindy and Beth took initiative and found solutions for a new way of life. If you want to see what a mother and daughter's love for life can accomplish, this book is a must read." ~ **Peggy Ewald, retired Swimming & Diving Head Coach at Ohio Northern University and Team USA Coach for 2008, 2012, and 2016 Paralympic Games**

"Cindy's story grabs you by the heart and holds on tight. It is a story of grace and forgiveness. Her daughter Beth's heroic, gentle optimism is a fitting tribute to Cindy and her ability to not only hang on but to steer the course of setting a perfect example for her child – and for all of us. As a mother of a child with a spinal cord injury and an advocate for this community, I can say I am truly honored to know Cindy. Even as Beth inspires and motivates people living with the injury, Cindy keeps it real for the moms and families learning to live a joyful life beyond our broken hearts." ~ **Debbie Flynn, Founder of the QUAD Foundation**

"Cindy has a remarkable ability to convey the complexity of a spinal cord injury and the ripple effect it has on everyone's lives. It's impossible to know what it's like unless you've been through it, but reading Cindy's honest and authentic account gives a window into what it's like." ~ **Brittany Déjean, Founder of AbleThrive**

"Everything about this story is beyond belief, and yet it's all true. How could one small mistake result in such calamity? How could a teenager possibly respond with calm confidence when faced with lifelong paralysis? How could any mother ever find the strength to deal with her child's needs and her own pain under these circumstances? Cindy Kolbe and her daughter Beth are made of the same astounding stuff. They do not whine, they do not ask for pity, they do not wait in helpless despair for miracles to happen. Minute by minute, day by day, stroke by stroke, word by word, they do the work before them with courage and determination. They create their own miracles, and this book is one of them. *Struggling with Serendipity* is a gift to all of us. I recommend it with gratitude and awe." ~ **Sandy Asher, Author and Playwright**

"Cindy is a passionate mother, advocate and talented writer who is not afraid to tackle the hard topics. Writing like this requires courage and commitment." ~ **Kay Ledson, Author of *Warrior Mom***

"We can live without many things, but living without hope is damn near impossible. Cindy and Beth's story reminds us that no matter the circumstances or diagnosis, with hope and love, joy is possible and life is worth living. I am simultaneously challenged and inspired by their shared journey." ~ **Terry McGuire, Founder of Giving Voice to Depression**

Struggling with Serendipity

By Cindy Kolbe

Eliezer Tristan Publishing
Portland, OR

All rights reserved

Copyright © 2019

No part of this book may be reproduced or transmitted in any form or by any means, electronic or mechanical, including photocopying, recording, or by an information storage or retrieval system, permitted by law. For information contact Eliezer Tristan Publishing, Portland, OR.

Cover design by Aaron Smith

Published with permission from the United States Olympic Committee.

Photo credits: front cover – Bob Gallagher; back cover – Aimee Custis.

❧ TABLE OF CONTENTS ❦

BREATHING LESSONS

RACING FORWARD

❧ FOREWORD ❧
Change, Devotion, and Reinvention

CINDY KOLBE AND her daughter Beth are two extraordinary women I was privileged to care for several years after the car accident that resulted in Beth's spinal cord injury. In *Struggling with Serendipity*, Cindy Kolbe brings readers into awareness that we will all face changes in our bodies, whether through injury, illness, or aging. Cindy transports us directly into her heart and mind as she negotiates the apparent catastrophe of the crash and her daughter's new tetraplegia—a rare story that she vividly conveys to readers of this book. In telling her story, Cindy eradicates "able vs. disabled" barriers, revealing our shared human experience.

Every day, cars are crashed and lives are changed. Every day, millions of people adapt their daily routines to accommodate a spinal cord injury. Over fifty million Americans have one or more disabilities, and this number has been rising every year. When our bodies do not function in the way they did before, will our world become bigger or smaller? Caring for Cindy and Beth in my work as a physiatrist in the Department of Physical Medicine & Rehabilitation at Spaulding Rehabilitation Hospital/Harvard Medical School, it was apparent that they made their worlds bigger. When I first met Beth, she was a successful undergraduate at Harvard University; she had been accepted to the Athens Paralympics for swimming, was training for the Beijing Paralympics, and was thoroughly enjoying her life.

Beth perennially focuses on what is possible, rather than what is not possible with a spinal cord injury. She has exceptional gifts of optimism, idealism, discipline, and tenacity. In addition to her considerable internal resources, she also has tremendous, unwavering support from her family. Her mother temporarily left her career to devote all her time and energy to her daughter's successful rehabilitation. She remained by her side—as long as necessary. Chapter 6 illustrates the on-call 24/7 experience when Beth returned home from the inpatient rehab facility. Her mother assisted with routine tasks like bathing and transferring, and was a tireless advocate for Beth's health and quality of life. Beth is also blessed to have spent her formative teenage years in a closely-knit community that had already known and loved her since her infancy and that adapted to change with her. Beth's internal state of resilience, combined with her supportive environment, facilitated her ability to define herself on her own terms and create her own path.

Beth and Cindy Kolbe are among the many individuals who function far beyond expectations despite unrelenting symptoms such as pain, spasticity or weakness. Human beings have the capacity to find greatness in spite of tremendous obstacles—Cindy and her daughter certainly have. However, we should be careful not to set their achievements as an unfair standard for individuals who lack Beth Kolbe's extraordinary internal resilience and social support. Compared with most young adults who compete for similar educational, athletic, and professional goals, Beth Kolbe has to spend more time and energy on her self-care routine and on regularly wrangling with inaccessibility. In Chapter 17, Cindy illustrates this vividly while describing Beth's first winter at college. Millions of people face persistent obstacles managing mundane, everyday tasks with limited accessibility, support and opportunities. The world becomes smaller for thousands of people who have sustained a spinal cord injury, and the reasons for this include inadequate access to rehabilitation care, limited resources, social isolation, and insufficient educational, workplace, and community accommodations.

Human beings have a long history of marginalizing all kinds of diversity. Perhaps, as Henri-Jacques Stiker writes, our ideology of sameness skews our vision. When encountering disability, uncomfortable with the reminder that our lives can change in a heartbeat, we may contrive an idea of distance: "That must not happen to me." Ray Lifchez writes, "Those among us who are able-bodied can no longer rationalise treating physically disabled people as 'them', an alien minority. This is not simply a matter of humanitarian bonhomie, for 'they' now include our parents, siblings, and children, our friends, neighbours, and colleagues, and—one day—ourselves." Our bodies are constantly changing, and all of us lose abilities that we had taken for granted, often accompanied by gaining abilities that we may not have imagined. Jerome Bickenbach writes that ability and disability are normal, fluid and continuous conditions that all of us experience at some stage of our lives. In other words, body diversity is an essential expression of our oneness.

In Chapter 7, Cindy Kolbe refers to a "new normal." Her life changed when she became a parent. It changed again when her daughter sustained a cervical spinal cord injury with tetraplegia, and her caretaking role increased exponentially. Her life changed again when her daughter became an independent adult. Who among us does not have to respond to change and define a new normal? Whether we are young or old, whether we ambulate with feet or wheels, whether we are free agents or become caregivers for our parents and children, we are more alike than different. Change and connection define our diverse human conditions.

With excruciating honesty, Cindy Kolbe takes readers into her life, and we are transformed as mother and daughter persevere and reinvent together. By the end of the book, the "able vs. disabled" lens has shattered, and our common humanity prevails. *Struggling with Serendipity* connects us to ourselves, to our constant state of change, and to each other.

Ariana Vora, MD
Assistant Professor, Dept. of Physical Medicine & Rehabilitation, Harvard Medical School
Staff Physiatrist, Spaulding Rehabilitation Hospital
Board Certified: Physical Medicine & Rehabilitation, Sports Medicine, Integrative & Holistic Medicine
@ArianaVoraMD
Boston, Massachusetts
December 12, 2018

❧ PREFACE ❧
Diving In

BEFORE, I BELIEVED in fairy tales. The ones dripping in hope and princess dreams, with dragons and sorcerers. And happy-ever-after endings for the good guys.

When I was a toddler, my dad called me Cinderelly. In grade school, I wrote poems about saving the kingdom. As a teenager, I dreamed of true love and having babies. I thought I would be a mom who always kept her child out of harm's way.

Now, I believe in unthinkable stories. The ones desperate for hope, with flawed heroes and likable villains. And happy-ever-after? The answer unfolded through an infinitely improbable story. My story.

This is not how my daughter Beth would write it. Beyond the facts of time and place, of encounters and events, the difference would be drastic. Her account would dismiss the endless progression of small goals battled and won. Stubborn teenage persistence would be simply a tool to gain independence. Volunteering and mentoring? To Beth, these were side effects of friendship and community. Roadblocks: opportunities for alternative routes. Success: the lucky convergence of unlikely detours. Perhaps the most telling would be the limits of severe disability: not important enough to mention. Instead, serendipity would be her focus and not just *one* fortunate accident—a wealth of happy coincidences.

But this is *my* story, woven with Beth's, but mine nonetheless. It begins with one regrettable moment. Is there a penance for a mom who is too busy, too tired, and too distracted?

Yes.

THE DEEP END
❧ Chapter 1 ❦
CRASHING

Beth: *The most defining—and, in many ways, positive—moment of my life might also be considered the most tragic by those who do not know me.*

MIDNIGHT CLOUDS blot out the nearly full moon on a night I'll never forget. On the home stretch of a two-hour drive, no streetlights shine on the lonely country road. Isolated houses loom on flat Ohio farmland, cloaked in shadows. Exhausted, I round a curve and notice a pay phone at the side of the road. I blink, and it's gone. The year is 2000, and I have no cell phone. I should turn around and use the pay phone to call my husband John. No. I can handle this. I'm only 10 minutes from home.

My three passengers sleep, my two daughters and a friend. I miss their usual teenage banter. I smile, remembering our shopping trip that afternoon. The girls laughing and teasing each other about being too old for Build-A-Bear. The long day ending, the car is dead quiet.

My familiar dull headache faintly echoes the beating of my heart. What's not familiar is a nagging urge to give in and let my eyes close. Yet, I don't question why this only vaguely worries me.

Maybe if I blare the radio. I reach to turn it on and stop. It would wake the girls. I try to think. I roll down my window and tip my head toward the rushing chill of the May night. Though only for a moment. I'm unwilling to disturb my daughters and their friend. My instincts as a mom had never let me down before.

My eyes blink open as the car crosses a white line. In slow motion. Tightening my grip on the steering wheel, I return to my lane. I nudge my youngest, 14, in the passenger seat next to me. Speaking requires concentrated effort.

"Beth, we're almost home . . . I'm way too tired. Talk to me, help me stay awake?"

"Okay," she agrees.

Time unravels in the pause that follows. Beth's next words muddle together in my mind. In a split second, the car veers to the right. A road sign appears directly ahead. I turn the wheel, but it's too late. The sign flattens on concrete with a sickening thud. Screams join mine to fill the car. As we lurch into a shallow ditch, the silence is sudden. Then . . . nothing.

I'm enclosed in an eerie stillness. Abruptly, I hear anxious voices. When I open my eyes, I see only Beth next to me. She hangs awkwardly, suspended upside down. Apparently, I am, too. My 15-year-old daughter Maria says something behind me. I glance her way. Why can't I see her? My eyes return to the front, fixed on Beth. She appears composed as she watches me.

"Are you both okay back there?" I say, my voice high and strange.

"I think so," Maria answers.

"Can you get out?"

"Yes, through my window."

"Go to the road! Get help!"

I desperately need all of us out of the car. In my jumbled brain, this will somehow render us unharmed. The two girls in the back seat escape through a shattered window.

The passenger side of the car is crushed, closed in. The skewed shadows make no sense. I take in Beth's worried gaze and extend my arms, but she's out of reach. I fumble with my seatbelt, another mystery. After an eternity, I drop down. Beth asks me to undo hers. In confusion, I comply, staring in disbelief as she slumps to her stomach on the ceiling. She is motionless on fractured glass, her neck at a disturbing angle. It's dark and cold. She calmly says that nothing hurts . . . and she can't feel her legs.

Everything—the whole world—twists and mutates. The life we knew falls to pieces, irrevocably broken.

Out of nowhere, a man's voice instructs me to turn off the engine. When I find the key, I can't figure out how to turn it. A hand reaches in to do it for me. The man says he's a volunteer fireman. As he introduces himself, I'm not listening. I crawl out headfirst through my smashed window onto shards of glass. I place my hands and knees on the jagged surface of a bare dirt field. I sit close by, impatiently waiting for the fireman to pull Beth out. Instead, he crawls into the car and takes my place. His flashlight alters the shadows.

For the first time, I notice how Beth's legs disappear in a cave of wreckage. Fear paralyzes me. I don't know what to do. The fireman chats with her about school and volleyball. A casual conversation that's beyond me. Minutes or hours pass. I interrupt them to say that I'll check on Maria. Struggling to stand, I lean on bent metal for support.

I stumble between the mangled car and the two girls standing by the road. Maria tells me a man driving behind us called for help. I hug her quickly. Then I step back. I need to inspect her, look her over. A small cut on her hand bleeds. Her friend appears unharmed.

Headlights push through dense blackness. The haunting scene burns in my memory with searing clarity. I go back and kneel next to the crash. Leaning into the narrow front space, I reach for Beth's hand. And ignore how her fingers don't close around mine in return. I intend to be comforting.

Unable to move, *Beth* reassures *me,* saying, "I'm okay. Everything will be okay." She sounds sure. My wrenching gut tells me nothing will ever be okay again.

When I return to Maria, I fall into the ditch that flipped the car. I forgot it was there. My knee hurts. The two girls sit on grass by the gravel of the road with gray blankets around their shoulders. A sheriff's deputy, our neighbor, shares with me her conversation with my husband. John is driving to the hospital. I ask our neighbor to call the friend's mom. My words catch and sputter. I lower my eyes to avoid her look of pity. Everyone must know that I am to blame.

A Life Flight helicopter is on the way. Someone reassures me that it's simply a routine precaution. It's not. The Jaws of Life tears into metal with bursts of harsh light and piercing squeals. A patrolman moves toward me. He talked to the man in the car behind us and learned that our car rolled three times. I think of Beth. Because I woke her up, I bestowed upon her a clear front row view of every traumatic detail.

"How fast were you going?" the patrolman asks.

"About 60." I purposely kept the speed up to get home faster. And there is no time for questions. I answer quickly, and I need to get back to Beth. Even though I am powerless, useless.

"Were you wearing your seat belt?"

"Yes."

"Were the passengers wearing seat belts?"

"Yes."

"Are you injured?"

"No." I hope he doesn't ask me about Beth.

"What do you think caused this crash?"

"Me, being sleepy." Yes, yes, yes! Undeniable, absolute, horrific guilt.

Life Flight descends. I tell Maria that Beth can't move "only because" her legs are pinned. The helicopter arrives only because it takes so long to get Beth out. Part of me recognizes the denial, my full rationalization mode.

The shrill screams of the Jaws of Life grind to a halt, exposing a gaping rip in the warped remains of our car. I hover nearby. Several men and women turn Beth s-l-o-w-l-y onto a long board in the dirt. An extensive neck brace is carefully positioned. They lift the board to a rolling cot.

I'm going with her. I push my way through the circle of bodies. I reach for the hand of my youngest, my baby. Someone says I can't go with her. In shock, I nod in agreement. I move closer into Beth's line of vision.

"I love you."

She responds with the same.

My sight blurs. I wipe my eyes.

"I'll be with you soon," I say. At least I think I did. I meant to.

The two girls by the road leave in an ambulance while medics rush Beth to the helicopter, its blades already spinning. The chopper rises into the jet black sky. I hate myself. For not demanding to go with her, and for more with a capital M.

Guided into an ambulance, I sit on a cot. "I'm fine."

Regardless, an attendant places a rigid brace around my neck. I wish him away, along with the thought of the car flipping and crushing. With my eyes closed, I see Beth lying too still, too flat.

After a short drive, I wave away a wheelchair and hurry into the emergency room. I find Maria sitting on a hospital bed, alone. She tells me she talked to John before he left for Toledo, Beth's destination. An hour's drive away.

On the other side of a curtain, I approach the mom of Maria's friend with reluctance. "I'm so, so sorry."

My apology feels so, so worthless.

I keep moving between my room and Maria's. I gently hold her bandaged hand as we head to radiology for her neck x-ray. The same hand she used to spike a ball over a net. The last few months, John and I drove on weekends to volleyball tournaments where Beth and Maria competed on club teams. I loved to watch them play.

I stop at a drinking fountain for a long time. A sour taste in my mouth remains. Hours before, I purposely bought a water bottle instead of a caffeinated drink because I wanted to sleep when I arrived home.

Back in my room, I wash my hands. The mirror reflects raw emotion. Some of the matted blood in my short brown hair found its way to a pale chin. I splash water on my face with trembling hands.

The doctor enters and abruptly asks, "Did you black out?"

Immediately, I say, "No," adding, "the blood in my hair isn't my own." I believe what I'm telling him in that moment.

"Does anything hurt?" he says. My hasty "no" follows. He nods. I mention the fall in the ditch and my knee, thinking this petty detail could help me leave faster. It might seem suspicious if nothing hurt. Unaware of my scheme, the doctor suggests a tetanus shot. I decline. After he tells me his uncle died of tetanus, I agree to the shot—*if* it can be done soon.

I'm wearing jeans and a Life is Good T-shirt with a peace sign. While the doctor cleans my scraped knee, I stare through the open door of the room. A nurse on the phone in the hallway keeps glancing my way. She walks in to say what I already know.

"You really need to get to Beth." I hear condescension, judgment. Desperate to know more, I'm terrified of what she might say. But, she won't tell me anything. She just repeats, "You *really* need to get to Beth."

I ask for a phone. Then I can't decide who to disturb at 1:30 in the morning. Calling my parents in daylight would be more kind, but their number is the only one I recall. Other digits refuse to come to mind. I call information for my brother's number, and it's unlisted. A frustrated groan erupts from my throat. "I can't remember!" I say, talking to no one. I rush into the hallway for a phone book, paper, and a pen.

My clumsy fingers dial the phone. Once, twice, three times. Finally, a connection. My dad answers the phone. I sugarcoat the accident and the damage done. I hang up so he and my mom can start the hour drive from the Lake Erie shore.

Next, I need someone to pick up Maria, take her home, and stay until my parents arrive. With a start, I realize I don't have a close friend in Tiffin. My good friends from high school lived far away. Instead, I call John's best friend Rich.

I jump when a technician calls my name for an x-ray. When I return, Maria's neck brace is removed. I spot blood in and below her ear when we hug, behind messy shoulder-length brown hair. Hair that is usually never messy. I ask the nurse about the blood. She dismisses my observation before even checking it. In an instant, I'm furious with the nurse. And with myself. Pressure builds and shrieks in my head. I wipe away tears and suppress an alarming desire to run.

Maria's friend has two hairline fractures in her neck. She sat on the same side of the car as Beth. Life Flight doctors arrive in the ER to take her and her mom to Toledo. Lightheaded, I retreat to my room and lean against the bed, fighting to breathe. My racing heart seems to belong to someone else.

The nurse unfastens my neck brace. It takes forever for the final paperwork. I sign it rapidly. Just get me out of here.

I watch Maria walk out of the hospital with Rich and his wife. I ride to Toledo with the father of Maria's friend. When he asks me about a street sign, I realize I'm not wearing my eyeglasses. Maybe that's why piercing throbs replace my usual tension headache. A deepening sting bangs and echoes with any slight shifting. I close my eyes. The left side of my head adds a new dimension to the pain. I touch an egg-size bump under hair stiff with dried blood. A wet cut at the base of my skull seeps. And something is wrong with my left thumb. I never received the tetanus shot though I couldn't care less.

For the first time, I relive every disturbing detail of the endless night. With my eyes open, the upside-down visions remain. A loop of regret starts a path in my head. I dread what I'll find in Toledo. Is Beth in pain? Is she bleeding internally? The very worst might happen, might already have happened. All because of me.

ᦇ Chapter 2 ᦇ
SHATTERING

Beth: *When I was injured, I really had no idea what was in store for me.*

THINGS THAT DON'T matter until they do: caffeine, a pay phone, rushing air, loud music, and a ditch in the dark. My experience the night of the accident differed from Beth's. She wrote about it soon after.

"I was, strangely, very calm. A nurse told me I was in shock. The doctors stuck many needles in me during the helicopter flight that seemed to last only a minute. I found out later these were high doses of medicine that slows the chain reaction of nerve damage. I landed at St. Vincent hospital in Toledo. I was taken to an exam room, and they cut off my clothes. They jokingly asked me if those were my favorite jeans and of course, they were. I had tests taken while I was trying to get some sleep. Through a speaker on the wall, they were yelling at me to stay awake. When I was taken to a room in intensive care, my dad asked me if I wanted to know what the doctors had just told him minutes before. I was paralyzed from the chest down. I believed it, but it did not scare me."

Hearing her diagnosis for the first time, Beth paused only a moment before simply responding, "Let's talk about what I *can* do." Sleepy, she added, "I can still sing."

A nurse at St. Vincent hospital met me at the entrance to take me to John. She mentioned he wasn't alone. Two members of the clergy also waited for me. My breath caught, and I cried. I wished I could wake up from the vivid nightmare. I walked into a dimly lit room and hugged John.

"Beth's paralyzed," he said. My tears fell freely on his shoulder. Breaking away, I couldn't listen to the clergy's spiel. Things will get better? I needed to see Beth.

I approached her, expecting the apparatus of intensive care. Something else floored me. Beth's small, welcoming smile when she first saw me, topped off with dimples and blue eyes. I stopped myself from losing it. I noticed a new chip in her front tooth. I attempted a hug around too many tubes, afraid to hurt her more than I already had. She lifted her arms slightly, with effort, then let them drop on the bed.

When she dozed off, I looked her over. Lying flat, Beth wore a large neck brace, her face swollen from steroid shots. Small glass cuts dotted her pale skin. A white hospital blanket covered her paralyzed legs.

I clung to John. "Everything will be okay," he said.

I looked into his eyes and said with certainty, "No, it won't."

John started to protest and stopped, in tears. The single fact that her legs no longer moved totally overwhelmed us. We had no clue about the far-reaching severity of her injury.

I thought of our son Ben, a freshman at Ohio State University. I remembered his Men's Glee Club concert only hours before, the reason for the long drive to and from Columbus. The girls and I heard the choir sing after shopping in the afternoon. We had bopped around Easton, all of us laughing when Maria suddenly joined in the chorus of a tune playing at a store. She sang her way through life.

We picked up Ben for dinner at a restaurant with OSU paraphernalia in every nook, stirring up fond memories of my time as a student there. I sat next to Ben and banked some extra hugs. After the concert, the girls and I dropped Ben off at the same dorm where I had lived and left Columbus for home at a late hour, confident we would sleep soundly in our own beds that night.

Beth looked small and helpless in the hospital bed at St. Vincent. We needed to call Ben. John picked up a hospital phone on a small table outside of Beth's room. As they talked, I suddenly realized how my son might feel. I interrupted the call, loud enough so Ben could hear me, "It's not your fault!"

"It's nobody's fault!" John said with conviction.

His words made no sense. Clearly, it was all on me.

Beth slept comfortably. I thought the worst was over. John looked weary, and I suggested he leave for home to take care of Maria. He left in the dark of the early morning. I pulled a chair close to Beth to start my vigil at her side.

A doctor entered our room with news of shattered bones in her neck. A punch to the gut. I struggled to catch my breath, to process questions I couldn't ask. A mess of bruises, glass cuts, and blood-matted hair, I let the neurosurgeon guide me to a chair. Splinters of bone cut Beth's spinal cord and caused the paralysis. First, he would try to realign her neck through traction. Two metal rods in her temples. If that didn't work, she needed surgery. The nightmare rippled on.

The surgeon insisted I leave the room as a nurse injected morphine into Beth's IV tube. They closed the door on me. I stood in the hallway, stunned and distraught. Incredulous. Before long, the doctor rushed out and told me traction didn't work. A team appeared out of the blue to take my sleeping daughter to surgery. The rods in her temples attached to a heavy weight at the head of the bed. Frightened by the quick action of the team, I stared at five people working together to move her bed extremely carefully down the hall. As they approached a red line on the floor, someone told me not to cross it. I obeyed and stood there until Beth disappeared.

A nurse suggested I go to the cafeteria. A strange thing for her to say, but I did need something for my parched throat. Not hungry, I picked up a water bottle and a soda in the cafeteria. I added a banana from a basket next to the cashier for later. I checked my jean pocket, relieved to find my wallet there.

Early Sunday, I paced alone in a cavernous, empty waiting room for several hours through the break of day. The hands of a wall clock moved erratically. Slow, fast, and slow again. I watched time unfold from a distance. Would the surgery never end? Terrified by the thought of losing Beth, I barely contained my fear only because she might need me.

When the surgeon finally appeared, I flinched. He led the way to a small consultation room even though no one was around. We both sat. Beth's vertebrae at C6-7 had shattered. The doctor had to cut bone out of her hip to support her neck. He attached two large titanium plates with 12 screws. He expressed relief as he declared the extensive surgery a success. If it hadn't worked, Beth wouldn't have been able to hold her head up on her own. He planned a second surgery on Friday to insert a smaller metal plate inside the front of her neck for additional support.

Some spinal injuries bruise the cord or cut a tiny bit of it. Not Beth's. The surgeon gently clarified that her cord appeared to be cut through, a complete injury, between the sixth and seventh cervical vertebrae in the neck (C6-7). Unlike bones, the spinal cord could not be fused or repaired. The broken cord caused her paralysis from the chest down. Chest down? Not just the legs? I couldn't find the words to ask what this actually meant.

When I hurried into the recovery room, Beth slept with a new stomach tube through her nose and a small red hole in each temple where the traction rods had been. To distract myself from how fragile she looked, I asked to use a phone to call John with a surgery update. After, I dialed the number of Beth's best friend. John had talked to Ellen earlier, but I wanted her to know about the surgery. Ellen's mom picked up on the first ring. She listened sympathetically to my good news that the surgery succeeded as if it negated the rest. When Beth and I returned to her room in intensive care, the nurses hooked up more tubes and wires.

I held her hand and watched her sleep. When I looked up, my parents surprised me. They walked in and stopped before reaching the bed, devastated to see their granddaughter in critical condition. Visibly shaken, they stepped back into the hallway to wipe tears away. The only other time I saw my dad cry was after his father died. When I fell asleep at the wheel, one colossal mistake hurt everyone I loved.

After my parents left, a highway patrolman gestured for me from the hallway and asked me to sign the accident report. The offense description listed, "Failure to Control." It should have read, "Failure to Protect."

The officer handed me my bent glasses. The other contents of the car had been delivered to our home. They included a box of perfectly-intact ceramic plates from shopping with the girls prior to the choir concert. Whole plates and a broken child.

Later, John brought me a bag of my clothes from home. Maria waited for me in the hallway and reached for a hug. Crying, she expressed a guilt all her own—the kind that emerges when you can walk away from an accident and someone you love cannot.

"Why," she said. "Why am I okay and they're not?"

"I'm so glad you're not hurt!" I said. "They will be fine. Beth's fine." Trying to convince myself. My girls grew up side by side, born a year and a half apart. As preschoolers, they loved to dress up as Snow White and Cinderella. They grew up in a fairy tale world of happy endings.

John stayed with Beth while Maria visited her injured friend in the room next to ours. I headed down the hall for a fast shower. I washed the blood out of my hair and threw on clean clothes. Not enough to make me feel better.

Sunday night, a nurse pointed out fresh blood at the base of my skull. She suggested stitches. I refused to leave intensive care, and she bandaged the cut.

I intended to lie down on the short couch next to Beth while she slept. I could not be still with every part of my head and body screaming silently in pain. A solid mass of hurting. I requested a pen and paper during one of the frequent checks by a nurse and channeled a fraction of my agitation into a complaint letter. I outlined the events at the ER the previous night. And rewrote them. Closer to daylight, a third letter for the final copy. I recommended that even small-town hospitals should require a basic physical exam for anyone in a serious accident, to rule out shock, concussion, and injury. I didn't care about myself. I worried about Maria. For all I knew, she had a health issue the ER doctor missed, in addition to the trauma etched in her memory. When the sun rose, my finished letter sat on the ledge, ready for John to mail.

On a typical Monday, I started a full workweek teaching literacy at the Tiffin Center, a state institution for adults with disabilities. Instead, I called my supervisor. After sharing news of the accident, I paced the hallway to calm down before returning to Beth's side. I had no clue what future Mondays would bring.

Bright and early, a stranger burst into the room saying, "So I hear you're a volleyball player!" I wanted to throw him out though I hesitated to upset Beth. He introduced himself as Jeff, a physical therapist. I hated his cheerful banter about a doctor with a similar injury. He had the nerve to quiz Beth on things she still could do, but he answered a few questions when she hesitated. Computer? Yes. College? Yes. Career? Children? Yes and yes.

Jeff set a high bar for a girl who lost everything. However, he redeemed himself by offering something more realistic: the hope of Laraine. She worked at a rehab center in Green Springs near our town. One of the best physical therapists for spinal cord injuries could work with Beth when we returned home.

Jeff continued to talk about our extreme good fortune. Despite Laraine, "lucky" did not remotely describe Beth. She lay flat and immobile with surgery incisions and tubes, pale and puffy, utterly dependent.

A steady flow of doctors examined Beth and added pieces to the puzzle of her disability. My pretty volleyball player acquired the new label of quadriplegia (also known as tetraplegia), a word plagued by ugly connotations. It simply described paralysis in all four limbs but implied more than that for many people.

I clearly recalled a high school psychology class in 1975 when my teacher ranted about quadriplegics. He questioned the value of such a life, using horrible words like crippled, disfigured, and retarded. He also told a lie, the old belief that children with Down syndrome died before reaching adulthood. I raised my hand to speak and challenged my teacher which I had never done before. A passionate teenager, I believed that every life had intrinsic worth. I also knew that people with physical disabilities could be very smart. In spite of these truths, many thought of quadriplegia as a dead end for the helpless. It made me sick that my own child would forever be defined by that word. Because of me.

Ironically, a cut spinal cord at C6-7 leaves victims fragile medically and completely powerless physically—at first. Beth's injury damaged her arm muscles and erased all leg and finger movement though partial feeling in her hands remained.

"I like it when you hold my hand," she said in a morphine haze. I struggled to hold back a wave of emotions.

A nurse brought a big call button for Beth to tap with her hand if she needed anything though I stayed close. The distant world beyond intensive care blurred. Her hospital room resonated with clear danger.

That night, I realized how incredibly easy it would be to curl up and lose myself under a blanket of guilt, just a slight letting go. I reclined on the couch to relieve my aching back. My head pounded. Tired to the bone, waves of panic kept my mind racing. What horrible thing would happen next?

Beth woke up from a nightmare of the car flipping. I hugged her until she fell back asleep. My tears flowed unbidden when I realized she couldn't reciprocate the hug or pat my back with her right hand, a hugging habit from her toddler days. As the room lightened, I concentrated hard on the things I could do in small moments. Help a nurse turn her to the side, adjust a pillow, stay in sight, hold her hand. Beth slept less during the day as the anesthesia wore off.

Somehow, she had already accepted her injury. Despite the uncertainty of her future, Beth's usual good-natured optimism was muted but alive, bolstered by Jeff's assurances she would eventually, slowly, learn how to do more. I knew what I saw, a deluge of paralysis and frail health. I feared the day, the hour, when she would fully realize what had happened to her.

On Tuesday, I assisted the nurse with a bed bath. Beth spiked a fever and developed congestion. A lung doctor ordered regular breathing treatments with a nebulizer and mask, familiar from her childhood asthma. I learned that if her injury had been one inch higher in the neck, she wouldn't be breathing on her own. Even so, the trauma paralyzed the lower part of her lungs, increasing her risk of pneumonia.

Another doctor mentioned paralysis research and dancing mice. I didn't want to hear about treatments that might help decades down the road. He left me with articles to read about quadriplegia. Grasping at straws, I desperately searched for a bright side.

The neurosurgeon checked in and talked to Beth about a complete injury, with the spinal cord cut through. I clung to a detail I read. Complete injuries generally caused less chronic pain compared to those with a partially cut or bruised spinal cord (an incomplete injury). Never mind that complete also meant no muscle function and no sensory perception from the chest down. No movement *and* no feeling.

Maria's friend walked in from the next room with her mom to visit us. Jeff joined them, announcing brightly how Beth would leave intensive care soon for a short stay in a rehab center. As though we were headed for summer camp. Soon? She had surgery on Friday. And a short stay? A doctor said months.

Our visitors shared good news. Test results showed no complications from the hairline fractures. Maria's friend would walk out of the hospital the next day with a temporary neck brace. Relieved, I couldn't help wishing Beth could walk out too. A nurse put boots on my daughter's feet to prevent foot drop caused by withering muscles.

John's parents and sister Jean arrived from Lorain at the same time he and Maria visited. More alert, Beth conversed pleasantly and didn't seem to notice her grandparents' tears. John told us about his decision to return to teaching to finish the last two weeks of the school year. Maria chose to complete ninth grade, supported by friends. Ben, alone in Columbus, had college finals to take.

John called family and close friends about the accident and received a memorable one. A fellow teacher called to say, "I don't have any words of wisdom, but I'm a good listener if you need me to be." John shared Beth's "I can still sing" comment, and a long, heavy silence followed. The caring choir director, Curtis King, was speechless.

Mr. King directed the choirs at the middle school and high school. He asked Maria to speak to her sister's eighth grade choir since many of them were upset about the accident. She told them Beth was fine! I realized that I was as guilty as Jeff for minimizing a cruel and severe disability. John also glossed it over. Lots of wishful thinking all around and in my case, denial too. However, when Maria said Beth was fine, she accurately described her sister's positive outlook.

"I remember my family always being there, and I remember not being afraid or worried," Beth recalled later. "My room was constantly full of people moving busily around. I didn't realize until a few days later how large and pretty the room was, because all I saw then were the white ceiling tiles since I had to lay flat and wear a rigid neck brace."

Plans evolved for a transfer to Toledo's Medical College of Ohio (MCO), the recommended rehab hospital. Beth needed to be medically stable first. A friendly MCO doctor completed her first strength test even though she literally had none to measure. He said the rehab nurses would teach me how to help with basic body functions.

Through the night, I watched the glowing numbers on beeping and buzzing machines. I checked Beth's forehead and held her limp hand. The nurse contacted a doctor when her fever spiked again. He examined her in the middle of the night and ordered more medicine.

Wednesday morning, a technician wheeled a portable x-ray machine into our room. Beth's back and neck x-rays were clear, meaning no complications from the complex surgery. Jeff and another therapist entered with a metal bed called a tilt table. They moved Beth onto it by lifting the cloth pad under her body. Straps over her hospital gown held her to the table. With the safety lock off, the table tipped on a central point to tilt her head higher than her feet. She described the experience in a school essay.

"At one point, they were amazed because I was still conscious even though my blood pressure took an unexpected plunge. They jokingly said I should become a fighter pilot but who knows, it could be a fun job. I thought it was funny at the time, but I also was on morphine."

With Beth back in her hospital bed, I raised the head in small increments for brief periods of time as instructed. John's sister Julie, a nurse, offered to stay to give me a break. Since I needed to hear the doctors' reports during the day, Julie arrived from Lorain with books to stay overnight with Beth on Wednesday. All the sleeping rooms for family had been taken, so a kind nurse allowed me to use a couch in an unoccupied room down a dim hallway. A deep, relentless headache eclipsed the aching of my left thumb and the rest of my body. No one heard me sobbing. My distress gave way to fitful sleep. Heartache weighed me down, a shroud of regret.

Thursday morning, a doctor reduced the number of breathing treatments and removed Beth's stomach tube. She started on soft food after days on an IV diet. An occupational therapist demonstrated how to hold a big spoon with a fat handle using a wrist reflex. Beth dropped the spoon a few times before she could control it enough to scoop Jell-O. I watched her struggle to lift her arm enough to get the spoon to her mouth, losing the contents on the way. Not easily deterred, she kept trying. I put on an encouraging face while I mourned her losses.

Rarely hungry and with my jeans fitting loosely, I literally ran downstairs to the hospital cafeteria twice a day, mainly for caffeine while Beth napped. Thursday afternoon in my absence, she upchucked the Jell-O. The call button had slipped out of her reach, a dangerous situation if she had choked. I added shame for not being there to my growing list of failures.

Later that day, I held a phone to Beth's ear. She talked to her best friends for the first time since the accident. They asked to visit on Monday, Memorial Day. She didn't hesitate to say yes. After the call, she admitted to being a little nervous. She calmed some of her concerns as only a 14-year-old could, even one who could not sit up in bed. Beth requested a shampoo since her hair had not been washed since the accident.

To move her on the hospital bed, I stood on one long side with a nurse on the other. We grabbed the heavy cloth pad under her and pulled upward until her shoulder-length brown hair hung down over the top edge. With a plastic bag under her head and a garbage can on the floor, I poured containers of warm water over her head. As water spilled everywhere, Beth laughed.

I remembered a toddler in her favorite costume and crown. Cinderella at the ball, giggling as she hopped and danced in a bumper car sort of way with Maria. Belly laughs followed as they tumbled and fell, entwined. Cinderella's magic shattered at midnight in the fairy tale—about the same time as our accident—and left her transformed. I lost the Beth who could walk through a long life. How would my changed Cinderella find her happy ending?

❧ Chapter 3 ❧
HOPING

Beth: *Accepting my new disability never was a real issue for me. The issue was what needed to be done next.*

I WATCHED different doctors come and go. I made a concerted effort to focus on their words. Each disclosure opened a door to unfamiliar landscapes, to new questions I couldn't have imagined before the accident. As another man in a white coat left Beth's room, I remembered my freshman orientation at Ohio State University. My mom and I met with an advisor who looked at my test scores and said enthusiastically, "You should be a doctor!" I shared a surprised look with my mom. It had never occurred to either of us.

I never would be a doctor who had all the answers. My career plan? I had wanted to be a physical therapist at a state institution, to shine a little light in a dark place. Even the best-laid plans have a way of changing and spinning out of control.

Terrible news, over and over, again and again. Not walking filled the small tip of the iceberg of quadriplegia. Below the surface, unseen, a knot of anxiety-inducing conditions twisted together. Nothing in Beth's body worked to its full capacity. Impaired lungs concerned me most, but other organs contributed to a multitude of problems. Add weak arms. Wasted hands. Useless legs. With poor circulation, her skin broke easily and healed slowly, including the open cut on her knee from the glass during the accident. Blood pooled in her feet and legs, causing swelling, splotches of color, and the risk of deadly blood clots. New fears settled in for a long stay.

In the mix of fatal threats for quads, autonomic dysreflexia stood out as the scariest. Blood pressure rose to a dangerous level. It was an early warning sign of a system gone wrong, often triggered by a health problem: big or small issues, from a broken leg to a slight temperature change, depending on the individual. Sometimes, a specific cause could be identified and treated. Otherwise, autonomic dysreflexia required an ambulance to the emergency room to bring down the blood pressure and avoid a stroke or death. As if that wasn't worrisome enough, a quad's unregulated body temperature could cause high fevers in hot weather because of the inability to sweat and cool down.

Friday's scheduled surgery added a small scar to the front of Beth's neck and a second titanium plate with screws, all hidden beneath the skin. John's sister Mary stayed with her overnight while I slept fitfully in a family sleeping room. I woke early with a painful jaw from clenching despite the bite plate I wore at night. When Mary left in the morning, Beth showed me her new pink manicure and teen magazines. More visitors over the weekend included her grandparents and brother. Ben had last seen Beth in a drastically different condition after his concert. I reached up and hugged him as long as he let me.

My boss from the Tiffin Center visited. Her unconditional support was heart-warming. I was the only employee hired under a literacy grant, and she didn't remind me about unfinished monthly and quarterly paperwork though I felt bad just the same. Also, she brought unexpected news of sick leave time donated by my generous co-workers and eased my foreboding of the high medical expenses ahead.

John completed his certification test to be a National Board Certified Teacher one week after the accident. The reason? Ohio teachers who earned the certification received an extra $10,000 a year for up to 10 years. He had stayed home the day of Ben's concert to study for the test. It looked like we'd need the extra income more than ever.

On Memorial Day, five unusually quiet teenage girls walked hesitantly into our hospital room with cards and gifts. They appeared startled and sad. As usual, Beth's smile greeted them. I left so the friends could visit. I huddled with the two moms in the hallway. Their worried faces probably included concerns about their daughters. I thought about that too, the ripple effect of Beth's injury. We had no way of knowing how profound the impact would be on friends and family.

"How is Beth?"

"She's paralyzed from the chest down." A sadly inadequate description, though I couldn't voice the terrible details. I defaulted to my natural tendency to look for the bright side. Was there one?

"Neck surgery went well," I said. I paused, not knowing what to say next. "She can still have children." My voice broke. I heard words of consolation as I immediately worked to regain control. I felt a hand on my shoulder.

"How are *you*?"

I avoided the question with something brief about sick leave time donated to me. One of the moms broke the silence that followed to share a struggle she experienced. "But, it's nothing like what you're going through," she said.

My usual well of empathy was empty, and I suggested we join the girls.

We walked into the room as Beth asked her friends about the week of eighth grade she missed. They laughed about my daughter getting A's on final exams she would never take. I listened to her first joke of many about the perks of disability. The friends and moms discovered that Beth was still Beth, with or without quadriplegia.

Within minutes after the visitors left, I read a new pile of cards while she fell asleep. Cheerful messages ignored the fact she would *not* get well soon. Researchers promised improvements in the future but complete cures for old injuries, ones with cut spinal cords in the neck? The odds for Beth seemed to be zero to none. Hallmark needed a new line of cards for quads with complete (and nearly complete) injuries. Instead of get well, get used to it.

The last night in intensive care, a nurse rushed into the room in response to an alarm. The tape fell off of a wire. "Instead of fixing it," Beth said, "she wanted to see if the other nurses were paying attention. She took off the wire connected to my heart monitor and tapped the wire so it looked like a heart attack. A few other nurses poked their heads in the door but when they saw us laughing they got the picture."

Beth fell back asleep easily while I stared at the shadows, my nerves raw and pulsing. In the morning, I packed up our few belongings. I left several bouquets for others to enjoy. Associating cut flowers with tragedy, I wished in vain to never see that many in one place again.

We drove away from intensive care in an ambulance. Beth's finger muscles had begun to shrink and tighten, atrophy and contract. Hands turned into loose fists. Involuntary muscle spasms started. They seemed to have a mind of their own with knees bending, feet jerking, and legs bouncing. With her morphine haze fading, Beth required help in every possible way. The one exception: breathing on her own.

The rehab wing for children at the Medical College of Ohio (MCO) consisted of a large gloomy room with six beds separated by curtains. Four of the beds already held patients and three of those children had their mom with them. In the bed next to Beth lay a little girl, all alone with an extensive brain injury. A prisoner enclosed in a special bed with high rails all around it.

Our landscape transformed from intensive care with constant activity to . . . waiting. Waiting for everything, anything. Waiting for a water pitcher and a cup. Waiting for a box of tissues to wipe away escaping tears. Waiting for something to happen.

At lunchtime, a nurse hurried in to tell us about meals served in the dining room down the hall. And as an afterthought, that she couldn't find a good chair. The nurse clumsily moved Beth into a much too large wheelchair. She leaned heavily, pitched to one side and uncomfortable. The nurse lifted the patient in the next bed into another wheelchair. I made a point to smile and say hello to the girl. She didn't make eye contact. I pushed Beth down the hallway while she fought the dizziness of being upright.

The bright lights in the dining room surpassed the pediatric wing though both places reflected misery. We sat next to a depressed stroke victim who didn't respond in any way to my friendly greeting. Another patient wailed loudly. Beth picked at soft food, and we left early. She asked me to transfer her into bed by myself, instead of waiting for a nurse.

I'd never moved Beth on my own. I double-checked each small step to keep my anxiety in check. Chair brakes securely locked, sliding board perfectly placed, bed adjusted to the best height. I tried to hold her knees in place with my own but with her inability to sit up or help at all, we nearly ended up on the floor. I could breathe freely once I shifted her position in the bed, an easier task after a week of practice in intensive care.

The empty afternoon held an eternity of disappointing moments. How was this the magical place where Beth would regain at least a little strength? Unfortunately, the friendly doctor who visited us in intensive care was on vacation. His replacement seemed distracted. Uninterested in the few TV channels, we requested books from John. At dinnertime, Beth asked me to bring her food tray to her bed. Staff disapproved, but I didn't care. We never returned to the dining room. Even so, there was no escaping my despair.

A nurse placed a cot next to Beth's bed that night. I closed my eyes, my body a fluid mass of pain, and listened to her small breaths. On the other side, our roommate with the brain injury moaned sadly. Trying hard not to add my own unhappy sounds, my guilt deepened in the darkness.

I remembered a Tiffin Center co-worker who returned from maternity leave and shared with me how becoming a mom changed her perspective. If she thought of the center residents as a son or daughter, she cared for them more—the same way she would want her own child treated. That's how I felt about the little girl surrounded by bed rails. I needed someone to give her the love and care she cried out for. I walked down the hall to find help for the child who couldn't even push a call button. After a nurse checked on her, the girl began to whimper again. I stayed on the cot, overwhelmed with my own injured child and hating my inability to do more. Be more.

I thought of my first visit to a state institution in 1974 with the Ohio youth group and hoped the little girl wouldn't end up living in one. A ward at Apple Creek had at least a dozen big cribs in one room and not for children. It saddened me for many reasons including the only staff in sight filling out paperwork at a desk. I dozed off into a new recurring nightmare.

In shadows, the high bars of a crib in the distance confined a child completely, mind and body. I hummed a lullaby as I approached and suddenly saw Beth in the cage. My scream made no sound as I woke and bolted upright, tangled in a sheet. I tried to console myself with the fact that Beth needed no high bed rails. A stab of guilt followed for the little girl who did. I closed my eyes again, haunted by images of the crushed car and the Jaws of Life, the dark field and a twisted neck.

The second day, I tilted Beth back in a better wheelchair and pushed her down the hall to her first physical therapy session. We waited a long time before the therapist, without explanation or saying much of anything, transferred my youngest from the wheelchair to a mat table in a sitting position. After the inevitable dizziness, instead of helping her lie back on the mat to relieve the vertigo, the therapist returned her to the wheelchair and tilted the chair back. So much for that.

For Beth's first shower since the accident, a nurse helped me move her to a white cloth chair on wheels. The seat had little support. The situation worsened when the nurse removed her neck brace temporarily, causing her to slouch awkwardly.

In the large open bathroom with a detached showerhead, Beth insisted on washing herself. She fumbled with the soap and washcloth, often dropping both. My tenacious daughter pushed the shampoo around with her fists for few seconds before agreeing to let me finish. She rested her shaky arms and felt better after the shower, but she didn't like wearing nothing but towels as a nurse pushed the white chair down a long hallway to her bed. I focused on my growing list of things to buy, including a bathrobe instead of the daunting thought of giving her a shower by myself at home.

Getting Beth into loose pajamas from home wore us both out. I rolled her back and forth too many times on a flat bed. We didn't know any tricks, like putting tops on from a sitting position in her chair. Since Beth could not help, my back and thumb ached. I had taken everything for granted before the accident.

I dreaded the never-ending nights when the floodgates opened wide. My headache dominated a litany of hurting. Every noise and movement throbbed in my head, pulsing with my heart. The night of the accident played on a loop.

In the hospital, I had apologized to the mom of Maria's friend for my poor choices. The night of the accident, I had bought water instead of a caffeine drink so I could sleep when I got home. I didn't stop at the pay phone to call John. I also told the girls in the backseat to crawl out. Would it have been better to stay put with hairline neck fractures? What if the car had exploded? I dwelled on pathetic apologies and staggering failures through bitter hours. Above all, paralyzing my youngest. I realized that if Beth or Maria hadn't survived the accident, I would've checked out permanently. Instead, Beth needed me. Heart pounding, I tried and failed to process the deadly risks of quadriplegia, terrified of losing her.

In the light of day, my only job was in jeopardy. The pressure intensified because Beth totally depended on me, and my composure slipped away. My sanity seemed at risk too. Life equaled pain, mental and physical. Privately, I asked a nurse for help. When John visited, I met with a rehab psychologist for a half hour, seeking any kind of advice on how to continue. No such luck. I faltered through my request for help, and the counselor said something about things getting better. When I explained my guilt, I couldn't stop sobbing.

Lesson learned. Don't ever talk about causing Beth's injury and try not to think about it. People said I should call if I needed to talk, but I knew that wasn't an option if I wanted to get through the days. I couldn't risk completely losing control because regaining it could be impossible.

When John hugged me, I didn't want to let go. We talked about other rehab options, and Beth agreed we should try a different place. John said he'd research rehab centers in the area. We didn't know about and never considered top-ranked facilities such as Boston's Spaulding Rehab, Minnesota's Mayo Clinic, or Chicago's Shriners Hospital.

Two days later, John visited to share news of an opening at the Green Springs rehab center where Laraine worked. No pediatrician worked on the staff, but they accepted teenagers. If we transferred there, Laraine would be Beth's physical therapist through inpatient rehab as well as outpatient therapy. If Laraine was merely half as good as we hoped, the move to Green Springs would be worthwhile.

John and I let our youngest decide. She said yes. Anticipating the move, I gained a bit more balance on my tightrope.

Beth waited for the mail to be delivered, surprised at the outpouring of well wishes from our small hometown. Flowers arrived from the coaches of high school volleyball, the team she had looked forward to playing on, and also from her club team. I loved traveling with my daughters to tournaments around the state where they sailed steady serves over the net.

I avoided talking about activities I thought Beth could no longer do: softball, soccer, swimming, summer camp, bird banding, trumpet, marching band, theater performances, painting stage sets, volleyball, and more. There wouldn't be another friend party to paint each wall of her bedroom a different color, with almost as much on the painters as on the walls. An avid reader, Beth might never be able to get a book off a library shelf on her own. She could barely hold one, let alone turn the pages, and I often read to her. She told me that dreams of playing volleyball replaced her nightmares of the flipping car. We assumed her future as an athlete was over.

A psychiatrist tested for brain damage, something I hadn't considered. After Beth passed the test, I learned she had worried about that possibility. Relieved, she felt genuinely grateful for her intact mental abilities despite her new physical reality. I was thankful for her positive attitude, certain it was simply a matter of time before that, too, would drain away.

An occupational therapist talked about relearning the most basic skills. She showed us soft fat tubes with holes through their centers. A toothbrush, pen, or handle of a hairbrush fit through the hole, and the thick tubes made them easier to hold without dropping. The therapist taught Beth how to brush her teeth. Every little step required practice, from holding the tube to picking up a cup of water.

To write, the therapist wedged a tube between unresponsive fingers. Beth touched the pen in the tube to paper. No mark appeared. She kept trying, over and over, until the faint letters of her first name appeared. She showed her dad the paper. We counted on him to show enthusiasm for each baby step.

On his last visit at MCO, John brought us a box of get well notes, cards for gas and restaurants, and news of an unusual gift. A principal who kept a cockatiel in her school office had started a collection. At one time, Beth owned small pet birds and told the principal about the African Gray parrot she wanted to own someday. Donations from staff and students in the Tiffin City Schools would buy a young parrot. A bird she could not take care of. I kept quiet while others welcomed the news.

On a Monday morning, Beth and I traveled by ambulance to the St. Francis Centre in Green Springs, much closer to home. The one teenager among many adult inpatients, she had a sunny room to herself. We soon met Laraine, the much-anticipated therapist. With a big heart and bigger personality, she did not disappoint.

৵ Chapter 4 ৶
HEALING

Beth: *I had to relearn how to do everything.*

WE HAD TOO MUCH to process. The first afternoon in Green Springs, Laraine made a good first impression. She tested Beth's absent strength, confirming the extensive permanent damage caused by the cut cord. An expert in muscle mechanics and the spinal cord, Laraine told us about specific muscles in the arms, shoulders, and trunk that could be strengthened. Damaged muscles could not respond normally to daily exercise. She spoke in a serious, confident way and emphasized the strenuous work required over months and years for Beth to be less dependent. I couldn't imagine my newly fragile daughter doing anything on her own though she believed. At that time, no one, not even Beth, could envision complete independence without a personal care assistant.

Surrounded by friendly, attentive staff, we welcomed the drastic change. Beth surprised me by suggesting I go home that night to sleep. John and Ben had left my little work car and keys at Green Springs. They had a rental car to drive until we decided on a vehicle to replace the one in the crash.

I questioned Beth's offer though I hoped she would insist. She said she was sure. Sleep felt like a rare treasure, intensely desired yet out of reach. I sat in the driver's seat for the first time since the accident, reluctant to turn on the car in the dark night. I considered sleeping in the back seat.

Ultimately, I realized I had no choice. Driving would be necessary for many doctor and therapy appointments after Beth came home. Even so, I drove too slowly, hyperaware. The familiar scenery was surreal. Stranger still, walking through the sameness of the house when everything else had changed.

I drove to Green Springs early in the morning and returned home late in the evening. Despite a new rehab center and somewhat better sleep, I agonized over life-threatening risks. Beth looked weak and vulnerable. My fears took on lives of their own. They swelled to layers of new losses that might occur anytime, anywhere, to anyone I loved. I felt powerless. I also couldn't give back one thing Beth had lost. Even with steady support from my family, I floundered privately. Deeply sad and hopelessly distracted. The future looked bleak. Because of me.

Days in rehab revolved around two long physical therapy sessions, morning and afternoon. The therapy room pulsed with activity, with several wide mat tables in a room the size of a small gymnasium. The first time on a mat table, Beth wore pajamas. I didn't expect to see other inpatients in street clothes. The next morning, I struggled for a long time to put on Beth's jeans, shirt, and gym shoes. I purposely had brought generic tops (not sports related) from home, to not remind Beth of what she couldn't do anymore. When she saw the generic ones, she specifically asked me to bring her volleyball T-shirts the next day. Those were the only shirts she chose to wear as an inpatient at the rehab hospital.

Close to retirement, Laraine stood out among the other therapists. With a sturdy frame, she wore her black curly hair short and radiated resolve. She taught patients how to move their bodies in a confident, no nonsense way that mirrored her personality. Laraine intimidated more than a few. However, many patients earned extended sessions, easy smiles, affectionate teasing, and a playful laugh as she pushed them forward.

Beth had essentially no strength, so I wheeled her to a mat table. Each session started the same. Remove footrests, angle chair to the mat, lock wheelchair wheels, position sliding board between wheelchair and mat table, slide her body over to the table, lift legs up on the mat, sit up, and take off shoes—with Beth unable to do one iota of it. Laraine's hands steered hers with total assistance, moved her across the sliding board, and kept her from falling.

Beth learned the steps to sit up. Lying flat on her back, the first step involved throwing one arm over the other to roll onto one side. The second step was pushing down on the mat with both hands to lift her body. Then, bracing the body in a sitting position by planting her hands on each side. However, knowing the process and having the strength to do it were two completely different things. When "long-sitting" with her legs straight out in front, she couldn't keep her balance without help. Another seemingly futile exercise placed her face down on her stomach, trying and failing to lift her body off the mat with powerless arms.

She wilted and wobbled by the end of each session. Her arms trembled. With Laraine's total guidance, hand over hand, they completed the closing routine together. Sit up, put on shoes, push feet over the edge of the mat, position sliding board, slide over to wheelchair, remove sliding board, put on foot rests, and unlock wheelchair wheels. Beth mandated an additional step in the routine.

My youngest somehow maintained an easygoing attitude about *almost* everything. It became imperative that the bottom of her jeans covered her ankles when she sat in a wheelchair. During transfers, her jeans slipped lower in the back and bunched up on her thighs. Immediately after, I grabbed the extra fabric on both sides of her knees and pulled down so that the bottom hem touched her shoe. Then, at her request, I adjusted it again. It usually required three or four tries to accomplish the task to her standards.

Next, I pushed Beth's wheelchair to a shorter occupational therapy session. Therapists explained the extreme challenge of relearning to do familiar tasks without hand function. It wasn't an exaggeration. She could move her wrists and arms but not her fingers.

Many quads used a reflex called the tenodesis to grip items though it required persistent practice to be effective. I tested it. I set an elbow on a table with my forearm straight up and my hand falling forward. Keeping my fingers loose, I pulled the hand backwards at the wrist. As my hand tilted back, the reflex automatically closed the space between my fingers and palm.

Beth sat in a wheelchair at a table, not able to grip a regular pen with the tenodesis reflex. A therapist inserted the pen into a foam tube. Beth tilted her right wrist back to hold the tube. She experimented on placement and settled on the space between the index and middle finger, her hand entirely closed. I noticed how she started to use her teeth for some tasks, like holding the top of the pen to accurately place it between specific fingers. The real difficulty of writing involved pressing the pen on the paper. After a week of practice, she could consistently press the pen downward with enough force for the ink to show. She attempted to manipulate a variety of small objects with patience.

We heard about the 1995 accident that left actor Christopher Reeve immobile and dependent on a breathing tube. His spinal cord injury occurred one inch higher in the neck than Beth's and required nursing care around the clock. I should've been grateful for her ability to breathe on her own and move her arms. Nevertheless, staring at the ceiling in the night, unable to sleep, I could not celebrate her shallow breathing or the arm movement that barely allowed her to brush her own teeth. I wanted so much more for her.

I judged and debated the pros and cons of disabilities as I observed other patients in therapy. A stroke to a spinal cord injury, paralysis to a missing limb, a brain injury to blindness. Countless factors played into my comparison game, all meaningless. Individual ages and attitudes seemed to tip the scales in one direction or another. Beth's outlook stayed hopeful but in a vague, trusting way. She had no idea what the future would bring.

Physical therapy, occupational therapy, doctors, nurses, aides, and visitors filled the hours during Beth's stay in inpatient rehab. Surgery scars healed slowly. She needed repeated rounds of antibiotics for frequent infections. Five baby African Gray parrots surprised us one evening with their owner. Propped up with pillows on the hospital bed, Beth cradled the noisy babies on her lap and picked the one that would be hers when she moved home. Another visitor, her softball coach, brought her a ball signed with well wishes from the team, including her sister's. I missed all of Maria's games.

Flowers arrived sporadically in Green Springs. Too many flowers died since Beth's injury though one bouquet arrived along with the sweetest stuffed bear I'd ever seen. About two feet tall, it had a striped body, bee wings, and two antennas with soft red hearts at the tips. She named it Honeybee Bear. He sat on the sunlit window ledge in her room with a perpetual smile, part of the improved view.

Beth wrote about Green Springs in a school essay. "At the rehab hospital, the simplest tasks of putting my shoes on or sitting up by myself were the hardest challenges of the day. Transferring from place to place was impossible for me to do on my own. Wheeling myself any distance was difficult. My life consisted of two long physical therapy sessions a day, where my therapists had no concept of being tired. They pushed me to exhaustion but I knew how much they were helping, and I appreciated it."

At Beth's request, I stayed close by during therapy sessions. I sat on a folding chair next to the mat table, reading about spinal cord injury, rewriting to-do lists, and trying to ignore her constant fight with her body. One morning, Laraine teased me about sitting there and said she'd take good care of my daughter.

If I left, was I letting Beth down? Making her feel uncomfortable in any way? Torn, I didn't know what to do. I claimed another folding chair on the far side of the big open room. I moved the chair farther back into shadows, stared blankly at my papers, and discreetly wiped away steady silent tears. Beth was fine, and I witnessed a baby step toward independence.

The therapy session ended in exhaustion. Arms that Beth had used awkwardly an hour before gave way. Her body tottered back and forth in a battle of balance. My mind flashed an image of Bambi on ice. My instincts screamed to hold her, support her. Instead, I turned away to regain my bearings.

She tried incredibly hard as though a cut spinal cord could be conquered through sheer force of will. Laraine still needed to cover and steer Beth's hands with her own to end the session and add the two footrest pieces to the wheelchair. I understood the technique well.

I taught with hand over hand guidance hundreds of times at the Tiffin Center, from touching a picture on a communication board to sounding out a word, and from brushing teeth to writing a name. With variable success. Laraine's consistent steps looked pointless to me when Beth's herculean efforts showed no results the first weeks, except for sitting upright without getting dizzy. Through continuous exertion with little progress, Beth's hope stayed at a high level.

Before the car accident, my awareness of disability had not been narrow. As a child, I yearned to help others and wept one afternoon. When asked why, I said, "I haven't done anything yet!" My mom should've earned an award for not laughing as she pointed out—with a straight face—that I was only 10 years old.

A few years later, I was a teenager compelled to try to make a difference. I joined my county's youth group to help those with developmental disabilities. We mainly hosted dances at the county school. I wanted to do more, so we started a countywide babysitting service for kids and adults with disabilities. I organized the training for babysitters and spent my free time playing with children with epilepsy, Down syndrome, cerebral palsy, and more.

In college in 1976, I stayed active with the Youth Ohio Association for Retarded Citizens and edited their monthly newsletter. (Even back then, my friends and I advocated for eliminating the word retarded.) As a freshman in college, I also fell in love with the friend I danced with at my senior prom, sort of the boy next door. Our parents lived across the street from each other in Lorain.

I lived in a dorm at Ohio State while John finished his last year at Heidelberg College in Tiffin, Ohio. We bridged the 85 miles between us each weekend. We sent letters in the mail on lonely weekdays. He wrote me moonstruck poems, and our kisses tasted of apples we shared. By October, two days a week together wasn't enough, and we planned to marry.

A few months before John would finish a teaching degree, we had an emotional debate about immediately dropping out of college and getting any kind of jobs—with only $40 between us. All that mattered was being together. A blink of time later, we married on June 18th, two weeks after John's college graduation and one week before my 19th birthday. In the years since, we've laughed about our difficult decision to not drop out, grateful we had a smidgen of common sense. Still, I hoped my children would experience that same kind of love. What were Beth's odds with quadriplegia?

Before our wedding, John signed a teaching contract, and Tiffin would be our new home. A few weeks later, we moved into a big house with four men with disabilities. John taught fourth graders, and I managed the group home.

My youngest child entered first grade 16 years later. I worked at the Tiffin Center, a state institution for adults with developmental disabilities. Many residents also battled mental illness and physical limitations. I thought I had seen it all. I thought I understood challenges.

Before the car accident, I felt confident I could make a small difference. I thought I lived in a world where cognitive impairments seemed worse than physical disabilities. Beth's injury changed my mind.

All the love and support in the world couldn't blot out brutal physical realities. At my paying jobs, everyone I worked with had a somewhat quantifiable disability, one with a wide range of realistic goals. In rehab, I couldn't see an array of potentials for quads. Even Beth seemed surprised by, and glad for, every little thing.

In intensive care, she had zero finger control but at Green Springs, she gradually realized one finger could move a little. Limited to a range of three inches, the ability of the left index did not allow the finger to straighten or to touch the palm. Nonetheless, it turned into a valuable gift, one that made her left hand the favored one for everything except her right-handed habit of writing.

Simple tasks remained complicated or unworkable.

The inability to put her hair up in a ponytail bothered Beth more than other barriers. Manipulating an elastic band seemed impossible and presented another major obstacle; she tipped forward to the floor if she raised her hands high.

Sitting in a wheelchair, Beth depended on the armrests to keep her upright and balanced. Laraine taught her how to push down on locked wheels with her palms to shift and move her bottom, inch by inch, to sit on the front edge of the wheelchair seat. Next, Beth leaned against the backrest for stability, preventing a tumble to the floor when she lifted her arms to her head. Every day, she tried and failed to find a way to put her hair up, over and over, until she couldn't hold her arms up anymore.

I bought a variety of elastic bands for Beth to try. I drove to the store a few times in the afternoons for anything she might need while John or Maria took my place at rehab. I returned once to find the sisters in the middle of a wheelchair race down a long hospital hallway. Ben worked full-time in a chemical lab for the summer and visited Green Springs when he could.

During my rushed shopping trips, I bought jeans for Beth to try on and ended up returning most of them. I also looked at sweatpants with elastic or Velcro, pleased to find an ideal design with snaps up and down both sides of the legs. We learned the hard way how polyester fabric slips too easily off a sliding board.

Jeans with zippers remained Beth's pants of choice and made transfers less precarious. One morning, she started to fall off the sliding board during a spasm. I grabbed the belt loops on her jeans instead of the extra fabric at the sides and almost dropped her when the loops ripped. She could live with broken belt loops but not high waters. Her jeans needed to touch her shoes. Always. Like many other teenagers, Beth's quest for perfect jeans never ended.

Weeks passed, and physical therapy ramped up. The exercise with Beth lying on her stomach evolved into baby push-ups as she lifted her trunk a few inches off the mat with her arms. She sat up by herself and put shoes on for the first time about six weeks after her injury. I applauded with John, Maria, and the therapists.

John's mom and dad watched Beth start on her back. She concentrated on the steps to roll over, making it after several tries, then slowly rose to a shaky sitting position. Beth swayed through clumsy minutes of strenuous effort to put on each shoe with uncooperative hands, and John's dad had to walk away so she wouldn't see her strong grandpa cry. For him, the long struggle eclipsed the small success.

I depended on regular visits from my parents. We watched her use the exercise equipment to strengthen her arms and shoulders. Together, we stayed on the sidelines and cheered for Beth, roles we would repeat often in other places. My dad told me that my voice sounded normal again. When I asked what he meant, he said that since the night of the accident, I'd talked too fast, manic, like my mouth couldn't keep up with my brain.

"Let us know if you need anything, okay? And take care of yourself," my mom ordered, hugging me goodbye with a soft pat on my back. I wanted to say that all I needed was to rewind the hands of time to before the accident. Meanwhile, Beth looked forward, not back.

"I learned how some people, given the same situations, react in opposite ways. I have seen how people take so much for granted," Beth explained in a school essay a few months later. "Some people had a tendency to stop. They wouldn't try to be independent. That's always been a goal of mine, to be independent."

We encountered several patients with spinal cord injuries in rehab. A middle-aged man with a wide-ranging injury (like Beth's) had lived his life in nursing homes and died of pneumonia in the next room. Another patient had a brain injury in addition to a bruised spinal cord. We met a boy who had been paralyzed during fusion surgery to correct scoliosis; he stayed home from school and blamed his mother for pushing the surgery. An older girl, a quad, worked with therapists to try to increase the tiny movement she had in one of her arms, without success. Dependent on others for everything, the girl greeted the world with a mischievous grin and sassy spunk. (Amused, Laraine teased that her mouth worked just fine!) A newly injured young man with paraplegia (paralysis of the legs) refused therapy and was scheduled to move to a nursing home. He had full use of his arms and hands. Before he left rehab, Laraine arranged a visit.

"I call on Beth to talk to newly-injured spinal cord patients," Laraine explained. "Her attitude is positive and motivating."

I watched as she pushed herself very slowly into his room. She tried to engage him in conversation and left when he didn't want to talk. She didn't understand why someone with the gift of full function in his arms and hands would give up.

Health insurance would not pay for rehab if a patient refused therapy, and knowing that, the young man with paraplegia chose to live in a nursing home. We hoped he would return to rehab later for the help he needed to be independent again. And what a wonderful thing, to take care of yourself, by yourself! It looked beyond the bounds of possibility for Beth.

The fact that no one talked to me about causing the accident amplified my guilt to an unspeakable level. Did they think I'd forget if it was never mentioned? Beth never forgave me because she never blamed me. There were times when I wished she had. I thought I didn't deserve a free pass for such a devastating injury.

Midsummer brought better news. Beth felt small sensations in her trunk and legs. Laraine called it a "return" that sometimes occurred after the shock of the initial trauma abated. Beth could feel a firm touch on the skin but not hot or cold or any degree of temperature. Translation: a tiny strand of her spinal cord remained connected at C6-7. This redefined her injury as sensory incomplete. Still, when we sat outside between therapy sessions, she couldn't feel the warmth of the sun on her legs.

"I've regained only partial feeling in my trunk and legs but still no movement," Beth explained. "I can move one finger on my left hand, and my handgrip is still weak."

Outdoors in Green Springs, one sense dominated all the others. One of the world's largest natural sulphur springs bubbled into a greenish pond next to the rehab hospital. Once thought to possess medicinal powers, the warm water of the spring showered the area with the distinctive smell of spoiled eggs. In times past, many had traveled there with false hopes, seeking miracles.

Beth's faith in the future seemed to be another false hope. Even so, when she reached her arms up for a hug, I felt grateful for arms and wrists that move. For lungs that breathe. For her ability to feel me pat her back in return.

John passed the test to be an official National Board Certified Teacher. He taught summer school and stayed on top of life at home with Ben and Maria. John also drove Beth and me to Toledo for a follow-up with the neurosurgeon. We struggled to lift Beth in the car for the first time. The angle and limited space made it difficult. Would it always be?

The doctor was happy to hear his diagnosis of complete injury had proved wrong. The connected strand in Beth's spinal cord translated to a big advantage. The ability to feel even limited sensations in the trunk significantly reduced the risk of pressure sores and other problems. She could sense when she needed to change her position on the wheelchair cushion, but pushing down on the big wheel rims to shift her weight still tested her slow-growing strength.

We viewed Beth's latest x-ray with the surgeon, a side view of the neck that showed six screws instead of 12 on the large titanium plate. The other set of six lined up perfectly behind. In spite of the doctor's impressive surgical skills, the motor (muscle) side of the equation remained absent (complete). Unattached to her spinal cord, the muscles in Beth's legs withered. No leg movement, besides spasms. No bearing weight on her legs. No standing. No walking.

No request for experimental treatments or cumbersome mechanical braces. No envy of those with expensive standers and stair climbers or those who spent long hours strapped to bicycles and machines. And no waiting for a miracle.

❧ Chapter 5 ❧
REBELLING

Bucyrus Telegraph Forum (3-24-2004): *Pressed if she has ever asked, "Why me?" Kolbe said, "No, I never did. I never did the whole grieving process thing. I was too busy during rehab. I had great physical therapists."*

THE DIRECTOR at the rehab hospital was a doctor who knew more about strokes than spinal cord injury. As she left a planning meeting about our transition to home, she told us Beth would walk out of the hospital. What? Beth and I exchanged an incredulous look. How wonderful if it were true, but it contradicted clear facts. A cut spinal cord at C6-7 and a motor complete injury meant no muscle function in the legs. Walking? Even standing would only be possible with mechanical braces—or a medical miracle in the future.

"Can you believe she said that?" Beth asked. Thankfully, it seemed to be a rhetorical question. Words failed me as I tamped down my rising anger.

"Let's go talk to Laraine," Beth said. I nodded. I wished I could read my daughter's mind. Was she getting her hopes up?

In the therapy room, Laraine paused after hearing the prediction. Her expression changed quickly and dramatically from a smile to a scowl, and she excused herself to find the director. Laraine had a few things to say about the thoughtless mistake, and the director lost my respect when no apology followed their talk.

The rest of the rehab center staff enthusiastically adopted Beth, the youngest inpatient by far. The evening aides held wheelchair races in the hallway and initiated shaving cream fights during shower time. They braided her hair. One afternoon during therapy, they emptied Beth's hospital room of her belongings, including Honeybee Bear. Just to surprise her when she wheeled into the empty room and make her laugh. The aides also teased my amiable 14-year-old about her new reputation as a rebel.

The director labeled her a "rebellious teenager" when Beth followed Laraine's advice over hers. Two issues involved white compression stockings (to improve circulation) and special boots worn at night (to prevent ankle joint contractures). Active during the days, Beth chose to wear the stockings at night instead of around the clock. Also, Laraine explained how foot drop occurred with quadriplegia regardless of footwear at night. Beth declined to wear the heavy boots, so she could roll over more easily in bed. Despite these victories of sorts, Beth lost one battle.

Laraine recommended physical therapy in warm water as a supplement to exercising on the mat and on the weight machines. The therapists who staffed the rehab pool had been trained to recognize possible health problems, yet the director refused to approve it.

"The director told me I should never get in a pool because my body would go into autonomic dysreflexia," Beth wrote. "My blood pressure would shoot up, my temperature would rise, and I could have a stroke. Luckily, my physical therapists disagreed with the doctor, but I had to wait until I was an outpatient to try their heated therapy pool."

The director also believed everyone with a spinal cord injury needed help for depression. Beth agreed to meet with a psychiatrist. After two sessions, she asked me if she had to keep talking to him. He told her she was in denial about her disability. It amazed me how easily she dismissed his judgment as a minor nuisance, with no need to argue or to change his mind. I asked about finding another professional for her, and Beth responded with a laugh and a firm no. We stopped the sessions.

"Her counselor seemed a little distressed because she didn't go through the textbook stages of depression, anger, and denial," John told a reporter later. "Beth's attitude has been positive from day one. I tell people that she is the one who carried me emotionally."

Beth talked openly about her injury. "I always knew I was just going to get stronger and get back to my life as soon as possible."

She asked about the details of her disability. Even with discouraging answers, she approached her life as a quad in a matter-of-fact way. Hour by hour and day by day. As though it were merely something she had to do.

"You don't really have time to cope with things," Beth said. "You just kind of get thrown back into the world."

The inpatient stay at rehab for those with new spinal cord injuries in the neck often exceeded three months. Beth decided to cut her stay short to start high school on time in late August. She planned to leave her Green Springs hospital room after only two months, with two weeks at home to adjust before school started. She refused to weigh the merits of tutoring, the easier option. No matter that she was pale, tired, and susceptible to infection. No matter that she could wheel herself a very short distance before her arms trembled and exhaustion set in.

"Life is about making choices," Beth said later in a speech. "At this point, some people may have taken a year off of school to rest and build their strength at home. I wanted to start at Tiffin Columbian High School with the rest of my freshman class."

I officially quit my job for what I thought would be a long-term role as a caregiver. One afternoon in early July,

John stayed with Beth while I turned in my work keys. At the Tiffin Center's workshop, I ducked into a little-used hallway and closed the door to my office. I organized my room and the literacy program for my replacement.

I filed incomplete projects, haunted by the dozens of residents I'd worked with. Most looked forward to our sessions, often a pleasant reprieve from monotonous days. I wished for more time to say goodbyes. Instead, I justified walking away. My other option, talking individually with many residents, would disrupt the routines and frustrate everyone. Residents lived with a revolving door of caregivers because staff left the center regularly for easier jobs. I took no comfort in the fact that I wasn't the last to leave.

A work friend knocked on my office door to express sympathy. She had a son in Beth's class. He questioned the parrot gift, because wouldn't Beth need a wheelchair more than a pet? In tears, I left co-workers, residents, and a meaningful job behind.

As I pulled into the rehab parking lot, John waited for me. I held my breath when I saw the look on his face. Awful scenarios flooded my imagination. More tragedy, more cut flowers dying slowly. I rushed out of the car, and he reassured me that nothing bad had occurred.

In my absence, Beth asked John to put her hair up, something he'd never done before. He could make a ponytail, just not the right way. She tried it herself, again and again, stopping only to wipe away tears of frustration. John felt worse than she did.

We held hands and watched afternoon therapy. One of the therapists had put Beth's hair up for her. Laraine leaned on her back during a push-up. With a contagious laugh, Laraine set a high bar and a new challenge. Once Beth could push her off, the need for physical therapy would end. Another unrealistic goal?

Therapists became trusted friends and advisors. Amy, Crystal, or Jill took over when Laraine moved on to another patient. Between therapy sessions, Beth and I sat outside in the summer sun. Since Beth was shy, Jill teased her about watching the cute mower boys working on the extensive grounds. The talents of the therapists included steady reassurance and constant reinforcement.

"Beth worked long hours in rehab," Laraine wrote later, "learning to feed and dress, move about in her wheelchair and moving from place to place from her chair. To do these tasks, innervated muscles need to be very strong and much of her day was spent weightlifting and exercising."

Beth weighed every decision on the metric of possibility, on whether or not it *might* advance her relentless goal to be less dependent. On weekends, she asked me to help her use the weight machine and cable pulleys in the empty therapy room. She included exercises for the trunk and abdomen, hoping to avoid the "quad belly" caused by weak stomach muscles. I resisted the urge to grab the pulley for her.

At our first wheelchair clinic at rehab, experts measured Beth for her own chair. I encouraged her to make the days easier with a motorized model for the freedom to go long distances independently. Most quads used heavy, bulky power chairs and then for back up, a smaller, lighter manual chair. Big motorized chairs required a van or another large vehicle with a lift. Manual chairs fit in cars.

Beth had one question. "Will I get stronger faster using only a manual chair?"

Laraine paused and smiled before answering with a simple yes, clinching the verdict. Beth's new manual wheelchair would fold at the seat to fit easily in the trunk of a car. I let her make important choices since between the two of us, she was the emotionally stable one. I also thought she needed to feel in charge of her life since so much of her body was out of her control.

At Beth's request, John replaced our vehicle in the crash with a car instead of a van with a lift. I suggested the Ford Taurus wagon, my favorite car in the Tiffin Center motor pool when I drove residents into the community. The front passenger door opened wider than most to accommodate a wheelchair.

Beth's friend Lizzy asked to have her birthday party at the rehab hospital. The staff agreed. Lizzy and her mom Deb decorated a meeting room with four other girls and brought in party treats. We sang around a cake with 14 candles.

Green Springs turned out to be a perfect fit.

"Rehab was a great experience," Beth wrote. "I was too busy to think about what had happened to me or to become depressed. Every new thing that I accomplished, like eating independently or lifting an extra five pounds during physical therapy, became a celebration. I was in another world. My family was always there. My best friends visited me often and even moved a birthday party to the rehab center so I could be there."

"The therapists and nurses became a second family to me. Everyone was so nice. My night nurses would always come in and talk to me."

After dinner, Beth and I took turns reading aloud from the brand new *The Goblet of Fire*, the fourth Harry Potter book and a gift from my former boss. We loved the earlier books in the series. Beth could hardly hold the book even though it rested on a small table over the bed. I used clothespins to keep it on the right page. At first, turning pages on her own was impossible. We put one of the fat tubes around a pencil, and Beth used the eraser end to turn a page. That worked until weeks later when she patiently figured out how to use her hands to accomplish the same job.

Ben's former English high school teacher, Betty Kizer, stopped by to visit after seeing us in the therapy room. She asked about the Harry Potter series and planned to read them herself.

"I first knew Beth Kolbe after the car accident when she was in the same rehabilitation center as my father," Mrs. Kizer wrote in a reference letter. "Beth was so pleasant that I stopped in to see her every time I visited my father."

Beth's shortened hospital stay added a sense of urgency. On productive days, I made a list in the morning and drew boxes before each task. Prioritized, of course, though the day often moved in another direction. I focused on what Beth needed and what to do next. Averse to pity, I avoided everyone except my family. Even with John, Maria, and Ben, the last thing I wanted was to cause them more worry. I made a heroic and ultimately futile attempt to bottle up my emotions.

I researched shower chairs and hospital beds while Laraine and Beth planned for therapy three times a week after school. Beth chose a bed without side guards and with a motor hidden underneath to raise the head or the foot. Elevating the head of the bed helped prevent respiratory infections. I realized later that I should have bought one that also raised the entire bed, to reduce my back strain.

The full-size hospital bed would fill our one first floor bedroom. Instead, we converted the living room to Beth's bedroom to give her more space. I sewed a lining on the window curtains. John removed the carpet and laid linoleum to make the floor less challenging to wheel across.

Our house had no air conditioning. Since Beth's body temperature didn't regulate, we replaced our old furnace and added central air. Spending or saving money seemed equally irrelevant to me.

My co-workers at the Tiffin Center built our first wheelchair ramp, a long one from the back door of our house to the door of the detached garage. We appreciated their amazing generosity.

"It felt like the entire town rallied around us," Beth told a reporter. "At the Tiffin Center where my mom worked, people donated months of their vacation time for her so she could stay with me, and my dad had meals cooked for him while we were at the hospital. We even had people come over and build a ramp at our house. Everyone kind of just pitched in."

A high school supervisor called me to set up a meeting at the school. I attended with Beth, John, and an occupational therapist from Green Springs. Beth expressed no concerns about her first year in the sprawling building or her inability to do almost anything. I obsessed over every aspect, trivial or not. Plain small tables for desks would be ordered, one for each of her classrooms. The therapist determined the perfect height for the adjustable table legs to accommodate her wheelchair.

With an elevator under construction, the first in the school, a few of Beth's classes would relocate temporarily to the ground floor. A new ramped side entrance would be ready for the start of school with automatic electric doors, right next to new handicapped parking spots. The construction surprised us. The principal said building accessibility had been long overdue. Our accident pressed the issue though others would benefit too.

At the meeting, I asked for an exception to the school's policy of no cell phones. Granted. I planned to meet her at school during lunch, and I requested a cot even though Beth didn't think it was necessary. She couldn't get on or off a cot by herself. The principal offered to convert a storage closet with an attached bathroom into her private locker room. They added a narrow mat table of cushioned vinyl to serve as a cot.

Beth's favorite idea of mine allowed her to choose a friend to sit next to her in each class. She couldn't stop the muscle spasms in her legs. When one or both bounced straight out, rigid, her best friends could safely bend the knee to break the spasm and put her foot back on the wheelchair footrest. They also agreed to photocopy their class notes and handle her books and backpack.

The high school staff offered extraordinary support. With over a thousand students in the building, the principal recommended that Beth leave each class five minutes early with an assigned friend to avoid the crowded hallways. He also suggested one set of her textbooks stay at school and a second set at home.

With medical absences anticipated, the special education teacher offered extra time to complete assignments and the use of pocket-sized tape recorders to record missed classes. Beth agreed to the recorders for two of her classes, Advanced Cell Biology and Spanish. Her modified schedule dropped physical education and band. Two study halls included one at the end of the day that she could skip to leave early. Three afternoons a week, we'd drive straight to Green Springs from school. The other two weekdays, she could nap at home.

Therapists visited our house to make recommendations. The greatest concern involved our one tiny bathroom, with no time for construction before Beth came home. They suggested a specific shower chair on wheels. It attached to a metal framework over the bathtub. Theoretically, she could slide in the shower chair over the tub and then back. I also purchased adaptive equipment to help with everything from zippers and buttons to handwriting and typing. I fastened forearm supports on the lip of the computer table. I didn't hesitate to buy anything that might help even though the sick leave pay donated by my co-workers ran out. I closed my only retirement account and deposited my pension in our checking account.

I signed our family's first contract for basic flip cell phones, one for me and one with enlarged buttons for Beth. Cell phones had been around for years, but there didn't seem to be a need before. I set up my number, our home phone, and her friends' numbers on speed dial. Beth pressed a phone button with the index finger she could move a little. When in school, she would turn off the sound and only use it to call me if she needed anything.

The same day, I received a call on our home phone from an acquaintance who worked at the Tiffin hospital. She mentioned my complaint letter and apologized for "my perception" of the night of the accident—then proceeded to confirm the events I wrote about. Polite, I repeated the purpose of my letter. Emergency doctors in small hospitals should perform a basic physical exam for anyone in a serious accident since patients may be in shock and be unaware of health problems. In response, she said I could stop by for the tetanus shot I should have received. She ended the call by apologizing again for "my perception." I said goodbye and hung up the phone, suddenly furious about her comments and upset at my intense reaction. I decided to avoid the local hospital in the future.

I talked to the therapists about our need for the best doctors after rehab. Laraine introduced us to Dr. Julie Miller, a Toledo pediatrician who specialized in physiatry, the study of physical medicine and rehabilitation. We liked her immediately. With an engaging smile and the ability to listen intently, Dr. Miller patiently addressed the issues on my long list. The widespread trauma of a spinal cord injury assaulted the body's immune system, making infections common initially.

I appreciated how she spoke thoughtfully, sometimes drawing on her experience with her husband, a quad. She agreed to be Beth's main doctor after inpatient rehab. At that time, Dr. Miller would write a prescription to try water exercise, and therapists would be prepared for the possibility of autonomic dysreflexia. After dealing with the Green Springs director, we welcomed the advice of an expert.

When Beth hugged the rehab nurses and aides goodbye, she could sit up for long periods of time in her own blue wheelchair, get a loose grip on the big wheel rims, and push the rims to slowly move the chair. With taxing exertion, she rolled her body on a flat bed to get more comfortable or to attempt getting dressed. Weak and wobbly, she sat up by herself and put her shoes on and off though she couldn't tie the laces. With effort, Beth could shift her bottom on the wheelchair cushion to prevent pressure sores. She ate and drank mostly on her own and kept trying to use her hands. She moved from the wheelchair to the bed more easily —with total help and an oak sliding board, newly made by my dad.

The sunny August day when we left the hospital room behind felt like a fresh start. In the back seat of the car, on top of medical supplies, the antenna of Honeybee Bear bobbed in the warm breeze. I returned Beth's smile, hiding my apprehension over what the future might bring. No longer needing the neck brace, the titanium plates fused to bone, Beth tilted her head toward the open car window, happy, as we turned up the radio and drove down the country road in the direction of home. A co-dependent team, we plunged into uncharted waters together.

❧ Chapter 6 ⚗
PUSHING

Beth: I had a small group of very close friends who helped me in many ways.

THE EXCITEMENT of leaving Green Springs evaporated with the realities of an inaccessible world. Home again after 12 weeks in the hospital, Beth couldn't wheel herself up the low incline of our ramp. Opening the refrigerator required colossal effort. She couldn't pick up anything heavier than a small water bottle. Still dropping things often, she drank from a plastic cup with a lid and straw. Her livable space shrunk without the second floor and basement. The hospital bed and a huge standing birdcage dominated the living room. From the top of a tall dresser, Honeybee Bear watched over us. A computer desk, couch, and TV crowded what had been our narrow dining room. The table in the kitchen left a tight path for a wheelchair, even with one less chair.

Beth requested a special dinner for her first night home. John grilled barbecue chicken while I cut a watermelon and made macaroni and cheese. After dinner, shower time. I set the frame of metal rails and legs in and out of the bathtub. A difficult transfer from the bed to the rolling shower chair wore me out. She slumped to one side in her new robe. The door of the bathroom opened into the kitchen and needed to stay open for me to attach the steel frame to the shower chair. So much for privacy. After I somehow managed to slide her over the bathtub, I stepped inside the rail frame to close the door.

I bunched the plastic curtain between the rails, leaving me little room to assist. Beth mostly washed herself, but she wasn't in the wide-open shower at rehab. When she dropped the soap or washcloth, I knelt down and reached around metal and human legs. Water soaked my jeans and the floor. Frustrated, she asked me to finish.

With the bathroom door open again, I fought with the rails to release the shower chair. I resisted the urge to give up and plop down in the flood. I babbled about a new bathroom, assuring Beth we'd enlarge the current one. A fantasy. Our house sat on a narrow lot, and a major addition required demolishing our one bathroom. We should have initiated construction right after the accident.

I slept in Beth's former single bed, relocated to the small first floor bedroom and close to the hospital bed several yards away. My responsibility doubled—tripled—without the safety net of rehab nurses. Everyone depended on me. In the dark, I recognized nothing of who I was before the accident. I'd become a diminished shell of a stranger. In the quiet, my heart broke again with the agony of regret. Self-pity shamed me. Sharply intense melodrama controlled my nights while Beth's shallow breathing whispered with the sighs of the old house. I watched her sleep, trusting and tranquil, her pretty face showing no trace of the swelling from the initial steroids or the glass cuts.

For her second shower at home, we tried a white plastic bench with a long seat. Two of the legs rested in the tub with the other two on the bathroom floor. Beth kept both hands planted on the bench and concentrated to stay in a wobbly sitting position, making it impossible for her to help. Creating more tension than the shower chair, the bench made the whole process worse, not better. Rushing to finish, I put her bathrobe on and asked Ben to help me carry her directly to bed where she'd be comfortable.

We lifted Beth awkwardly with her wet legs slipping in spasm. She looked away, tears welling. I swiped at my eyes and resolved to try harder, to be better. When Ben walked away after, he probably had tears of his own. Life challenged all of us. I stored the plastic bench in the basement and practiced on my own with the metal shower chair and rails. At bedtime, I hugged everyone until they pushed away.

Three days after Beth left the hospital, her new pet arrived to stay. The intelligence of African Gray parrots has been compared to that of a three-year-old child. Emotionally, the "terrible twos" aptly described our newest member of the family.

Beth chose the name Timber since he could not perch well, sometimes falling from a hand to a lap (tim-berrrr!). She also had a crush on Justin Timberlake, the boy band heartthrob. The parrot baby stood nearly a foot high with striking gray and white shading. He demanded frequent attention.

Three times a week in physical therapy, and every day at home, Beth tried to do more and more. She resolutely pursued vague, elusive benefits that might or might not materialize in the long run. I felt pathetic in comparison. I created a few short-term goals for myself with guaranteed rewards, goals like aerobic workouts or replacing soda with water. I failed. I possessed a fraction of her tenacity at my very best, and an eon had passed since the last time I felt at my best . . . . all the way back to when Beth was born.

I remembered clearly the day she arrived. When I held my youngest for the first time, I embraced the euphoria. I had not expected the pregnancy to end well. Surgery to close the cervix with a band in the first trimester preceded bed rest, bleeding, contractions, and hospital stays. My mom called Beth a miracle. I knew she would be my last baby, and I paid more attention. To baby sounds and smiles, yes, but also to the intricate petals on my African violets and daily bursts of joy with Maria and Ben. What a privilege to be home with them.

My young children shared their magical world with me while a mild tension headache quietly crept in and out of my days. I anticipated a simple cure and wouldn't take any medicine, over-the-counter or otherwise. Dire causes came to mind. Determined not to be a hypochondriac, I nevertheless established my first life insurance policy. I tried massage, biofeedback, chiropractic, allergy shots, homeopathy, vitamins, diet changes, and a new bite plate. The results of blood work and an MRI of the head were normal. I had my eyes checked and saw an ear, nose, and throat doctor.

The doctor suggested a same-day procedure at the hospital to clear a sinus blockage that might be contributing to the headache. I should have said no. In the recovery room afterward, I sensed something was wrong. I told the nurse. The doctor returned, and when he helped me sit up, blood flowed freely from my nostrils. I lost too much blood before the emergency surgery that required an additional week in the hospital.

When Ben started first grade, I babysat six little girls in addition to my two, every school day. Hours looped in a crescendo pattern around a constant mild headache. By the time my youngest entered first grade, I worked full-time at the Tiffin Center, unable to appreciate the low level of an endless headache and unaware it would progress. The beauty of small moments faded as my ability to multitask grew. I tapped into that skill after the accident by preparing for worst-case scenarios.

Before I drove Beth anywhere, I filled a backpack with a thermometer, Tylenol, Band-Aids, antibiotic cream, water bottles, extra clothes, and more. I added quarters and a list of emergency numbers in case our cell phones didn't work, and I needed to use a pay phone. I checked and double-checked before putting the pack over the back handles of her wheelchair. One afternoon, I added her gym shoes with the rest. Beth's chair tipped backward on an incline with the too-heavy pack, and I barely caught it in time.

A sludge of sad emotions filled my aching head. I acquired the diagnosis of depression at 23 as a new mom, but my Tiffin doctor didn't tell me. He wrote it down instead. When I read the diagnosis later, I thought it labeled me weak and ungrateful. The doctor had to be wrong.

Over the years that followed, I realized he was right. Extended times of melancholy brought more than just sadness. I lost interest in reading, sewing, walks, and other things I usually enjoyed. Most episodes began with no apparent reason. Others had a trigger, like when my favorite grandma died. My headache also flared, a band of pressure around my head and aching across and behind my eyes. I drove to Columbus to my first pain clinic after refusing to take any drugs for years, even Tylenol or Advil.

A doctor at the pain clinic diagnosed me with a mental illness again. Still, I rationalized it away. My excuse for depression? The headache. And vice versa. I needed an excuse since the diagnosis created a conflict in my mind. How could I be depressed when I cherished my family and felt loved? I also had a meaningful job and many other reasons to be thankful. Part of me understood the connection between body chemistry and depression. I ignored that part and clung to the belief that I'd be fine—as soon as all my ducks lined up in a row. Better sleep, better food, better exercising, better relaxing, better thinking, etc., etc. Healthier, tougher, wiser. Or something.

Around the same time, I joined a chronic pain support group in Tiffin. Affiliated with the American Chronic Pain Association, a basic tenet emphasized the need to accept pain. I dropped out after a few months. Accepting pain clashed with my belief that around the corner, I would beat it. I minimized my headache with my family, and the support group didn't understand. When my unruly ducks finally cooperated, my headache would evaporate.

My new doctor at the pain clinic didn't understand, either. He talked about my depression, fibromyalgia, and chronic fatigue, all things I did my best to deny and ignore. Struggling with a high headache, I agreed to try prescriptions for the first time. I started with Celebrex, an anti-inflammatory, along with two antidepressants. Nothing eliminated the headache completely.

My mood improved with the antidepressants, and Celebrex lowered the base level of my head pain. Until Beth's injury.

Weeks after the car accident, my doctor doubled the medication doses, ordered an x-ray of my left thumb, and made two referrals. One to a psychologist for counseling and one to a surgeon for my dislocated thumb. With more immediate concerns, I put his referrals on hold. I also declined physical therapy for my sore neck. The medicine fell short, even with twice as much.

Deep depression equals real pain. The fervent need to care for Beth was the only thing pushing me out of bed every morning. I braced myself for recurring waves of anxiety and guilt. Steady support from my family kept me upright.

My days revolved around disability. I watched Maria come and go to band camp, volleyball, softball, and voice lessons. I missed the trips to Taco Bell with my girls where we talked over burritos and sodas. Ben finished his summer job as a research assistant and packed to return to OSU.

Before Ben left for his second year of college, we gathered for a family dinner. I carried a bowl to the table of Hungarian paprikash with dumplings, a favorite, while John teased, "How was your good day?" It was the question he asked at our dinner table most days when our children were small, followed by sharing the positives of the day. John and I also had insisted on politeness with word choices like "please be quiet" instead of "shut up" and no colorful language. After the accident, those rules melted away, trivial in the face of loss.

John organized his new sixth grade classroom at the middle school for a new school year while I shopped with my girls. We searched for the holy grail of school clothes: the perfect jeans. High-rise, low-rise, baggy, not baggy, long, extra-long. I helped Beth try on zippered jeans while she sat in her wheelchair inside the fitting rooms. A major workout for me. It was much easier for me to change her clothes when she was in bed. She exhausted herself in efforts to help me, but her strength had increased only marginally. After fighting to try on two pairs of jeans at the store, I bought ones that *might* work to try on later at home in bed.

I hated how people stared openly in public. Before we left the mall, a woman asked Maria about her sister's wheelchair.

"Some people assume I'm not intelligent because I am in a wheelchair," Beth wrote in ninth grade. "They talk loud and slow when they first see me. When I do normal things such as moving around or crossing a threshold, some people will tell me 'good job' like it is the most amazing thing."

Beth replied to the lady's question with a matter-of-fact statement about the accident. The woman responded with pity and the mindless phrase about God not giving anyone more than they could handle. What? How could anyone say that, ever? At any single moment, millions and millions of people on our planet dealt with much more than they could handle. The numbers of suicides kept growing. I assumed the rude woman meant well, but her God seemed devoid of compassion.

Platitudes failed on many levels as we frequently heard, "Everything happens for a reason." Really? Even if Beth's life turned out to be happy and fulfilling, fate and miracles would have nothing to do with it. Many quads lived in isolation, ignored and forgotten.

A gentleman from the Tiffin Shriners organization met with us. Local members drove patients and parents in an accessible van to and from the Shriners Hospitals. The Chicago hospital, a five-hour drive each way, included a specialized clinic for children with spinal cord injuries.

A week before the start of school, I dropped off a summary of Beth's medical status to the principal to be shared with her teachers. The serious document detailed deadly health risks. The principal asked me if I had a current teaching aide license. I did, and he offered me a part-time position in a program for at-risk students. A job at the high school where I could be available to Beth. I paused, surprised, before accepting on the spot. He asked me to meet with a supervisor on the first morning of school.

I hurried away, suddenly winded with a tightening chest, thudding heart, throbbing head, and dizzying view. Why did I say yes? I had none of Beth's courage. How much would she need me? How many school days would be missed?

At home, Timber screeched and squawked in an impressive range of piercing, demanding sounds. We attempted to take him out of the cage only when he wasn't yelling, but he would not be ignored. I cared for the needy bird baby the most since I wouldn't ask for help. The moody parrot had a tougher time adjusting to being home than his owner.

Beth hosted a Saturday movie and popcorn party at our house with her favorite friends. Ellen had been her best since the year I picked them both up from morning kindergarten and babysat in the afternoon. Ellen had a beautiful voice and shined in choir. Beth and Ellen met Lizzy in junior high, all of them shy and quiet. Lizzy shared the same name as Beth, Elizabeth Anne, with the middle one spelled differently. A natural nurturer, Lizzy loved children and dogs and babysat often. The fourth was Jackie. With a fun sense of humor, her strengths aligned with art and drama.

"My friends have been very positive," Beth said, "and treated me just like everyone else."

Lizzy and her mom Deb surprised Beth with an extraordinary gift, an elegant silver and gold ring with a small diamond. The word HOPE had been engraved inside the band. Five friends wore identical rings and had planned to pay for their own and share the cost of Beth's. Instead, the Osterman Jeweler's manager in Tiffin donated all six rings.

I wondered about the meaning of the inscription. For Beth's friends, perhaps the hope of her walking again? For Beth? Probably the general hope for a happy future. And for me? Small, specific hopes like fewer infections and antibiotics. Anything more could be wishful thinking.

A typical teenager in many ways, my youngest wanted to look her best for the start of school. Our dentist put a cap on the tooth chipped in the accident. Beth asked for a haircut and her first highlights. I made an appointment at my usual salon where the entrance had a few steps.

Laraine taught me how to bump the wheelchair up steps. Positioning myself behind Beth's chair, I stood at the bottom with my back to the steps. Next, I tipped the chair back slightly, stepped up and back, and pulled up on the chair handles, letting just the big back wheels roll up the steps to the top landing. Going down, we repeated the process, both of us facing backward. I let gravity roll the big wheels down the steps. Beth didn't think twice about the details of access.

At the salon, staff fussed with a rickety ramp. Inside, we squeezed through several staring hairdressers and customers as Beth's legs bounced in spasm. Our stylist pushed the usual rotating seat out of the way to make room for the wheelchair. After foil strips added blonde strands, inches of thin brown and blonde hair fell to the floor. The length stopped at her chin with long fringed bangs to one side.

That evening, my daughters posed with Timber for pictures. Beth looked starkly pale compared to her sister. Maria spent the summer on the softball field as well as the football field where she played drums in the high school band. I wrote thank you notes for the gifts we received after the accident and mailed them with a picture of Timber and the smiling girls. My tendency to minimize included the injury and its impact.

A rare intense storm ushered in the first day of school, complete with hard driving rain, lightning, thunder, and high winds. I planned for extra time but when I parked near the new automatic doors, most students had already arrived. I pulled the wheelchair from the trunk, unfolded the seat, plopped the cushion on, dashed to Beth's open door, scooped her legs over the doorway, grabbed the outside seam of her pants, and lifted her to the wheelchair. Beth still wanted me to fix her jeans in the gusty downpour, but Maria said she would adjust them inside. The umbrella Maria held broke so when the girls hurried into school, they left a trail of water down the hall. I needed to meet with my supervisor, but I rushed back home first to change out of soaked clothes.

Frazzled and sick to my stomach, I grabbed a dry towel to sit on before I drove back to school.

My new boss asked me to fill out papers at the employment office to allow me to start the next day. I checked my phone often, waiting for Beth to call. Returning to school at lunchtime, I exhaled when I found a smiling teenager waiting for me by her private locker room. She couldn't turn the round doorknob or unlock the door with a plastic key holder. Even if she could, she'd have to ram her chair forward into the door with enough force to keep it open as she wheeled through the threshold. I returned her smile, grateful for her forgiving view of the world.

"Kids stared a lot at first," Beth said in an interview later. "They wanted to get my attention, to talk to me, to see how I had changed. I was already used to being stared at. They thought they would offend me by confirming that I use a wheelchair, as if I didn't know. Most of my classmates only knew me as the shy volleyball player that I was before my car accident, but everyone was welcoming and supportive."

The strand of sensation that remained connected to Beth's spinal cord caused aching in her low back from sitting too long in one position, even with shifting her weight on the cushion. She looked paler than usual and completely drained. I suggested leaving early with me for home, a futile request. After school, I moved her to bed where she fell asleep quickly. While she napped, I ordered a textured grip cover for the locker room doorknob and a different kind of key holder.

The second day of school, I followed both girls down the hall from a distance, purposely looking at the floor on the way to my job. Most people avoided me. Perhaps they didn't know what to say or maybe they respected my obvious desire to be left alone. Checking in at the school office, I noticed the photo of my girls and Timber posted on a bulletin board with one of my thank you notes.

I followed my supervisor's lead in the classroom as instructed. I usually tutored 10th graders in math. Glad to not have more responsibility, I genuinely liked the students. Under different circumstances, I'd seek connections and ways to be a positive influence. I'd be concerned about their choices and advocate for their future. Instead, I kept my distance, my well of worry already overflowing. Would Beth attend school enough days for me to keep my job? And how soon would we be rushing to the hospital in a crisis?

❧ Chapter 7 ❧
EXHAUSTING

Beth: *I began high school as a different person than I was in junior high.*

DEADLY RISKS of quadriplegia threatened. Imminent. Waiting. I called off work for Beth's high fevers and doctor visits. Humbled by the physical onslaught of shortened school days, she worked ahead on assignments whenever possible, determined not to fall behind. With hours of homework most nights, she stubbornly refused to accept extra time, partly because it would accumulate.

Every morning exposed a higher than usual level of congestion or coughing or fever or fatigue or infection or nausea or spasms or swelling. The days cast a vulnerable light on my students and Beth, on family and friends, on humanity and me. At school, my thoughts vacillated from tutoring to tragedies that could happen any moment. I jumped and hurried to the door when Beth sometimes knocked on it for my help. My supervisor didn't object to the extra breaks. A few times I left work early to take Beth home or to the doctor though most school days, we shared a lunch break while she melted into the cot, both of us stretched too thin. She appreciated the cot—the same one she thought wouldn't be needed. After the first month, she could unlock the door with a key holder, turn the round knob covered with a textured cover using both hands, and push the door open with her chair.

At about 2:15 p.m. on weekdays, I collected my coat and headed to the automatic doors of the high school. The same double sliding doors they installed for Beth. A memorable day in mid-September, the doors opened and wind misted my glasses with rain. I stepped back in the building, away from the door sensor, to wait for Beth.

I watched her wheel down the hall toward me, slower than usual and without her usual smile. And, more pale than earlier that day at lunchtime. Not a Green Springs therapy day, she could nap before an appointment that evening. A reporter had asked to interview her for a feature in the local newspaper.

At home, I transferred her to bed. Her fever prompted a debate since infections could escalate quickly.

I read a thermometer. "It's 101°. Let's get it checked out here in Tiffin." She understood that I meant driving to the local pediatrician's office instead of the hour drive to Toledo to see the physiatrist.

"No," she said pleasantly, but firmly. "Help me up. I need to start my trig homework."

"You need a nap more," I said.

"I want to get up!"

I stood still as we stared at each other.

"Please," Beth added. I was about to help when she added, "I'll do it myself."

Not on my watch, I thought.

It was my turn to say no. If she tried to get up by herself, she would fall. She had poor balance and little strength. So, I played the mom card. Must nap. Stubborn, she started the difficult process to sit up in bed, the first steps for the transfer.

Whatever patience I started the day with was long gone. In a fierce burst of frustration, I grabbed the wheelchair and moved it away from the bed, out of reach. I left the room while she protested. Not a proud moment for me.

She gave in and fell asleep a few minutes later. Relieved, I wiped my eyes and pulled a blanket over her shoulders. I also moved her wheelchair back to the bed.

That evening, a reporter interviewed Beth and also asked me a few questions. The article that followed in the local paper included my quote. "She has a great future ahead of her. We're feeling like things are going to be okay."

The quote haunted me with words I wished were true. Great future? Would she even survive the first year? And when I said, "We're," it accurately described the rest of the family but not me. Okay? Not okay. My identity? Gone, along with the world I knew. My fears sharpened on Beth's poor health and my dismal expectations including the impending demise of her optimism.

Four months after her injury, she asked to go out and away from me for the first time. We met Ellen, Jackie, and Lizzy at Tiffin's Heritage Festival, a tribute to pioneer days with booths winding around Rock Creek through Hedges Boyer Park. Beth and I agreed on a plan to separate and reunite later, our cell phones within easy reach. I quietly recommended the concrete path to Beth instead of wheeling on grass. John and I talked to another parent and watched the girls.

They walked next to Beth down a grassy slope, knowing she preferred to push herself. A wheel caught on uneven terrain. Eager to help, one of the friends pushed the handles at the back of the chair and tried to overpower the bump instead of tilting the front wheels over it. Beth tumbled forward to the ground. John and I rushed over and lifted her back in the chair. She seemed breakable though not hurt. That time. I reluctantly watched her leave again down the same grassy slope. From the apprehensive faces, it appeared to bother all of us except Beth. More trial and error would be needed to navigate the wheelchair safely around Tiffin and beyond.

Another day, Lizzy's mom picked Beth up. "The first time I took the girls to the mall," Deb said. "Beth's wheel fell off her chair, and we had to use one of the mall's wheelchairs which was awful. I was a wreck and all the girls could do was laugh!"

The friends commenced a long tradition of meeting most weekends, with Beth's time away from me limited unless they gathered at our house. I sometimes drove the girls to and from their homes. I wondered if the other parents worried about my driving.

Jackie's dad made a wood ramp to cover their front porch steps. I maneuvered the wheelchair in and out of houses until Beth taught Ellen, Lizzy, and Jackie the safest way to handle a few steps: an extra spotter for safety and *not* facing the bottom, a sure way to fall for a new quad in a manual chair. We couldn't imagine the flights of stairs they would learn to master.

Beth preferred to sit on the couch or floor in living rooms, leaving her wheelchair empty. Her friends learned wheelies. My youngest didn't have the strength or balance to roll back and forth on only the big back wheels. When the girls lifted Beth back into the wheelchair, they automatically pulled down the extra fabric at her knees. Her focus on jean to foot perfection did not lessen though she tended to be more particular with family than with friends. Inexplicably, other aspects of disability did not faze her.

In choir, Jackie bumped Beth down two wide steps in the music room. One morning, a wheel turned, tipping sideways. After a flop to the floor, they burst out laughing. My 14-year-old daughter described the scene that autumn. "My choir teacher pretty much freaked out at first and he got me back into my chair really fast. It was funny!"

Curtis King, the concerned music director, offered to change where she sat to avoid the steps though Beth declined. He had called John after the car crash to offer a sympathetic ear, touched by her "I can still sing" comment.

Beth, Maria, and Ben had inherited perfect pitch. Their grandmothers sang for weddings in times gone by. During long drives, including trips to volleyball tournaments, my girls belted out favorite songs with the radio. After the accident, Beth's lung capacity limited the strength of her voice but not her love of music and singing.

Time blurred. At physical therapy, Laraine and Jill talked to my exhausted daughter about taking care of herself. Weekends focused on recovery and sleep. One Saturday, we helped with a training seminar for therapists at Laraine's request, the first of many. Beth shared her transition from her inpatient days in Green Springs.

"Wheelchairs were the most common sights, everyone was completely accepting, and nothing about my injury seemed out of the ordinary. High school was different."

After answering questions, Beth moved to the mat table. She followed the same steps preceding each workout while Laraine described the muscle mechanics of the exercises. Five months after the accident, progress showed with less hand over hand guidance. Even so, Laraine caught Beth when she tipped too far forward as she tried to release the brake lever. She needed several boosts to scoot over on the sliding board and then sat up on the mat independently.

We received a gift at our first appointment with Dr. Miller, a prescription to try physical therapy in the warm water pool. We agreed to put off scheduling the sessions as Beth started a different antibiotic for another respiratory infection. I asked about the spinal cord injury clinic at the Chicago Shriners Hospital. Dr. Miller encouraged us to go. I hoped the clinic would put a few of my fears to rest. Wrong again.

In Green Springs for outpatient therapy, I noticed a wheelchair with painted plastic discs covering the spokes. I bought a clear set of discs online and hosted a party to decorate the covers. New to high school, the friends chose to paint blue and gold designs to display school spirit. Go TCHS, Columbian Tornadoes, #1. At Beth's request, I attached the covers on the big wheels with Velcro for a football game. I sat with John at the game and watched Maria play drums with the band. The stadium had no wheelchair access in the stands, so Beth stayed with two friends near the cheerleaders on the track surrounding the field. She didn't ask to attend any more football games that season.

The fall Homecoming Dance introduced the logistics of dressing up in a wheelchair. Many aspects required consideration. The length and width of the skirt. The placement of any ribbon to avoid the spokes. The style of the dress and how it draped over the body. I bought an earlier version of Spanx at Beth's request. I sewed a wide elastic strap in a circle to hold her knees together under the dress — a few years before crossing one leg over the other served the same purpose. Most dressy shoes slipped off during leg spasms and transfers, and we shopped at several stores to find a perfect pair with a strap along the back.

The evening of the dance, John and I dropped Beth off at the high school. Her sister and friends were already inside. Beth's new fancy shoes fell off during the transfer from the car to her chair despite the back strap. With the shoes back on again, I adjusted the sleeveless black dress several times. I worried more about social aspects than physical details, concerned about Beth's expectations. She refused our help to wheel up the sidewalk to the main entrance of the school even though she couldn't begin to open the heavy glass doors.

From the car, John and I observed Beth's slow, labored ascent on the long incline. Another little action turned into a grueling challenge. He expressed amazement at her tenacity and how easily she took the leap of faith that someone would let her in. Someone did. At home, waiting for her phone call, I braced for a negative outcome. Was this a turning point? How much vulnerability could she carry as a new quad and as a new freshman at her first high school dance?

After, Beth wheeled to the car with barely worn shoes on her lap and her three best friends alongside. Bursting with enthusiasm, the beaming girls talked nonstop. They all wore the HOPE rings. Most had not been taken off for weeks. I dropped off her friends, then asked Beth if she danced. Silly question. She *loved* the new experience of dancing in her wheelchair. I had stressed needlessly again. I pushed my pessimism down the road with the crisis of the moment averted.

Maria arrived home later that evening and told me how Beth danced most of the night in groups that included boys. Maria and I had shared tears over the shock of the accident, survivor's guilt, and the limits of a C6-7 injury. The night of the dance, after Beth's pure joy in life, we hugged and cried again.

Our new normal continued to feel strange. My typical school day started before dawn. One morning before school, Beth's favorite jeans weren't clean. Maria spoke up in my defense and helped me diffuse her sister's frustration, a feeling expressed only with small things not related to her disability.

With one bathroom and two teenage girls, I set up a hair and makeup station by the utility sink in our small laundry room with two mirrors, one on the wall for Maria and a smaller one on a table. I put on Beth's jeans and shirt and drove the girls to school. I waited until they entered the building before I followed. The classes I helped in varied from calm to crazy. I talked to a manic girl determined to beat up another student. I tutored an angry boy through an in-school suspension.

During my lunch break, I shared peanut butter sandwiches with Beth in her private room. She left marks near the bottom of the heavy door with her dogged determination to hold it open enough to wheel through. After two more classes, I met her at the car about 2:15 p.m. On Tuesdays and Thursdays, she fell asleep at home by 2:30 p.m. The other three weekdays, I drove straight to outpatient rehab.

Beth started with 30 minutes of occupational therapy, then exercised much longer on the mat and machines in physical therapy. I usually walked around the sulphur pond, a little less smelly in the cool fall weather compared to summer. How many moms had walked the same path before me, hoping for healing? We usually left Green Springs about 5:30 p.m. in the dark.

Driving at night triggered new anxiety for Beth. She watched the road nervously and overreacted to every small thing. I reassured her that I must be the safest person to drive with. Knowing what it felt like to be too tired, I would never let that happen again. Regardless, her fear generously encompassed anyone behind the wheel at night. Even so, she didn't let it prevent her from going where she wanted or needed to go. I encouraged her to close her eyes and rest in the car but at night, her fears kept her eyes open. Hyper-vigilant.

Beth's anxiety made me sad, knowing I caused it. She couldn't relax until we pulled in the driveway at home.

Another new worry focused on the gasoline level in the car. If she noticed the low gaslight, she asked me to fill the tank right away and remained uneasy and frustrated until I did.

After therapy, we arrived home tired and ready to eat. Not a focus for either of us that fall, food merely served to shut down hunger. We ate simply and gradually lost weight. Boxes of Kraft macaroni and cheese, Beth's former staple, no longer filled my cupboards.

Essays, lab reports, and other assignments filled the time after dinner on weekdays. Initially, I typed while Beth dictated. After a few weeks, she typed herself, aiming for specific keys with the one finger she could move a little, the left index, with help from her thumb and the built-in mouse. She didn't like the typing aids with rubber tips I bought, one for each hand. She also asked me to remove the forearm supports attached to the computer table.

I interrupted homework for the time-consuming shower routine with the annoying metal chair and rails. I asked Beth about selling the house to buy one with a better bathroom for a wheelchair. She insisted we stay in the only home she'd known. Some nights, I passed out after 10 p.m. with her working on homework in bed. She couldn't turn off the lamp on the nightstand until I replaced the usual on/off switch with a piece of plastic in the shape of a big plus sign.

Left alone most days, a crabby parrot greeted us when we returned. Timber directed his complaints at me. He woke at the same time each day, a noisy alarm clock. With his cage near Beth's bed, John and I alternated freeing him early on weekends so the girls could sleep in. During my turn to babysit, Timber sat on my shoulder while I folded laundry or cleaned or rewrote my to-do list.

Always a step behind, my personal goal each day involved getting through the hours without crying in front of anyone. I walked a tightrope, afraid of a long fall. All the while, Beth set unnecessarily high standards for herself. Pushing herself around in the manual wheelchair sapped her stamina. She continued to grope with uncooperative hands to attempt zippers, buttons, and shoelaces. I stepped back when she tried something on her own.

Beth needed help almost all of the time. Resolved to be whatever she needed me to be, I waited and watched for subtle signs to assist—a pause or a sigh or a look. I played a guessing game to anticipate the variations from morning to night and day to day. One thing she *always* attempted first: putting her hair up in a ponytail. I found no magic elastic. She fumbled with a typical round band several times before handing it to me. I tried to be patient even though my personality bent toward lists, to more work and less rest. Productive. Check. Efficient. Check. Too busy. Check. The same traits that contributed to my ultimate sin of falling asleep at the wheel.

For the first OSU choir concert since the night of the accident, John drove us to Columbus on a different route to avoid the crash site. When another car cut in front of us, I shrieked involuntarily, instantly deluged by fear and sorrow. I apologized for my overreaction before closing my eyes and pretending to rest, breathing deep until I couldn't feel the rhythm of my heart in my head.

I watched and listened at dinner before the concert, grateful John could easily carry the conversation. Ben told us about his change of majors from honors engineering to physics and English. Beth and Maria called him a genius because he aced the Advanced Placement Calculus test and the math section of the ACT, with every answer correct. I loved to listen to Ben as a child on taped recordings, reminders of the joy of being a new mom with a beautiful and busy little boy. We shared the best conversations about his number charts and projects including a re-creation of the

Sesame Street movie, "Follow That Bird." He called it "Follow Your Bird."

During Ben's last year of high school, my depression had intensified, knowing he would leave home for college. I wasn't ready for him to go. I needed tissues through each senior event, from concerts to plays to ceremonies. Instead of appreciating every moment with him, John and I overreacted when he asked for a later curfew and argued unnecessarily. Letting go was hard.

I talked to Ben privately before his concert since he seemed down. It was reassuring to hear he'd started counseling at the college health center. Everyone in my family struggled in different ways after the accident. I asked Maria about counseling, but she declined. I wished I could do more for them. I had changed all of us.

When we hugged, I reminded him, "Let us know if you need anything, okay?" I realized my mom said the same thing when we parted.

Ben tended to be quiet like me and didn't like to talk long on the phone. I stayed in touch with occasional care packages and emails. I read books on the syllabus of his New Zealand Literature class and asked him for book recommendations from other classes. My favorite, "The Things They Carried" by Tim O'Brien, was sad but reinforced my pacifism through stories about soldiers in Vietnam. My holiday cards always focused on peace. Every year when snow started to fall, I stitched together felt dove ornaments by hand to give away as gifts, a tradition from my first winter at home with a baby. After the accident, my streak of 19 years ended.

One cold morning before school, Beth had a low fever accompanied by congestion and a shallow small cough that clearly indicated the weakness of her lungs. We argued when I asked her to stay home even though I didn't want to call off work again. She insisted on going to school. When I transferred her from the car to her chair, I hit an ice patch, and we both slipped to the ground. Maria helped me lift Beth back up, but my rocky composure tipped over a sharp edge.

I tried to hide unrelenting tears. A few people noticed. I told them my head ached, no big deal. If pressed, I gave assurances that it would let up soon. My head did hurt, but that wasn't the biggest problem.

At home after school, I checked her temperature and scheduled a doctor's appointment for the next morning. I moved a wheezing Beth into bed, elevated the head, and rushed to give her medicine and water before she fell asleep. She repeated the frequent request to not let her sleep too long. A stack of homework waited. She needed the rest more, but I rarely won that battle.

Alone in the quiet, my control collapsed. More than anything else, I needed to function day to day. Beth depended on me. No one could care for her as I did—beyond guilt, beyond love.

When John arrived home, I shared the immediate problem: my low odds of getting through another school day without falling apart. He knew about the headache and nightmares, but I had worked hard to mask the rest. Always a good listener, John pushed me to quit the aide job and call the psychologist. I agreed, with relief. He suggested going out for dinner. No, thank you. He offered to call for a massage appointment for me. No, thanks. John made dinner while I scheduled my first session. We thought counseling would help.

❧ Chapter 8 ❧
FLOATING

Beth: *I immediately loved the water and the freedom I had in it.*

DURING A BRIEF respite from antibiotics, Beth set in motion a far-reaching odyssey. One that would encompass extraordinary events in and out of the water.

Two therapists held her up in the warm water rehab pool, one on each side and both on the lookout for autonomic dysreflexia that did not occur. After basic stretches, Beth asked to float on her back, a complicated endeavor with no command of the lower body. Fully supported on her back, she wanted them to let go. They resisted but eventually agreed to move their hands a few inches away. Hands that swiftly rescued her a moment later. They tactfully suggested shoulder exercises. Beth talked them into more floating attempts.

The second time at the pool, the therapists bent to Beth's pleasant persuasion again, positioning her body horizontally and letting go, over and over. They also demonstrated how to roll over after being face down, but she couldn't do that or anything else in the water.

Jill assisted by herself at the third session. Experimenting, Beth discovered that waving her arms underwater allowed her to float for a few seconds, with the bonus of moving in the direction of her head at the same time. Kind of like a backstroke without the stroke. Even so, she tipped under after a short distance and she couldn't get to the edge of the pool by herself—or back up to breathe.

With more sessions, more practice, and more sinking, Beth floated incrementally longer on her back through sheer force of will. She also figured out how to work her arms with a flurry of effort to pop her head up and take a quick breath before going under a second later. At the edge of the pool, she held herself up with both hands on the wall, then tried and failed repeatedly to get on her back without help. Weeks later, Laraine and Jill watched on the pool deck as another therapist stayed close to Beth for the last water therapy session.

At one end, she attempted to float on her own, unsuccessfully. Sinking, she awkwardly worked her arms, raised her head, reached up to the wall, and caught her breath. After another try, she positioned herself on her back. She waved her arms underwater to stay afloat and to move very slowly across the small pool. Eventually reaching the opposite wall, she grabbed the ledge with effort, using both hands. In an impressive feat of balance, she achieved a floating position independently again and dragged along a sinking trunk and legs through another lap.

"Once she entered the water, wow," Jill said. "It was awesome!"

"I discovered I had good water technique and was able to keep myself afloat pretty well," Beth told a reporter years later. "Not at the beginning. It obviously took me awhile to learn how to swim."

At a time when every movement on land required focused exertion, she found unexpected freedom in the water.

I expected to find help at my first counseling session. I thought the psychologist would bestow at least a smidgen of peace, with more promised on the horizon. I hadn't talked about causing the accident since the half hour with the therapist at rehab in Toledo.

I hesitantly walked up stairs to a small office. I sat on a plain couch across from a woman in a chair who wrote on a clipboard. As the floodgates opened, I tore off a seeping scab of guilt. I felt like *I* should've been injured instead of Beth, but no deity had intervened. With no faith in fate, I carried the blame. The defining mistake of a bad mom with a cruel penance.

Even as a little girl playing with dolls, I somehow knew that being a mom would be my leading role. Life revolved around that certainty. Encouraged to write at a young age, I had imagined typing at a desk while young children played at my feet. Utopia, where the ideal mom loved, nurtured, and protected. When the car flipped in the field, my identity as a mom shattered along with the bones in Beth's neck.

The therapy session exposed a raw nerve and a dark abyss. Tears offered no healing. When the sad hour drained out, I sat in the car in the parking lot and sobbed, haunted by Beth's fragility and my own. Completely losing control terrified me, especially when I needed to take care of her more than anything else. I dreaded the future and expected her outlook to cloud and crash. When it did, would I be able to function at all? I hoped for help at my next appointment or maybe the one after that.

A community of support waited in an unlikely place. Beth and I entered MCO's rehab unit on a school night. The look we shared validated her earlier decision to go to rehab at Green Springs instead.

The Northwest Ohio Chapter of the National Spinal Cord Injury Association gathered in the therapy room. (The nonprofit changed its name later to United Spinal.) Family centered, the large group included several Laraine alumni and others of all ages and abilities including members of the Raptors wheelchair sports team. Deb O. extended a warm welcome to us and introduced Beth to the other teenagers. Most had spina bifida from birth, making them wheelchair masters from an early age. Timid through the meeting, Beth listened with interest about annual events including the wheelchair games and a summer fishing trip. I also overheard a hushed conversation between two parents about a young quad who died on the way to the hospital from a stroke caused by autonomic dysreflexia.

The holiday season lost its appeal. Prolonged efforts to look normal sapped my energy. Life hurt in every possible way. I fought to hold back tears. I avoided people and neglected friendships. I dreaded the social interactions required at choir concerts and other school events.

"How are you?" echoed from well-intentioned acquaintances. How did they expect me to respond? I would never share my regret in the high school lobby. I refused to be a lightning rod for pity. When questioned about Beth, deadly risks came to mind. Instead, I briefly commented on her attitude and found an excuse to retreat. How many people looked beyond Beth's big smile? Did they think the stars aligned to illuminate an easy path for her?

Timber screamed when I pushed his cage into a corner to make room for our artificial pine tree. With everyone busy, I decorated most of it myself. A red glass cardinal topped the tree. Instead of nostalgia, the sweet ornaments made by my kids reflected lost innocence in a ruthless world.

Not accustomed to my company during school days, Timber cried out for my time and for a major behavior plan. I made another attempt to reward him when he wasn't yelling, a rare occurrence. I never let my babies cry though I eventually gave up on our neurotic bird toddler. I fed him and cleaned up after a growing irritation. I'm sure he felt the same way about me.

One Saturday before Christmas, the party of the spinal cord injury group filled a big hall in Toledo. Beth asked me not to park in a handicapped space, to leave it for those who needed it more. It turned into a common request.

Beth and her new friends freely used the words quad or para (paraplegic) to refer to themselves, an affirmation of sorts, a belonging within an accepting community. No one at the party reacted to the slurred speech of cerebral palsy or jerking limbs or a urine bag showing below a pant leg. Scars showed, some healed, others not. In view of that litany of limitations, my private battles paled in significance. Despite the obvious perspective, my negativity wouldn't budge and generated senseless comparisons.

A wide gulf separated two typical hands with 10 functioning digits from two damaged hands like Beth's with one finger that moved a bit. It seemed like miles between standing for a few moments and her inability to bear any amount of weight. Standing made transfers and changing clothes a cinch in comparison. The people at the party understood the complexity of movement. They also knew my daughter's dimpled smile did not erase the challenges of quadriplegia.

In the buffet line, I expected to hold Beth's plate. She put one on her lap and let me help only with items she couldn't reach. For the first time, she picked up an open cup full of punch. It dripped over the top as her left hand compressed the plastic with the tenodesis grip. The bottom side of the same hand slightly pushed one of the big wheels while the right hand moved the chair forward since one-handed wheeling turned a chair in circles. She willingly, almost defiantly, accepted the inevitability of small spills along the way and the bigger risk of dropping it. Tense, I followed her slow progress to a table where she concentrated on releasing the cup with care. Someone else had brought his own cup with a lid and straw. A minute later, Beth picked up the wet cup to take a drink. It slipped from her grasp, the liquid pooling on and off the table. Since her clothes stayed dry, no big deal. I cleaned it up and grabbed a new drink cup without asking her first.

Other parents offered me mostly effortless conversation. We lived in the same world, one with the added dimension of disability. I heard stories of spina bifida at birth and the onset of multiple sclerosis, of wins and losses. When asked about Beth, I sidestepped the question of blame. They enthusiastically shared details of the Ohio Wheelchair Games in May when the Raptors paid for a hotel room for each member of the team. In a rare display of caution, Beth chose not to participate. Instead, she asked to visit Ben in Columbus the same weekend, so we also could watch the Ohio Wheelchair Games at OSU.

Christmas arrived, normally my favorite family time. Beth played N'Sync holiday music, Ben beat us in Scrabble, John called me Cindy Lou Who, and Maria created music mixes on CDs. We also visited grandparents, aunts, uncles, and cousins on the Lake Erie shore.

After my grandma passed away in 1995, my parents moved from Lorain to the family homestead in Vermilion. Built by my great-grandfather in 1885, it never failed to invoke broad chords of memory. For me, the farm would always be a haven tinged with sadness without Grandma Henning. The farmhouse also was inaccessible in every possible way, from the stone driveway to the tiny bathroom that didn't fit a small wheelchair.

The house in Lorain where my in-laws lived also was inaccessible. Avoiding stress on my sore thumb, I let others bump Beth up and down many steps. John's oldest sister Jean greeted us at the door. She liked the wheelchair and wanted one of her own. Jean, born with Down syndrome, counted down the days to each family birthday and holiday. She knew her January birthday arrived before John's in February.

Every Christmas, he teased her that his birthday was next, both of them mischievous.

Back in Tiffin, Timber welcomed us home. I printed photographs from the holidays to put in an album. My smile in pictures contradicted my outlook but not my goal. I wouldn't give the people I loved more to worry about, especially after I accomplished that spectacularly well with the accident.

Hell-bent on making sure everyone enjoyed the holiday break, I accompanied Maria and Beth to the mall and Taco Bell. We made popcorn and watched "The Princess Bride" again. John and I planned a date night at a nearby restaurant where I set my phone on the table next to my plate. He said a principal informed him that many families don't stay together when something like Beth's injury happens. The comment irritated John because it made no sense at all to him. I felt the same way. I kept the rest of the conversation safely away from my headache or guilt or sadness. Sometimes I wished he could read my mind but not at the risk of bringing him down. He deserved better.

John and I played bridge with Ben and Beth using new bigger playing cards. A piece of molded plastic held her cards vertical in front of her. By the end of the evening, she put the plastic to the side and experimented. When Beth held the cards in her right hand with the tenodesis grip, she could lift up a specific card with her lips and use her one moving finger from the left hand to set the card on the table and adjust the others.

Beth and I created a mess in the kitchen with my grandma's brownies from scratch recipe, and her best friends arrived to usher in the New Year. She christened her new fondue set with a pot of chocolate and an elaborate spread that included brownies, marshmallows, pretzels, and fresh fruit. They camped out in sleeping bags. How easily the girls laughed while they watched a new movie, *The Grinch*, played with Timber, and ate dipped treats. It seemed as though none of them had a harsh disability.

The New Year brimmed with brewing threats, with an emergency only a heartbeat away. My initial flash of fear when the phone rang waned only after I heard appointment confirmations or band fundraiser details. For the first time, I understood the compulsion to feel better through food. That didn't work but not for lack of trying. I joined the ranks of emotional eaters and had to buy clothes in the next size up.

During my weekdays alone at home, the TV stayed off. No reading or resting or relaxing. I turned into a certifiable detail queen. The family planner and medical coordinator. The laundress and maid. The errand runner and cook. The supply tactician and insurance whisperer. So much to do. So many emotions to suppress.

Even small tasks seemed daunting through the lens of depression. Endlessly busy, by obligation and necessity. Emotion slammed me with sharp dichotomies. I appeared calm while I imagined disasters. I loved my family but drowned in heartache. I had no spinal cord injury and fought with disabling pain every day. I returned Beth's smiles but waited to cry alone, the guilt spilling over in waves. How could I contain it? My psychologist had no clue.

Each session, my answers to innocent questions inevitably spiraled down to raw fears about everything out of my control. The floodgates opened every session and didn't wash away any guilt or pain. I convinced myself that one day, one not-too-far-off day, a session would help me. It had to.

At the end of each day in a quiet house, I checked off final details. Restful sleep had been a problem for years. After the accident, I relied on medicine to help me fall asleep. I woke up several times through the night, always aware of the headache before I opened my eyes. Part of a chorus with other pain. Dismal thoughts warned me not to lose control. I checked on Beth, grateful she slept well.

Eager to get back in the water, she asked for a schedule of open swim times at Green Springs. I never—ever—suggested going to a pool. Life felt too overwhelming without it. However, I rarely questioned or discouraged her ideas. I was the last person who should say no.

In the warm water pool at rehab with me instead of a therapist, Beth moved from the wall into a floating position by herself after tipping and sinking twice. Far from mastery. She asked me to let her go in the middle of the pool. Without a wall to hang onto, she tried to keep her head above water and get on her back. A teenager willing to take risks (overestimating her abilities?) and feeling invulnerable. A parent hanging on tight and hesitating to allow failure for a task with little or no hope of success. I compromised and limited underwater dips to critical seconds.

After, the rehab locker room overflowed with elderly ladies in various stages of undress, getting ready for a class. Beth asked me to pick up a pool schedule at our local YMCA. I talked to Laraine to find out if a typical pool with a cooler temperature could trigger autonomic dysreflexia. She said yes. I needed to be alert for flushing skin, a pounding headache, sudden changes in heart rate, dizziness, and more. I put a blood pressure monitor in the swim bag.

At Tiffin's one indoor pool, I lowered Beth from the wheelchair by myself to the deck and into the cool water. No scary symptoms surfaced. The pounding headache belonged to me. I stayed nearby in the water and followed her leisurely motion back and forth, arms waving under the surface. It appeared to be somewhat smooth sailing, but I knew better. Turning around at the wall alone required strenuous exertion. Less than 10 minutes with frequent long breaks made her arms tremble.

The lifeguard didn't know how to operate the sling lift. I faced the pool and squatted at the edge of the deck. With Beth's back to the wall, I reached under both of her arms and pulled up, thoroughly scraping her back. I couldn't lift her from the deck to the wheelchair and had to ask the lifeguard to grab her knees while I lifted under her shoulders. Others stared as both legs extended in bouncing spasms. I bent her knees and put her feet back on the footrests as quickly as possible.

The second time at the YMCA pool, Beth's foot twisted in the metal of the wheelchair when I lowered her to sit on the deck. She felt no pain. However, spasms intensified in her legs, her body's indicator of a problem. Too early for a stress fracture to show, Dr. Miller examined the swollen foot and a clear x-ray. The doctor told us the foot would heal on its own since Beth could not put weight on it. Dr. Miller also prescribed a muscle relaxant to tone down strong spasms that made falls more of a risk. Because spasms also could be useful, the low dose would not eliminate them.

Laraine showed Beth how to shift her trunk to trigger a leg spasm that bent her knees, an invaluable skill for changing clothes in bed. Lying on her back with knees bent, Beth hugged her legs up and over her body. Feet in the air, she put a pant leg over one foot to begin, the opposite of what most of us do (putting a foot into a pant). After the pants bunched at her knees, she pushed down on her thighs to straighten her legs. Rolling from side to side with effort, she pulled up the fabric a little at a time by hooking a belt loop with her left index finger—the one finger she could partly command.

She let me take over for the final stretch after trying and failing to budge the zipper and hook the button. She refused to wear clothing with alterations except for flip-flops, her preferred footwear. I added a piece of thin elastic around the back heel and sewed it to the side straps to hold them on. Getting in and out of cars sometimes scraped and smudged her unprotected feet, a consequence she judged as acceptable under the circumstances.

When her legs swelled, purplish and puffy, Beth used her new skill to deliberately trigger a leg spasm to stretch the muscles, move the blood, and reduce the risk of blood clots. Staying active, she cast aside the white compression stockings. Except for hospital stays.

The first crisis struck on a brittle January morning, eight months after the accident. The nurse at our pediatrician's office took one look at Beth and led the way to the doctor. He ordered chest x-rays at the local hospital, the place I vowed to avoid. I relented to get a quick diagnosis, still resolved to never let my family be treated there. After the x-rays, we waited while they called our pediatrician. He told me on the phone about Beth's pneumonia. I interrupted his plan to admit her to the Tiffin hospital. With his consent, I immediately called Dr. Miller who sent us to Toledo. I focused on the icy roads to keep my breathing steady.

Admitted to intensive care at the Toledo Hospital, Beth had never been so sick before. Her childhood asthma returned stronger than it had ever been. Extreme, relentless, uncomfortable symptoms alarmed us. Every labored breath ended in a wheeze. Her weak cough could not clear her lungs. Her fever spiked too high repeatedly despite strong IV medicine. Her blood pressure, low since the accident, jumped higher, a close call with autonomic dysreflexia.

A team of pediatric lung doctors closely supervised Beth's care during the days with breathing treatments six times around the clock. At night, a nurse checked on her frequently and called a doctor more than once to increase her medication.

Four bad days melted together with no improvement and little rest. I fixed pillows, offered fluids, and read aloud, unnerved at how little I could do. A nurse carried the few get-well flowers out of the room to remove possible allergens. A doctor talked about surgery to dislodge the mass in the lower lung. He also showed me how to do physiotherapy by pounding her chest and back with a cupped hand.

On the fifth day, Beth could breathe a bit easier. John had dropped off homework, and she asked to see the pile for the first time that week, a testimony to how sick she had been. She never wanted to fall behind. The sixth day, an x-ray showed a smaller pocket of pneumonia. The doctor made a discharge plan for the seventh day and ordered strong IV antibiotics to be given by a nurse at our home through a PICC line.

An intern started to thread a tiny tube through a vein in Beth's right arm to her heart—with no pain medication. Even though she didn't have full feeling or function in her arm, the discomfort was intense. Her left hand suddenly touched mine, her eyes wide. I questioned the pain and was told that the procedure was almost over. I hugged one side of Beth, both of us in tears, through 10 more minutes. Pure exhaustion amplified our apprehension about leaving the hospital.

The first evening at home, a nurse connected the IV antibiotics to the PICC line and left before it finished draining. Beth's upper right arm heated, swelled, and reddened. My fears came to life, and I called Dr. Miller in a panic. I couldn't stop myself from crying on the phone. She told me to disconnect the IV. If the swelling went down, we should drive to Toledo in the morning to take out the PICC line. If it didn't, Beth would need an emergency room that night. After stopping the IV and turning on the nebulizer for a breathing treatment, I lay down on the hospital bed beside Beth. I hugged the arm with the PICC line, afraid of another crisis. Would she be admitted to the hospital again? Would the leaking vein cause other problems? Would her pneumonia clear without IV antibiotics? Would I lose her over this? I checked her arm through the night.

Dr. Miller met us in Toledo on a Saturday morning to remove the line and prescribe strong oral antibiotics. I apologized for my embarrassing phone call the night before. I made a poor joke, placing the blame for crying on a week with little sleep. I asked Dr. Miller and other doctors a critical question, "How can Beth be as healthy as possible?"

The lung doctors recommended the flu shot and pneumonia vaccine. They all agreed on the priorities: stay active, sleep and eat well, drink enough water, treat congestion, watch for signs of infection, avoid skin breaks, treat skin issues seriously, and go for regular checkups.

My only personal health goal was to stop gaining weight. I convinced myself that if I drank enough diet soda, I could maintain my weight despite the unhealthy habit. Since the accident, Beth gradually lost a little extra weight without trying.

After two lost weeks, I carried a nebulizer to school at lunchtime for her breathing treatment. Pneumonia set back her stamina by months. A shortened day of school wiped her out again.

The completed elevator led to second floor classes. I wrote a detailed fire drill procedure on how to carry Beth down the stairs and helped a therapist from Green Springs lead the staff training. Several teachers volunteered to attend. The principal had bought a heavy vinyl sheet like firemen used. Beth described the process in a homework assignment, an essay about chemistry in daily life.

"With the vinyl sheet on the floor next to my chair, two teachers lower me onto it, careful to keep my neck supported as I lay down. They really don't need to be so careful. After my car accident, doctors reinforced my neck bones using titanium plates and screws. Four teachers lift the vinyl sheet using four sets of handles, two on each side, and down the stairs we go. Behind us, another teacher carries my chair."

Mrs. Kizer, our new friend from rehab, volunteered to lead the process. Beth's Spanish teacher wore a football helmet to make her laugh. Concerned about hitting her head on a step, they lifted the sheet high with extreme caution.

"It took a while for them to realize I don't break," Beth said, reminding me of her new favorite saying, "I'm not broken and I don't need to be fixed."

She put up with fire drills but disliked being carried outside on the vinyl sheet into a crowd of students. Sometimes when teachers knew about the drill ahead of time, Beth talked them into bending the rules with an unplanned stop at the bottom of the stairs to lift her into the wheelchair. From there, she pushed herself outside.

A close friend changed classes with her so riding the new elevator turned into entertainment. Beth accidentally bumped the alarm button and nothing happened. Hitting the alarm on purpose became a joke as well as wishing for elevator music or singing N'Sync's latest hits. The girls also flirted with cute boys on crutches, injured athletes who also used the elevator.

Draining school days and demanding assignments persisted. Beth's essay about the vinyl sheet and the titanium in her neck won first place in a National Chemistry Council contest. Happy about the $500 prize more than the national win, she bought two tickets for us to attend a summer concert of her favorite boy band, N'Sync. Plus a hotel night after the Michigan show with another mom, four friends, and me.

I convinced Beth to take a day off of school to go to the Shriners Hospital. I expected to find reassurance. I also hoped it would help me come to terms with the health risks of quadriplegia. Instead, it added more.

❧ Chapter 9 ❧
BREATHING

Beth: *When I began water therapy as part of my physical therapy, no one expected me, a quadriplegic, to ever move in the water without someone holding me up.*

OUR PNEUMONIA WINTER gave way to spring before Beth felt well enough to request swimming at the YMCA. At home, she attempted to put on a bathing suit by herself, much harder than other clothing but accepted my help to pull it up. At the pool, I stayed with her in the water, watching as she floated on her back and waved her arms gently underwater. She stayed at the walls for frequent breaks and increased the number of laps little by little. I lifted her out of the water carefully to avoid scraping her back. Even so, the concrete walls left her lower extremities with slow-healing abrasions. She wouldn't consider any kind of protective coverings for her legs or feet, except for waterproof Band-Aids on the worst of the scrapes.

Early on a chilly morning, Beth and I met two Shriners volunteers in Toledo where we left our car and boarded their van. The friendly drivers, one the grandfather of Beth's friend, lived in Tiffin. The drive to the Chicago Shriners Hospital lasted four hours. They went out of their way to make us comfortable.

The van stopped at the front doors of the hospital. We parted ways with the drivers at the lobby check-in desk after their promise to find us at the end of the day to drive us home. The receptionist apologized for the extensive renovations underway on each level. Beth and I sat with

other parents and children in a colorful waiting area with
toys and books.

The friendly head of the spinal cord injury clinic
explained the routine at our first appointment. We would
meet individually with each member of a large team
including a physiatrist, urologist, orthopedic surgeon, social
worker, occupational therapist, and physical therapist. At the
end of the day, the entire team would convene with us to
make recommendations.

After initial appointments and x-rays, we learned
about more health risks for quads. Damaged back muscles
changed the spine and worsened curvatures. Beth acquired
two new diagnoses. I'd never heard of kyphosis, an outward
bowing of the back. I understood scoliosis, a curvature
sometimes resembling the letter S. As a teenager, I wore the
Milwaukee back brace, a now-antiquated treatment for
scoliosis. Leather pads covered most of my pelvis and
connected to a metal bar that curved out in the front to end
with a chinrest. I wore the brace 23 hours a day, making three
years of middle school and high school more awkward than
usual.

The day at the Shriners Hospital ended with a
meeting with all the experts. They had plenty to say. If the
curving and bowing of Beth's back continued to worsen, her
organs could be damaged. Major surgery would be needed
to straighten the spine with a metal rod. The urologist talked
about common problems with surgery recommended down
the road. The occupational therapist suggested hand splints
be worn every night; she custom-made ones for Beth with
bright colored Velcro earlier that day. The doctors also told
me to contact a Tiffin dermatologist to remove a mole on her
neck next to her long scar. Overwhelmed, I agreed to return
to Chicago with Beth in six months. In the meantime, I
needed to schedule visits with Dr. Miller, a dermatologist,

and the Toledo lung doctors. We would also need to see the local pediatrician for recurring infections.

Instead of alleviating my stress, the Shriners visit added to it, though I appreciated the doctors' honesty. I added skin cancer, a metal rod, and more surgeries to my ocean of anxiety. Through long nights at home, I had a new recurring nightmare. I ran through a fog, alone and desperate to get to a very urgent destination, to a loved one in distress. Then, my legs suddenly buckle, too weak to carry me. I can't move.

The dream left me unsettled and shaken, but I didn't wake up John in the basement bedroom. A light sleeper, he often had trouble falling back asleep and a teaching job in the morning. I also didn't want to worry him.

Beth's therapy continued at Green Springs after school. The occupational therapists agreed with the Shriners therapist who recommended hand splints. We met another young woman with quadriplegia who proudly showed us her hands on the padded armrests of a power chair. She had straight fingers, the result of a long, concerted effort with hand splints and stretching exercises.

Beth's new rigid splints extended from fingers to elbows and interfered with her sleep. She asked her favorite therapist for advice. As always, we heard both sides of the issue.

Laraine explained how some people slept well with hand splints and wore them religiously, with straighter fingers to show for it. However, for C6-7 quads like Beth with no hand function, straight fingers could hinder the ability to grasp items well with the tenodesis reflex. That fact made it an easy decision for Beth. She threw away the splints and chose more function over form.

She owned wheelchair gloves but rarely used them since she preferred the ones with individual fingers that exposed the tips of her fingers and required extended time to put in place. With growing confidence, she never hesitated to extend her contracted fingers and calloused palm when meeting new people, not concerned about how her hands looked or felt.

In sharp contrast, I worried for Beth, for me, for the rest of our family, and for the world. About everything, endlessly. I couldn't fully appreciate the occasional good news, like the normal skin biopsy results from Beth's removed mole. In the car, I couldn't stop myself from crying out when anything startled me, regardless of who drove. In those moments, fear instantly transported me to the anguish of the accident. John pointed out that the things I reacted to were minor. I agreed, but I couldn't control my instant visceral reaction.

The relentless headache dug in deeper, filling the space behind my eyes. Sadness and regret spilled over. I talked to the psychologist about pain. The wild melodrama in my mind created real fear of losing control, losing my mind, and losing a loved one. She told me guilt could resemble grief and offered some advice: find things to look forward to. In other words, stop waiting for a tragedy. Stop imagining Beth in her wheelchair answering phones in a dingy office cubicle.

Certain I'd ruined Beth's life, I needed a way to erase the injury and her losses. I wanted nothing less than the world at her fingertips, with digits she could feel and move. At the same time, her optimism spread to encompass any number of paths in the future. She talked to Laraine's physical therapy students in Toledo every few months.

"I was one of a few panelists who shared our experiences and answered many questions," Beth wrote in a school essay. "I also participated in the hands on part with Laraine showing specific techniques. Then the seminar participants tried the exercises with me while we talked. I hope it helped them understand a patient's perspective a little better and also to see that a quadriplegic can do more than is usually expected."

The panel included a young married quad who showed the students her intricate embroidery while her adorable toddler played nearby. Another quad, an older man, seemed annoyed when his leg straightened suddenly. He broke the spasm by leaning forward and pressing a fisted hand at the back of the knee on the same leg. A process my daughter would practice and duplicate endless times.

"Beth's insights and down to earth presentations enlighten students and motivate them to challenge the spinal cord injury patients in their care," Laraine wrote in a reference letter.

After the panel, Beth started her physical therapy routine. Transfer out of her wheelchair with help, lift an inert leg onto the mat table with a now-stronger arm, and sit up slowly on her own. As she sat in the long-sitting position with her hands in her lap, Laraine gently pushed and prodded her trunk. Beth stayed upright most of the time, winning the battle of balance. The students clapped.

To end the demonstration, Beth wobbled through the steps of the ending routine independently. She slowly tied the laces of her shoes by using her teeth to tighten the bow.

Laraine asked her to share the progress on her ongoing ponytail quest. Beth scooted forward in her chair before leaning back to anchor herself. She put a standard elastic band around her left index finger and left thumb. Her right wrist lifted the hair up from the nape of her neck. With effort, she used her head as an anchor for her hand to push the hair through the elastic band. It worked, but it wasn't tight enough. She kept trying to find a way to loop the band around a second time to hold the ponytail in place, determined to do it on her own.

A dinner at a restaurant followed the seminar. It felt good to laugh with Beth and her extraordinary therapist. I couldn't imagine where we'd be without Laraine.

Against my advice, Beth sang at tryouts for the high school musical, *Guys and Dolls*. I stressed about her taking on too much, the week in the hospital fresh on my mind. During tryouts with Ellen and Jackie, she bypassed the stage steps and wheeled the long way to the stage through the choir room.

I drove Beth and Maria to and from musical rehearsals, and we shopped for costumes at Goodwill. When a tornado watch started with a rehearsal underway, I returned to school early to pick them up and hurry to our basement.

Ohio's annual tornado season escalated in significance for my family. Before the accident, John monitored the weather during watches, and we rarely camped out in our partially finished basement. No more. Beth felt compelled to heed each warning and watch at once, so we carried her down the steep basement steps. She couldn't relax until everyone stayed in the basement, including Timber. The growing parrot sat heavily on her shoulder and played with her hair while she finished homework. When Timber hopped onto the papers in her lap, she prompted with his first words, "up up," for him to jump on her hand.

One stormy midnight, Beth insisted on a family trek to the basement during a long tornado warning, not a watch. She admitted her tornado anxiety was similar to her response to the low gasoline light in the car and driving at night. I suggested we ask Dr. Miller to recommend a good counselor, but she emphatically declined.

One weekday afternoon while Beth stayed home with John, I sat in the bleachers at a softball field watching Maria play on the high school team. A hard hit ball connected with the head of a girl from the other school. An ambulance drove right onto the outfield with lights blazing and sirens wailing. A friend told me Maria was upset. The ambulance brought back unwelcome memories. We hugged behind the bleachers in tears.

The first anniversary of Beth's injury came and went without discussion. It didn't seem to faze her, other than an appreciation of how far she had come.

The annual regional choir contest had been at Tiffin Columbian on the date of the car accident. Early that morning, I set up the concession stand in the cafeteria. I heard my girls sing, then we left for Columbus. A year later, the choir contest took place out of town.

Curtis King, the director, complained when he couldn't reserve a handicapped-accessible school bus. Beth didn't mind driving with me. I brought a book along and opened it as I leaned against a wall at the school—to discourage other parents from talking to me. I also perfected the art of hovering at a distance to be available for Beth. She sang with her ninth grade choir, and Maria had a solo in the Women's Chorus. The Tiffin choirs earned high marks as usual. Without being asked, Mr. King and his father built a portable ramp to the lowest riser, so Beth wouldn't be the only choir member on the stage floor. His unexpected kindness would be repeated by many in other times and places.

I drove to Columbus on a Saturday in May for an event marked on our calendar for months: the first Ohio Wheelchair Games since her accident. The Toledo Raptors team stayed two nights in a hotel. We visited Ben and watched some of the games.

With frequent accessibility problems of one kind or another, we witnessed an impressive exception at the new Jesse Owens Memorial Stadium at Ohio State. Beth had no trouble wheeling in the stadium stands by herself to watch the track events. Lower than usual inclines allowed for independent wheeling. On other ramps, I walked next to her, holding the closest handle on the back of her chair and discreetly helping while she pushed the big wheels.

From the stands, we cheered loudly for our team. They raced on the new track in specially designed racing chairs built low and long. A teammate offered to let Beth use his racing chair. I smiled when I heard her say she'd compete in the track events at the next games, in one year. Beth didn't consider races in the pool since she couldn't actually swim a stroke. Yet.

The high school's Individual Education Plan for Beth focused on access. Special desks, leaving class early, the private locker room, and getting down the steps during fire drills. At an IEP meeting at the end of the school year, the principal asked her what she needed. She surprised me with a request: a place for a wheelchair in the student section of the stadium for home football games. She also mentioned the problem of others being too helpful. When someone grabbed a push handle on the back of her wheelchair, she reached around and lightly smacked their hand with her fist.

"I realized that my biggest challenge would be to insist on doing things myself and to become independent again," she said. "At the risk of sounding corny, people are generally kind, so it was my responsibility to speak up for myself."

As summer vacation began, we recruited our relatives for a Beth-inspired project. We built an extended deck beyond our garage and 130 feet of raised wooden walkways through her dad's large backyard garden.

A cookout coincided with a workday as aunts, uncles, and grandparents arrived to help. John and Ben grilled barbecue chicken. Maria made a strawberry pretzel dessert. Beth handed out a steady supply of cold drinks from the coolers. She also shared her enthusiasm for floating at the YMCA.

Beth prioritized friend time during her first summer at home with a spinal cord injury. The girls made N'Sync posters and wrote "2001 Pop Odyssey N'Sync" in bright paint on a van's back window. Lizzy's mom drove us in the van to the concert in Michigan. Near Detroit, a traffic jam on I-75 turned into a party. Teenage girls blared music, waved signs, and shouted to other fans across the highway lanes. It might have been fun except for temperatures in the nineties with high humidity. The van had no air conditioning as we inched along and no breeze. Beth flushed with fever, her body unable to sweat to cool down. I brought Tylenol but nothing to drink it down with since we didn't anticipate the traffic. I encouraged her to take it without water. Beth chose to wait.

Finally approaching the stadium, I waved the handicapped parking placard out the window at the traffic cop to avoid another jam of cars. As soon as we parked, I rushed Beth out of the van to the first drink stand for cold water. She swallowed the Tylenol with water and drank two bottles before finding our seats. I inhaled as much cold soda as I could. In a shaded spot at the concert, Beth felt better and danced in the pulsing lights of the show, dominated by 20-year-old Justin Timberlake.

Soon after the concert, my outpatient surgery repaired my dislocated thumb and left me with pins and a cast up to my elbows. It put my left arm out of commission for weeks. I scheduled the surgery for summer vacation when John and Maria would be more available to help. Ben worked in research at the Air Force base in Dayton and came home on a weekend to watch both of his sisters onstage in a musical at Tiffin's beautiful Ritz Theatre. He knew some of the cast from his earlier shows.

"Auditions for the show required all performers to act, sing, and dance," Director James Koehl said in a reference letter. "But we were going to waive the dance for Beth. She informed us that she wanted to take part in all of the audition, including the dance, and with her wheelchair and use of arm movements, it was obvious that she was going to fit right in with our concept of the show."

"I have been in other plays, but this was the first since my injury," Beth said. "Most everything about my play experience was the same, everything that is, except the dancing. The wooden set they built was difficult to move on since everything was on a slant, but I stayed on the flat part of the stage. The theater was recently renovated to include an accessible backstage, so it was easy to get around, apart from the time when the elevator was broken, and I had to be bumped down the steps in my wheelchair."

All of my kids earned award pins from the Ritz for volunteering more than a hundred hours to paint sets and act in shows from a young age. Beth's first time onstage at 12, she played the barrister of the Munchkins in "The Wizard of Oz." A fitting role for our "little lawyer," the nickname she earned as a toddler by pleasantly talking her way in or out of most anything with a big dimpled smile.

Our summer comings and goings confused Beth's high-strung African Gray. He plucked out feathers and injured his skin. A vet put a plastic cone around his neck, making him more miserable. A friend wondered if Timber had been taken from his parents too soon and recommended a bird sanctuary in Cleveland. A woman at the sanctuary offered to adopt Timber. Beth agreed it would be the best home for him though she still cried when she said goodbye. I cried too. It felt like another way I had failed. Regardless, the parrot toddler needed more help than we could give. I drove him to the sanctuary with an extensive outdoor aviary and other African Grays. I left with mixed emotions. We were happy to hear that Timber recovered quickly, delighted in his new home.

At Beth's request, John and I moved her hospital bed out of the living room and into the small first floor bedroom. The full-sized bed and nightstand filled the room with just enough open space for the wheelchair next to the bed. I added length to the pull cord on the ceiling light, so Beth could reach it. Honeybee Bear moved to a closet shelf. We restored our living and dining rooms as they were before the accident. With the new arrangement, I slept in the basement bedroom with John since Beth rarely needed me through the night. When she did, we both had cell phones within reach.

She often stayed up later than I did to read, and I placed the table lamp with the big switch within reach. She checked books off her list of the top hundred classics and highlighted ones to pick up next at the library. We also continued physical and occupational therapy through the summer.

Early on an August Saturday, firemen lifted Beth in her wheelchair onto a boat at a Sandusky pier on the Lake Erie shore. I skipped the fishing part of the Fishing Has No Boundaries event. When the boats returned, my daughter had caught more perch and walleye than John in the lake waters. The boat's young first mate watched three fishing poles and handed one to Beth whenever he had a nibble. She reeled in about two dozen fish and let someone else take the fish off the hook.

A friendly crowd gathered for a picnic when all the boats returned to the dock. A mom told me how children at school made fun of her daughter who grew up feeling like a victim. A man shared his ongoing battle with pressure sores, reminding me of an article I read. A woman had both legs and part of her trunk amputated because of pressure sore infections.

The comparison game ran through my head without my consent, pitting mobility factors against attitudes. How could not having something define anyone? We were friends and strangers unified by community, too complex to label. Listening to the teenagers laugh, I wondered if Beth could avoid depression entirely.

Beth asked to go to the YMCA about once a week. She wanted to be in the pool without needing me or anyone else nearby, but she could tread water only briefly with hands that couldn't cup the water. In the center of the pool, she struggled to achieve a floating position. I stayed close, rescuing her from time to time.

"I slowly progressed to swimming laps at the YMCA," Beth said.

I didn't point out that floating on her back with her hands underwater wasn't technically swimming a stroke. Her optimism ran deep.

Eventually, gradually, Beth could tread water for about five seconds and get to a floating position on her back by herself from anywhere in the small pool. I left my swimsuit at home and sat on the deck bleachers, watching her float through slow, unhurried laps. Her arms waved gently below the surface. No rush, no race. No expectations and no destinations. Yet.

STAYING AFLOAT
✎ Chapter 10 ✎
SHIFTING

Beth: *Early on, I decided that I was going to become completely independent no matter how long it took.*

HIGH SCHOOL and physical therapy. Friends and surprises. The first football game of her sophomore year, Beth wheeled up an incline to a new concrete platform in the stadium stands. Large enough to share with an elderly couple, it also included a bench for friends and a front railing to prevent tumbling into the student section below. The novelty of the space attracted a steady flow of young children. Beth and her friends didn't mind. John and I sat several rows above the platform and watched Maria perform in the flag squad with the band. I welcomed our occasional forays into normalcy. We didn't interfere with popcorn fights on the new platform. Beth asked to go to all the home football games that season.

"I really liked my little spot," she said.

At friends' houses on the weekend, she gravitated to the couch or floor. Lizzy would ask her to get something in another room, and Beth responded she was tired from too much walking. At school, she smiled when Ellen scolded her for not standing up during the Pledge of Allegiance. Being a quad also meant you couldn't flip someone off with a middle finger and raising a fist instead became a joke. John, a Star Trek fan, bought her a T-shirt that said, "Stairs, the Final Frontier."

"Everyone I know with an injury who is doing well has a sense of humor about it," Beth said as a freshman in high school. "You need that."

Asked about school, she replied, "My small group of really close friends in high school helped me in many ways including breaking my leg spasms and carrying my book bag. By the second year, I had those things under control, but a friend continued to sit by me in class only because it was more fun that way."

On September 11th at lunchtime, I took a short cut through the school cafeteria and paused by a strange crowd of silent students in front of the television screen. I caught my first glimpse of unthinkable tragedy. I rushed to the locker room, relieved to find both Beth and Maria waiting for me. We hugged, close and safe for the moment anyway.

My worst-case scenarios amplified after 9/11. I grieved with the nation for the horrific losses including children who'd never grow up. In my mind, terrorism took on a life of its own, growing and mutating into an ongoing and imminent threat. I tried to tamp down the fear by storing bottled water in the basement and packing an emergency duffle bag. I wrote phone numbers and a meeting place on a small rectangle of paper. I laminated copies for my immediate family to carry in their wallet. They humored me.

My psychologist moved away and another took over. I read an article about the nuclear age, about how my generation changed with the terrible knowledge that nuclear weapons might be used again. My heightened fears grouped nuclear weapons with terrorism and deadly viruses. Add in toxic chemical spills, a high risk in Ohio with the heavy truck traffic. Add also a personal, selfish anxiety about any number of alarming events that could restrict prescription drugs. Acutely aware of my dependency on antidepressants and an anti-inflammatory, who would I be without the prescriptions? How would I help Beth?

I attempted to describe how powerless I felt to the psychologist. I couldn't protect my family. He patiently explained that widespread catastrophe would be highly unlikely, as if that would comfort me. The 9/11 tragedy had been highly unlikely. Our car accident and Beth's injury also had been highly unlikely.

I longed to be optimistic and picked up books at the library with positive messages. During my hours alone, I struggled with indecision. Even small choices felt monumental. I kept myself busy. I fervently wished that getting rid of anxiety could be as easy as making a choice not to worry. Simply choosing to have hope. Simply deciding not to fear each day and what would happen next.

Beth continued to ask to go to the YMCA a few times a month. I read books on the pool deck while she moved slowly on her back with her arms underwater. I no longer needed to watch continually for her head dipping too long under the water. One fall Sunday, I joined Beth in the water at her request. She tried the backstroke, and the effort to rotate her arms out of the water caused her to sink. I splashed my face to hide my tears as I lifted her up.

I drove to Green Springs after school for physical therapy two times a week, and the therapists encouraged her to keep swimming. Technically, she floated.

At a follow-up visit to the Chicago Shriners Hospital, we met other patients and parents. One discussion touched on college. Beth assumed she'd attend, the result of deliberate indoctrination. Since her preschool years, "When you go to college . . ." started random conversations at our house.

Another teenager planned on Wright State University in Dayton, Ohio, a top choice for wheelchair users in the

Midwest because of underground walkways to avoid winter weather. At Wright State, when pressure sores required one student to stay on his side or stomach, an able-bodied friend pushed his hospital bed down the street to class. Was that a good thing?

A bubbly nurse guided us on a tour of the hospital with the renovations complete. Large open spaces combined with bright colors, effectively designed to welcome families. She pointed out a display for the Make-A-Wish Foundation for children with life-threatening medical conditions. The nurse casually offered to make a referral for Beth and introduced us to another quad and her mom who recently returned from a cruise in Alaska through Make-A-Wish. My children had rarely traveled. I had saved my income from the Tiffin Center to pay for our biggest vacation to Florida's Disney World eight years before.

The referral offer bothered Beth. Between appointments, we talked. Make-A-Wish clashed with her wholehearted belief that her condition would get better, not worse, on the only scale that mattered to her—one of maximizing available strength and decreasing dependence. The frightening severity of her pneumonia and other deadly risks did not factor into her decision. Certain that others needed Make-A-Wish more, she turned down the nurse's offer. Beth led and I followed. I trusted her judgment over my own.

A specialist at the hospital confirmed the absence of Beth's asthma symptoms, leading to less medicine and longer intervals between visits to the lung doctors. The orthopedic surgeon told us the angles of her scoliosis and kyphosis progressed as expected, making the metal rod fusion surgery more likely in the future. The unyielding rod would hinder movement and add to her limitations.

Despite all the odds stacked against her, Beth's general goal shifted from *more* independence to *complete* independence, an extremely rare feat for quads. In a world where wishes came true, I wanted all of that and more for her. The brass ring looked too high.

On the advice of a social worker, Beth and I met with a Tiffin Rehabilitation Services counselor. He asked about a career. At 15, she expressed an interest in Dr. Miller's job as a rehab doctor. Surprised, he chose his words carefully and voiced objections. The counselor doubted her physical abilities, but to be fair, he didn't know how persistent she could be in finding ways to use her hands for fine motor tasks.

Beth didn't like being told she couldn't do something. With the exception of standing, walking, and jumping, she regarded most physical obstacles as surmountable in some way. She asked for my opinion. I shared my certainty that she could be a great doctor—after proving herself every step of the way in the face of resistance from some who would see the wheelchair first.

"I have always wanted to do something important with my life," she wrote. "After my injury, this goal became more focused. I want to make a difference from the start of my career."

In 10th grade, Beth wrote, "I think it would be fun to work on stem cell research. Finding new or better medications would also be something I might do after college. Science has always been my favorite subject."

We added DragonSpeak software to our computer. The early version required time to teach the program to recognize your individual voice. Growing comfortable with typing, she gave up on DragonSpeak. Learning to drive piqued her interest much more.

Beth passed the written test for her learner's permit using one of her favorite Dr. Grip pens with a cushion near the tip. She had thrown away the foam tubes long before. The counselor guided us through the next steps. A specialist recommended individualized car modifications. The major issue: getting in and out of the vehicle.

A van with a lift would easily solve that problem. Instead, Beth bought a little blue Ford Focus hatchback with insurance money from the accident. Mechanics added several modifications, and she practiced driving with an instructor from Toledo.

Sitting in the driver's seat, she used her right hand to grip a large knob attached to an easy-to-turn steering wheel. Her other hand pushed or pulled a bar on the left side of the steering wheel to apply brakes or accelerate. After testing that her spasms would not hit the pedals, the gas and brake pedals on the floor worked, which meant I also could drive the car the usual way. To top it off, a large motorized box on the roof lifted and stored a folding wheelchair, by using a control box within the driver's reach.

"My newest challenges are learning how to drive a car with adapted hand controls," she said, "and how to transfer in and out of the driver's seat independently."

Beth enjoyed driving but not getting in and out of the car. She chose not to use a sliding board. She scooted to the far right edge of the chair cushion and put one hand on the driver's seat and the other on the chair cushion. Her goal? To lift her trunk high enough with her arms to bridge the gap. It looked impossible, but Beth kept trying. Each time.

I stood right behind her and grabbed the extra fabric of her jeans by her upper thighs. I intervened with a boost to prevent a fall. When others accompanied Beth, they often grabbed belt loops to help. At first, I sewed up rips and the holes they left. When they just ripped again, I gave up. Her shirts covered the holes, like the bottom of her jeans always hid her socks. Important things to my usually easygoing daughter.

Once Beth settled in the driver's seat, the empty wheelchair created another problem. She liked the idea of taking the wheels off the chair and lifting the pieces across her body to the passenger seat. Unfortunately, the high back of the chair and her level of arm strength nixed that idea.

The mechanized topper on her car seemed to be a good alternative. However, the wheelchair needed to be folded and positioned perfectly on the hook. Also, the chair didn't always fall into place properly in the topper which meant the car wouldn't start.

To go anywhere in the car by herself, Beth would need to open the door to the driver's seat, remove the foot rests, position the wheelchair, lock it, place the sliding board to bridge the gap to the car, slowly shift over, put away the sliding board, grab the remote control, release the hook from the top, take off the chair cushion, fold the wheelchair, catch the folded seat with the hook, and push the toggle to lift and store the chair. With anything less than perfection, the car would not start and Beth couldn't fix it. We rarely used the topper. I flattened one of the back seats, so I could set the chair into the hatchback without folding it or taking the wheels off. One small shortcut in days that felt too complicated.

Beth resigned herself to the fact that driving wasn't a completely independent activity. Even so, she had no regrets about her decision to purchase a car instead of a van with a lift.

I rehashed with a new psychiatrist, a man who listened and rarely spoke. I started to feel like a lost cause. I concluded privately that I failed at counseling. At life. I dwelled on the accident. I couldn't find a way to forgive myself. I felt disconnected and scattered. In my weakest moments, I feared death, of not being there for Beth. I tried too hard to put up a good front that felt disingenuous. Yet, how else could I avoid pity? I also didn't want to worry my family. I waited on edge for the next crisis.

When snow started to fall, I pulled my sewing bag out of the closet. I made my favorite peace doves out of felt with embroidered accents and lacy wings for Laraine, Jill, and other therapists at Green Springs, part of our extended family. I loved how they loved Beth. I mailed Christmas cards decorated with doves, wishing for peace. For the world, for our country, and for me.

John drove with Beth, Maria, and me to the holiday party of the Toledo spinal cord injury group. Talking to other parents, I could answer the question of who was to blame for the car accident without crying. Progress, of sorts, after a year and a half. Still, my guilt was alive and well, so I quickly steered conversations away from the accident. I talked to other quads, some with serious health issues that increased my sense of foreboding. I wanted to be positive and optimistic, but I couldn't see the way.

John often said, "Everyone has a story." In his element at the party, he started conversations and listened to the journeys of others. He also shared our family's story. We teased him that all of Ohio knew about Beth's injury and her progress.

Maria and Beth sat at the cool kids table with the teenagers while the younger children watched them. I heard part of a conversation about the first Harry Potter movie, *The Sorcerer's Stone*, in theaters a few weeks earlier. Most had watched it more than once, including my girls.

After the party, I sighed in relief when Beth dozed off in the car, avoiding her anxiety of driving in the dark. Her worries stayed specific and situational.

Maria already had a driver's license and one clear Saturday afternoon, my girls shopped at the Findlay mall. On the way home, Beth noticed the low gas indicator on the dashboard, right when they entered a 15-minute stretch on Rt. 224 with no gas stations. The conversation started civil.

"Maria, please turn around and go back to Findlay for gas."

"We have plenty to get home."

"The light is on! We really need to get gas now!"

"Beth, I'm not turning around. I have to be at work soon. We'll be fine, trust me!" Though it wasn't about trust. Running out of gas seemed to trigger Beth's fears of a problem she couldn't fix by herself. Just like getting down the basement during a tornado.

My daughters have always been close, and both had stubborn streaks that usually served them well. That afternoon, their streaks clashed in an epic way. They burst into the kitchen, frustrated and talking at the same time. I played peacekeeper until they calmed down, and Maria left for her job at a video store.

The girls left their car dispute behind, and Ben arrived home for the holidays. It was beginning to look a lot like Christmas as it had been before the accident. I held brief conversations with other parents after the holiday choir concert, always a lovely highlight of the season. I listened to music, decorated the house, baked cookies, played card games, watched movies with popcorn, and made new memories to add to many heartfelt ones at the Henning homestead. Sitting around the big dining room table at the farmhouse, I missed my grandma and grandpa, reminded again how life can change in a moment. All the more reason to hug loved ones close.

Another New Year's Eve arrived with Beth's best friends at our house. Soon after, Dr. Miller asked her to exchange emails with a new teenage quad while I talked to the overwhelmed mom on the phone. I listened but shared little, focusing on slow improvements and the hope of more progress. I didn't feel like a good role model for other parents.

What would the future hold? The New Year and the time beyond seemed impossibly uncertain. Since 9/11, my nightmares evolved to include terrorism and nuclear weapons. Hope eluded me. Health problems threatened Beth and everyone I loved. My concerns encompassed the global, the trivial, and everything in between. I was an equal opportunity worrier.

At a meeting in Toledo, Beth registered for the wheelchair games in May with the Raptors. She thought she wasn't good enough to sign up for races in the pool, but others convinced her to try. Some of her friends talked about their earlier trips to another sports event, the National Junior Disability Championships, held each summer for kids from across the country.

In February, Beth elected to have abdominal surgery to pave the way for independence. A Toledo urologist performed the successful eight-hour surgery. As a result, I'd no longer need to be with her every few hours. A week after she left the hospital, against my advice, she agreed to help Laraine with a new class of physical therapy students. Beth wore loose clothes to cover two temporary tubes from the surgery that protruded from her abdomen, along with a separate small rubber bulb.

Laraine teased about going easy on her during the mat exercises. When Beth transferred with help, she moved out of her new orange wheelchair, more stable than a folding chair. On the mat, she sat with hands in her lap, wobbling less than she had at the last demonstration. Careful with the tubes, Laraine refrained from pushing hard to test her balance.

Beth also shared her ponytail progress with the students though she still couldn't complete an additional loop of the elastic to keep it in place. Yet.

At the follow-up appointment with the urologist, he removed the bulb and all the tubes for good, leaving bare skin and a long vertical surgery scar below her belly button. We celebrated with a shopping trip. She had fun picking out cute underwear and a bikini swimsuit. Part of the scar would be visible with a bikini. She didn't care. However, no swimming for six weeks. Not negotiable.

With growing confidence, Beth filled her time with the school newspaper, homework, volunteering, clubs, Raptors, and another high school musical. Some weeks we made it to physical therapy once instead of twice. She also decided to get back in the pool as soon as the doctor's ban ended.

Sweet 16 on her early April birthday, Beth returned to the water. At a previous seminar with Laraine, a physical therapy student offered to meet us at the University of Toledo pool on a Saturday. A college swimmer, Colleen observed my daughter's usual floating with arms underwater. She provided advice and a hand of support under Beth's back while she rotated her arms, one at a time. Next, they tried circling both arms together, causing her head to dip under water.

None of it came naturally. With only water safety lessons as a toddler, Beth had not been a swimmer before the accident. We met Colleen a second time with the first wheelchair games a week away. They focused on the traditional, alternating backstroke, taxing muscles and stamina. For the first time, Beth could swim the backstroke.

A clumsy and faltering backstroke. She slept through the hour ride home.

The Michigan Wheelchair Games took place at an old high school complex, two and a half hours away by car. We joined several dozen participants and family members. Beth lined up with a few other first-timers for classification that attempted to even the playing field. Officials measured Beth's muscle strength, tested her in the water, and assigned her the S2 classification on a scale of S1 to S14. Those labeled S1 and S2 had severe disabilities and the least amount of physical function, compared to the higher numbered classifications.

First, the track events. Beth didn't have a racing chair, and her friends' chairs didn't fit, so she stayed in her own and pushed herself around the track. I joined a small group of enthusiastic, cheering spectators.

In the afternoon, the atmosphere at the old pool could hardly be called competitive. Races included both sexes with any classification and age. Beth's times would be compared with other S2 female teenagers. Since there weren't any others at the meet, she automatically took first place in each of her races. That served as our first hint that most quads couldn't move independently in the water.

Following the lead of other swimmers, I lowered Beth to a gym mat at the side of the pool and then into the water. Minutes before, we asked how the lane numbers corresponded to the lanes. For the first time, she dunked under plastic lane lines with difficulty to get to her assigned lane.

For the first race at her first meet, Beth swam a sloppy backstroke for 50 yards, two lengths of the pool. She didn't know how to push off at the start, how to turn at the wall, or how to approach the finish. Another teenager, also in her first race, had never been alone in the water before and couldn't swim any strokes. She moved on her back, kicking her legs with her arms underwater. I painfully watched her struggle.

Sadly unprepared, the girl zigzagged in her lane before gently bumping her head on the ending wall, panicking and going under. Her father immediately jumped in with his clothes and shoes on when he could've reached her easily from the low deck. I wondered if parents of children born with a disability tended to be overprotective. Though I had no right to judge anyone, especially after failing to protect Beth the night of the accident.

"At my first swim meet," Beth told a reporter. "I met Cheryl, a Paralympic swimmer, and her husband Shawn, a Paralympic coach. They encouraged me to compete nationally."

The annual USA Swimming Disability Championships would take place in Seattle just five weeks away. Shawn and Cheryl encouraged Beth to attend and "see the possibilities," a clear invitation to adventure. They opened a door we didn't know existed, a door that changed everything.

Shawn hedged a bit when another swimmer asked if she should go too. I jumped to the conclusion that Beth possessed some kind of exceptional swimming skill not apparent to me.

Our world shifted again as it had the night of the car accident. During the drive home from the Michigan games, Beth played John Mayer's Room for Squares CD and sang along with her new favorite tune, "No Such Thing." It became her buoyant anthem to the future, replayed again and again. The lyrics etched in our memories, infused with the essence of vague but powerful anticipation.

"I just found out there's no such thing as the real world," Beth belted out with John Mayer. "Just a lie you got to rise above. I am invincible!"

A self-fulfilling prophecy. Invincible.

❧ Chapter 11 ❧
VISUALIZING

Beth: *I really didn't expect to ever be able to compete, so that surprised me.*

BETH STARTED TO identify as a swimmer, even though she could barely swim one stroke for short distances. I could not—should not, would not—dampen her excitement. Still. We had no travel budget for Seattle. We knew nothing about competitive swimming, with or without a disability. Flying with a wheelchair? No idea. Beth didn't worry, and I stressed enough for both of us.

I shopped for flights, a hotel, and a rental car. Only Beth and I would go, to save money. Her classification and swim times from the wheelchair games would not count for the national meet, so Shawn pointed us in the right direction. I signed Beth up for her first USA Swimming membership and filled out the registration form for the USA Swimming Disability Championships. We requested the needed classification appointment for the day before the Seattle meet began. Next, Beth needed qualifying times for the championships in short order. Shawn suggested a USA Swimming meet in early June.

The second anniversary of the accident approached on May 20th and was barely noticed at our house. Beth focused on progress made. She wheeled herself—on easy surfaces and low inclines. She moved from the higher bed to the lower wheelchair seat on her own—sometimes. She completed the easiest steps of getting dressed in bed—when she had extra time. In her wheelchair, she hooked one elbow under a push handle to anchor her body while reaching down with the opposite hand to pick items up from the floor—easy to grip, light things. She tried to get in and out of the car—with help always needed over the threshold. She attempted to put on a swim cap—before handing it to me.

Maria's friend, the one injured in our accident, planned a sleepover on the anniversary of the trauma for solace and support. My oldest daughter was indignant. Beth responded, "Whatever," and didn't give it a second thought.

At one and a half years old, Maria christened her newborn sister with the name "Ber." When the baby fussed, Maria joined in. Always musical, her first original song repeated the words, "My Ber-rrrrrr!" She sang her way through the next 16 years. My strong and sensitive Maria wrote and gave a letter to her friend, with the gist that if Beth could handle quadriplegia with humility and humor, then others had no excuse for drama. I didn't hear about the letter until after the fact.

The friend's mom called me the same evening, upset. I apologized for Maria's letter, and we cried together on the phone. When I couldn't sleep that night, I sat at the kitchen table and wrote to the mom, a note I never sent.

I wish you could really see how Beth has dealt with her disability. In so many ways, she is more able than most of us. She accepted her paralysis before she understood it. She never cried in intensive care.

Beth focuses on what needs to be done next and works incredibly hard to be less dependent. And in her view, there's no reason to not enjoy the moments along the way.

You look at her and assume that not walking is the worst thing. You have no idea how much more she's lost, but you won't hear her complain or ask for pity. She feels genuinely grateful for the arm movement the injury left her with, for friends and family, and for the amazing people she's met since the accident.

Before Beth's sophomore year ended, we met the Toledo Raptors in Columbus for the Ohio Wheelchair Games, much larger and more organized than the one in Michigan. We stayed two nights in a hotel near the OSU campus. In the lobby, one of the teenage boys showed off with extreme wheelies. When his manual chair tipped backwards to the floor, the front desk staff rushed over while Beth and her friends laughed to tears. (Meanwhile as he fell, the para tipped his head safely forward, chin to chest before righting the chair and climbing back into it.) Karaoke in the hotel lounge turned a bit wild.

Returning to the Jesse Owens stadium, this time as a participant, Beth sat with her friends near the track while they waited for their races. I watched from the stands with other family members. I noticed some athletes who utilized extensive supports, things like power wheelchairs, when they seemed to have full use of their hands, arms, and trunk. If I had a disability, I probably would too. Something else bothered me. A few sat on absorbent white pads with a blue backing. I understood why, but I wished they would tuck the extra part of the pads out of sight. Or better yet, use an alternative in public. Even on the grounds of the state institution where I had worked, appearances mattered. Dignity mattered. Negative stereotypes of disability needed no reinforcement.

Beth wheeled around the track in her manual chair. She also tried field events and threw a discus for the first time. She laughed when it plopped nearby.

Before the table tennis competition, she practiced holding the paddle with the tenodesis grip. She used her wrist to move her left hand back, perpendicular to her forearm. Other quads strapped the paddle to their hand. Beth depended on the armrests of her wheelchair to balance as she reached from side to side. If she leaned over to pick up something off the floor, she fell unless she first hooked the opposite elbow on a push handle. The paddle dropped to the floor twice and she picked it up. Some watched closely, perhaps thinking they might try the same thing later on their own.

Beth drew on ping-pong skills learned as a child from my mom Helen Barnes, the first woman in Lorain County to teach physical education back in the early 1950s. My mom also had played field hockey and basketball at OSU where she met my dad. He liked to point out Beth's double dimples and blue eyes, both of which she shared with him, along with freckles and a stubborn streak.

For the weightlifting competition in a gym, I helped Beth recline face up on a narrow elevated bench with a barbell suspended over her chest. For quads, the officials started with no weight added to the barbell. Beth's arms were not strong enough to budge it from the rack. At all. Despite nearly two years of intense physical therapy, swimming, and pushing herself in a manual wheelchair. A reality check. Another reminder of the severity of her disability.

Embarrassed a bit, Beth moved on to her new favorite sport. Her fan section at the OSU pool consisted of John and me, my parents, Ben, Laraine, and Colleen. My mom and dad had never seen Beth in the water and were amazed as they watched her during warm ups. Swimmers gathered for their races, most not aiming for a specific time. No announcer at the meet meant that the results of races were anybody's guess. Someone might touch the ending wall first while another in the same race might set a new games record based on their age, gender, and classification. It didn't matter. Encouragement reigned.

"I advanced from being held up or sinking to basically falling in and swimming laps," Beth said.

We all met for lunch on Lane Avenue at Laraine's favorite restaurant, Tommy's Pizza, famous for subs. After a rowdy lunch with much laughter, Beth hugged Laraine and Colleen goodbye. Tired from the late night of karaoke, we napped at the hotel. At the banquet that evening to end the games, a Raptors mom enthusiastically congratulated my smiling daughter for winning a ping-pong match against a para. The crowd in the ballroom applauded when the announcer surprised Beth with the Rookie of the Year award. She set several new games records for her classification and age group in track and field, swimming, and table tennis.

On June 8th, we experienced a different kind of competition. The sheer size of the USA Swimming meet intimidated us. At Oakland University in Michigan, the 50-meter long course pool stretched on and on. Able-bodied teenagers packed the large deck, and I led the way when we needed to pass through. In the upper bleachers, the audience filled every seat, with others standing.

I wore a deck pass on a cord around from my neck, giving me access with the other adults. All coaches or officials. The elevated deck by the starting blocks added significant distance to the water. I literally dropped Beth into her lane.

Any stroke could be used during a freestyle race. She had one option, the backstroke. The other girls in the same race swam the forward freestyle, their fastest stroke. They finished and waited at the wall while Beth swam the last 50-meter length by herself. The extra 60 seconds abruptly stopped the fast pace of the meet. Teenagers in the next race waited impatiently, ready to step up on the blocks with ease and dive in.

Beth swam 100 meters without rest breaks for the first time, swerving from side to side through the last long slow length of the pool and sometimes hitting a lane line with her hand. I thought back to the girl at the Michigan games who had never been in a pool by herself. It had been easy for me to judge the girl's parents as I watched her unhappy struggle to finish a race. After Beth's last swerving lap, I questioned my own parenting. Had she been prepared to compete in a 50-meter pool? Sadly, no. Despite this, would she enjoy the experience? Miraculously, yes.

I felt the stares of several hundred spectators and swimmers as I bent forward very low from the elevated deck to reach her shoulders. My deck pass dangled in my face. I lost my balance and almost fell on top of her. Staring continued as Shawn and I each grabbed a shoulder to lift Beth out of the water to the deck. And into the wheelchair with her legs straight out and bouncing. I broke the spasms since I could do it faster. The electronic timing system clocked her at a plodding three and a half minutes for 50 meters, enough to qualify for the Seattle nationals as an S2 swimmer. On the long drive back home, Beth played her favorite John Mayer CD, singing along and dancing. Invincible?

The school year ended, making way for our first West Coast adventure. An entire trip of firsts. At the Detroit airport, a clerk asked about Beth's wheelchair. No, she could not walk to her seat on the plane. No, she could not stand. An aisle chair? What was that?

I helped Beth into one of the airport's clunky wheelchairs. I folded her blue chair, duct taped it together and watched it disappear on the conveyer belt with the luggage. Not my best idea.

High security since 9/11 quieted Beth's excited chatter. At the gate, we learned that we would board first. Down the jet bridge, near the open door of the plane, I transferred Beth to an aisle chair, an odd seat with a width of about 15 inches that rolls on four little wheels. An employee fastened an abundance of straps before he pulled her backwards down the middle of the plane. We lifted her over the armrest to her seat.

Things that don't matter until they do: worrying about autonomic dysreflexia triggered by cabin pressure, bruising her lower legs from spasms hitting the bottom of the seat in front of her, apologizing to the passenger who had to crawl over Beth to get to their window seat, and staying seated for five hours. She held my hand while the plane ascended. On our first flight after Beth's injury, neither one of us thought to lift and move her legs to reduce the risk of blood clots.

The process reversed when we deboarded in Seattle. We waited for an aisle chair after the other passengers left. On the jet bridge, we borrowed another airline wheelchair to transport her to baggage claim. I grabbed her blue wheelchair from the conveyor, the chair that had traveled cross-country with luggage piled on top of it. The travel gods smiled on us. No major damage, just one bent brake lever. And no blood clots.

I rented a car through the cheapest company and found out their shuttle was inaccessible. Rather than being carried aboard or taking a taxi together, Beth chose to stay at the airport while I left to get the car. It didn't take long, and I hurried back to pick her up.

I removed the big wheels of her chair and put them in the backseat. The rest barely fit in the trunk of the economy car. With only flip phones and no GPS, I handed Beth printed Google map directions to help me navigate, nervous about my first rental car. She pointed out a striking sign.

"I saw a billboard with a girl in a power chair and a Harvard graduation cap on," Beth told a reporter. The caption simply said, "Quadriplegia at Harvard: A+."

We arrived at the pool in the afternoon for the classification appointment that attempted to even the playing field. Theoretically, competition approached fairness by grouping those with similar physical function. The devil was in the details.

Parallel to the Olympics, U.S. Paralympics supported athletes with impairments. Classification compared the absence of function between those with limb differences, spinal injuries, spina bifida, multiple sclerosis, cerebral palsy, osteogenesis imperfecta, and more. The specific criteria to classify a swimmer often left little room for debate or error—with one notable exception. The categories for the most severe disabilities (S1 to S3) had less precise guidelines. To complicate matters, individuals with the same diagnosis often possessed different motor abilities.

On June 12th, international classifiers asked Beth questions on the wide deck of the nearly empty pool. Her sincere answers minimized her quadriplegia. I thought about interrupting but with muscle testing next, I hoped they would get a more accurate picture of her limitations.

For the last assessment, I lowered Beth from her chair to the pool deck. She scooted to the edge before falling into the water. Classifiers observed closely as she did her best to comply with their requests. When asked to swim the breaststroke, she kept her arms in front of her in a variation of treading water. Her head dipped underwater after several seconds. Trying to swim the butterfly and freestyle strokes, she valiantly moved her arms out of the water. Before sinking a few seconds later. Swimming forward on her stomach seemed impossible.

The classifiers openly debated between S2 and S3 before settling on S3. Beth looked down and paused before thanking them. If they had said S2, her swim times rocked. Those same times would not qualify for the current meet as an S3, but newly classified swimmers could race regardless. It made sense that a novice who had never worked with a swim coach would need to improve before ranking among the best.

Beth and I stayed at the pool complex for the picnic dinner to kick off the meet. We sat out of the way and watched the friendly crowd. It amazed me how few used a wheelchair. In street clothes, most had invisible disabilities.

We returned to the pool the next morning for the first of the three-day meet. Swimsuits revealed a wide range of physical differences though no one stared or judged. Paralympic rules banned artificial limbs and other supports in the water. Prosthetic legs propped casually on the bleachers underscored the unspoken acceptance of disability.

The only people we recognized had been at the Michigan games. Shawn and his wife as well as another teenager and her mom. Beth wheeled around groups of friends on the deck. We noticed a couple more wheelchairs in use compared to the night before. One girl, minus her prosthetic leg, pushed a manual wheelchair with strong arms, instead of using crutches on the wet deck.

"There were about two hundred athletes from eight different countries," Beth said. "The entire Australian and Mexican National Teams were there."

Swimmers warmed up in the pool to the beats of pop music before the morning's prelims (preliminary races). An announcement designated a specific end lane for those classified S1, S2, and S3, with no explanation because the reason was obvious. To avoid collisions with peers in crowded lanes where they streaked down the right side of the lane, flipped to change direction, pushed off the wall with their feet, and swam back on the opposite side, making a circle. Beth shared the slower lane with a few others for the first time and spent more time hanging on the wall than warming up. On the deck, many attentive coaches supervised warm ups. Small fish in a big pond, we only had each other.

The meet overwhelmed me at first with the visual overload of a crowded disability competition with international teams. The beeps and buzzes of back-to-back events. The stress of having to be in the right place at the right time. The sweat running down my face and back, a combination of humidity and nerves. The thirst that had to wait since Beth didn't want to be left alone.

Most swimmers dove off the blocks from a standing or sitting position with no assistance. Others started races in the water. One coach reached over the edge to hold a swimmer's feet to the wall. Another coach held an arm before the buzzer sounded. A man with no arms floated on his back, with his feet touching the wall and a cord in his teeth. The coach at the other end of the taut cord dropped it at the start.

We clapped for the first American Record of the meet, a neck and neck race. It quickly became evident that I had misunderstood Shawn in Michigan. Beth had no exceptional swimming talent. His invitation had been based on the fact that a tiny percentage of quads around the world could be alone in a pool without drowning. Even rarer: quads who could swim.

Beth had the dubious honor of being the only S3 female from the United States at the meet, a distinction that would reoccur many times. The fastest athletes during prelims would return to race in the early evening *if* they beat the cut times for finals.

For Beth's first race at her first nationals, swimmers on both sides entered the water without a mother's help and surged ahead at the start. My daughter merely sought to prevail over the seemingly endless distance of the 50-meter pool. Twice. The only one weaving down the lane in the last stretch, she did not make the cut for finals as expected. I put my deck pass in the pocket of my jeans before I lifted her out of the pool.

In the women's locker room, swimmers showered and changed on their own. Beth chose an out-of-the-way spot by the back lockers because she needed my help. Our hotel had no accessible rooms available to us so instead of being lifted in and out of a bathtub, she decided to shower at the pool in her wheelchair for the first time. I pulled off the cushion and backpack ahead of time, adjusted the tight water handle, and picked up the soap when it slipped from her grip. I squeezed out the shampoo, and as she moved it around in her hair, her arms trembled slightly from the exertion of racing. The wheelchair left drips of water on the concrete on the way to the rental car. After a quick lunch and a nap at the hotel, we had the rest of the day free to explore.

"The trip was truly amazing," Beth wrote. "Seattle was beautiful. My mom and I were able to tour the city in the afternoons and evenings after I swam."

Beth read from my maps while I drove from the fisherman's wharf to the Space Needle. We rode the elevator to see the panoramic vista, and found an unusual store. For Maria's birthday, I bought her a Snow White mirror about a foot wide with elaborate metalwork, hoping I could get it home in one piece. My girls would always be princesses who believed in happy endings.

As toddlers, the girls often wore special dresses I made for them. Maria often played in her Snow White gown, and Beth had a Cinderella dress. They wore the ankle-length costumes until the bottom hem reached their knees. At five, Maria decreed that we would live together forever in our Tiffin castle. Our tiny corner of a big world.

When I drove to the pool the second day of the meet, we loved how Mount Rainier seemed to float in a pillow of clouds on the eastern horizon. At the meet, a friendly official introduced herself and a coach, along with a talented swimmer, another Beth. They extended a warm invitation to join their Toledo club team. We also heard about the next Paralympics in Greece, held shortly after the summer Olympics in the same venues.

"I was hooked," Beth wrote in an essay. "I knew it wasn't going to be my last national meet."

I borrowed a page from Laraine's book and assumed the role of a foil, reflecting and questioning, not encouraging or discouraging. Should we pause and contact a Tiffin swim coach? Were swim coaches like medical specialists in the sense that they tended to be better in big cities compared to small towns? We had no clue. I worried about Beth taking on too much, especially learning new strokes that looked like an exercise in futility. Wouldn't life be easier if she settled for a leisurely backstroke?

Her next 50-meter race with one length and no turn felt less intimidating, but her time did not qualify for finals again. That afternoon, we boarded a boat in the harbor and saw Seattle from a different vantage point. We treated ourselves and shared a fancy ice cream dessert with chocolate shavings and extra whipped cream.

The third morning of the meet, we tried to sort out a jumble of criteria on the lists posted at the pool. Unreasonably fast times to make the U.S. National Team. Absurd times for American Records and ludicrous times for World Records. All broken down into events, classifications, and genders. Almost every American Record for S3 women had a blank line where a name should be, along with a fast, arbitrary time that no one had yet achieved.

The last evening, we returned to the pool to watch the finals races. Beth officially enlisted the help of the Toledo coach to find out what she could do in the water. She told him that one year ahead, at the next national championships, her swim times would be fast enough to qualify as an S3 *and* make the cut for finals. Not stopping there, she set a goal to swim *all* the strokes in the next 12 months. She visualized a fast, smooth forward freestyle. As always, Beth underestimated real challenges.

I arrived back in Tiffin with a missing push handle on the wheelchair, Maria's unbroken Snow White mirror, and a 16-year-old intent on learning to swim. Occasionally floating across the pool had been a pleasant pastime before Seattle. After, she raised the bar to the sky for her first swimming summer.

The World Rankings of the International Paralympic Committee (IPC) compared individual swimmers. Beth's three slow races in Seattle placed her on the rankings at 15th, 17th, and 21st in the world. A testament to the rarity of S3 swimmers.

"For the first time, I began training with swim coaches," she explained. "I am one of two swimmers with a disability on GTAC (Greater Toledo Aquatic Club)."

We drove to Toledo for her first morning swim practice with a coach. The small locker room at their pool proved to be difficult with no accessible toilets or private spaces. The only mom in the locker room, I pulled on her swimsuit and then helped her into the pool.

A coach jumped in the water with Beth to better direct and experiment since no instructions existed for teaching a quad to swim. They focused on the backstroke. The afternoon of the same day, we drove to St. Vincent, the hospital where she had stayed in intensive care after the accident. Her idea, not mine.

"After attending the orientation," Beth wrote, "I volunteered in the outpatient physical therapy department for one afternoon a week. This was a particularly interesting assignment for me since I was still going to outpatient physical therapy as a patient at a different hospital closer to my home. I liked being busy with bed-making and clerical work, and it was easy to relate to the staff and patients."

Beth initiated regular visits to the Tiffin YMCA pool with me. She approached each practice on her own with a singular focus: swimming forward, not back. With hands that couldn't cup the water and useless legs dragging behind, she propelled herself with arms moving underwater in front of her body. Not attempting a swim stroke, she concentrated on forward motion several seconds/inches at a time, undeterred by the sheer difficulty of what looked impossible. When her arms faltered, and she couldn't keep her head above water, she rolled on her back to breathe. When she reached the wall, she took a break before trying again—and failing again. And again.

We stopped for an extra swim practice in Toledo before a meeting of the spinal cord injury group. We learned about adapted equipment made by engineering students from the University of Toledo. Beth considered a low racing chair. Her need for more independence prevailed, and she requested a specialized lift chair instead. The goal was to get from her wheelchair to the pool deck without help, and vice versa. I filled out the project application.

After only a handful of GTAC practices, we drove to her first competition as a member of the club. The Ohio Senior Meet took place one month after Seattle. Beth hadn't practiced with swimmers her own age in Toledo. Still shy, she stayed close to me at the meet instead of hanging out with other members of the team.

Teenagers amassed everywhere. Beth took the lead for the first time when we passed through the crowd. She repeated the phrase "excuse me" until she said it loudly enough to roll by. Sometimes she reached up and tapped someone lightly with her fist to get his or her attention.

Beth's only option at her first Ohio Senior Meet? The backstroke. During the first race, she swam the final leg by herself. She didn't swerve in the lane as she had in Seattle four weeks before. The crowd applauded when she finished.

Some of the moms sitting in the packed bleachers looked perfectly coiffed and dressed to a T, part of a lingering swim culture that implied privilege. I usually didn't fuss with my hair and makeup, and I felt intimidated in my jeans and T-shirt. I quickly learned that swim club memberships involved expensive dues, swim gear, meet fees, and a wide range of travel-related costs. Though to be fair, many club teams helped with costs for those who couldn't pay.

For Beth, a packed school year with two Advanced Placement classes approached, plus the school newspaper and swim practices on top of volunteering and mentoring.

"Laraine said that when therapy gets in the way of life, then it is time to move on," Beth wrote. "I continued physical therapy as an outpatient for two years. Three times a week at first, then going twice and then once a week, we drove to St. Francis after school to work out for about two hours. I recently graduated from physical therapy since I get plenty of exercise on my own now, and I am always extremely busy."

The last physical therapy session, a little over two years post-injury, ended with Laraine's anticipated rite of passage. The final test. With her favorite therapist leaning on her back, Beth finished her pushups with a dramatic thrust, causing Laraine to dramatically step away. Everyone cheered. A happy and sad day, the end of an era.

"Beth still faces many new challenges," Laraine said. "I know she is up to the task."

We met Laraine in Toledo for another seminar for physical therapy students. Beth enthusiastically shared a milestone. She pulled off the elastic band on her wrist with her teeth and held it there. Both hands planted on each side of the wheelchair seat as she scooted her bottom forward. She leaned back. From that stable position, she reclaimed the elastic with the one finger she could move. Her smile wavered a moment as she concentrated on intricate degrees of progress. The second loop secured a messy ponytail, followed by her bow with a flourish and a triumphant ta-dah!

Our application for the lift chair approved, we met with senior students from the University of Toledo who measured Beth and discussed the design. My niece Meghan attended UT and her boyfriend Phil volunteered for the chair when he saw our name on an application. They would build a standard seat with back support and a toggle switch powered by a motor with a rechargeable battery. Sitting on the seat, Beth would push or pull a toggle switch to get down to the floor or back up.

We drove five hours one way for the last meet of the summer with GTAC for Sectionals at Indiana University. As we passed Indianapolis, Beth pointed out the unusual billboard again. Quadriplegia at Harvard: A+.

At the crowded meet, able-bodied swimmers stood on the raised blocks to begin races for all the strokes except one: the back which always started in the water. Most used their feet and legs to surge at the start. Beth gained a slight bit of momentum with her hands pushing off the wall.

With rare exceptions, backstroke swimmers alternated their arms simply because it was faster. For Beth, moving both arms at the same time in the double-arm backstroke resulted in a better time despite her head dipping under. She improved slightly on her swim times but aimed higher.

Beth planned for a GTAC practice late afternoon on Fridays through the new school year. With the pool filled to capacity, she learned to share a lane while a coach supervised her backstroke laps. At the end of practice, Beth tried to get out of the pool by herself. She pressed her back into a corner of the pool and put her hands up on the ledge behind her, attempting to lift herself out of the water. She rose an inch or two before falling forward, but she kept trying regardless. At every practice.

Beth asked to go to the Tiffin YMCA once or twice a week. I helped her into the water. Her practices without a coach always focused on forward motion, the first step in her plan to master all of the swim strokes. I watched her closely from the deck bleachers since she spent more time under water than on top. With a few short bursts to the surface for rapid breaths, she could get herself almost to the halfway point of the 25-yard length. At that point, she had to give her arms a break and roll onto her back to breathe deeply.

Even if by some miracle Beth could progress continuously on her stomach, a bigger hurdle waited. She needed to learn the mechanics of the butterfly, breaststroke, and freestyle, with legal modifications for legs that dragged and hands that could not cup the water.

I thought the inevitable failure would tip her over the edge to depression. It made my head hurt more just thinking about it. Without Beth's buoyant optimism, would we be able to move forward?

Anxiety plagued my days and nights. What if overused antibiotics lost their effectiveness? The quad in the room next to Beth in Green Springs had died of pneumonia when antibiotics failed. Or would a blood clot travel to her heart or brain? I obsessed, sadly stuck in worst-case scenarios. Thankfully, Beth was not.

"My next goal," she said, "is to make the U.S. National Team that will attend the 2004 Paralympics in Athens, Greece."

❧ Chapter 12 ❧
TESTING

Beth: *I started doing the backstroke. Then, learning to swim on my stomach and still breathe was a big challenge initially.*

A SURPRISING REVELATION would absolve my guilt, but I expected a gradual catharsis with counseling which never came to pass. I had to be doing something wrong since I couldn't find the mom I had been before the accident. She was long gone, and I didn't know how to glue the new pieces together. Weekly sessions stirred up tearful regrets and ugly smatterings of self-pity. I sat in the car after, breathing deep, until I carried no visible baggage home. I scheduled more therapy, determined to redeem myself with Beth though others needed me too. And I needed them.

I waited impatiently for my gratitude for the people in my life to win the battle over my negativity. When worst-case scenarios controlled my thoughts, the effort to look normal doubled. I didn't want to pretend to be okay anymore. Unfortunately, it would take more than a positive attitude to defeat my fear and depression. Often distracted, paying attention in the moment required hard concentration, even with my immediate family despite no lack of love or genuine interest. My brain just wouldn't cooperate.

John shared a conversation at work. His boss asked him how he did it.

"Did what?" I asked.

"Forgive you," John said. He told his boss that forgiving me was never a choice for him—it had been a given from the start.

Forgiveness from anyone other than Beth? I had taken John's for granted. I appreciated how he understood. After the car accident, my best friend waited patiently for my attention as he had when I immersed myself in the care of a new baby. His forgiveness added to countless thoughtful overtures, from making me laugh to hugging me spontaneously. I vowed not to take John for granted again.

Unlike Beth, I had no grand goals. After magically erasing her injury, what I desired most? The absence of pain. No headache. No guilt. No depression. I read about how repetitive pain left untreated could hardwire into nervous systems. Maybe I should have taken Tylenol a decade earlier instead of refusing all medicine. I had tried to be healthy and hoped for a simple cure.

When noises around me echoed in my head, I resolved to ignore the pain though I religiously filled the Celebrex prescription month after month to lower the base level. It embarrassed me to admit I had a constant headache. The few times I mentioned it in the past, friends offered advice on another plane from where I found myself. A single pressure point to press for a cure or a few drops of essential oils to eliminate the headache. I loved that they wanted to help. I debated about sharing more about the entrenched head and neck pain or about the endless list of things I've tried. I cringed at the thought of that long, painful conversation. I obviously failed at getting my ducks in a row.

My headache seemed like a solid, singular entity that embodied my weaknesses. I concluded I had a low tolerance for pain, a costly flaw. I chose not to talk about it with anyone other than a doctor and avoided them whenever possible. Complaining served no purpose other than asking for pity which I refused to do.

Years before, my doctor had given me a prescription for a strong opiate painkiller to try to completely eliminate the headache. I picked it up at the pharmacy, then remembered my favorite grandmother's last months and decided not to use them.

My beloved Grandma Henning had taken Percocet (an opiate) for back pain for many years. A heating pad stayed plugged in on her couch, ready for her to lean against. Through her last months in 1995, the strongest narcotics had little effect, and unrelenting agony left her broken and altered.

At her funeral, I made a radical decision; if I lived to be elderly, I would choose my time to die long before that shocking level of suffering. My fear of pain ran deep and dark. I hoped my odds without an opiate addiction would be better than my grandma's. As it turned out, opiates wouldn't be an option for me.

My headache cycled between lower and higher levels, the typical aching almost welcome in contrast to the rare deep pounding. It bothered me that mental illness also cycled sometimes. The worst pain caused insomnia. Poor sleep aggravated everything.

One miserable night, I opened my new bottle to take the opiate oxycodone for the first time. My headache remained through the hours until dawn, with an added dimension of disturbing confusion. Self-pity swirled through the haze. My heart raced with unbidden thoughts of a heart attack, stroke, or cancer. And fears of dying, of abandoning Beth when she needed me.

In the morning, I threw away the rest of the opiates. If it had worked to eliminate my headache without confusion, I probably would be an addict. I settled for keeping my muddle of ducks afloat and breathing, barely above water.

After Beth's injury, my anxiety, depression, and guilt ebbed and flowed, like the headache. Pain combined to contract and expand on a whim. Some days, Beth emanated vulnerability, a lifelong quad forever haunted by scary health risks: autonomic dysreflexia, serious infections, bladder stones, blood clots, pneumonia, and pressure sores. Not to mention imminent depression. Other times, she looked to me like a typical teenager, which was closer to the truth.

I followed Beth wherever, whenever. On her forward motion quest at the YMCA, she progressed to spending more time with her head above water than under it. She could roll on her back to breathe and move to the edge, even if a leg or body spasm occurred. I started reading while I sat on the bleachers, instead of watching every minute. One evening, she finished a backstroke lap as her high school's swim team arrived to practice.

A few friends stopped to say hello to her. Their head coach, Peggy Ewald, introduced herself to Beth. Neither of them sensed the serendipity of the encounter.

I started a volunteer position as Adapted Chairperson on the Ohio Swimming Board of Directors. I provided information for coaches, swimmers, and families and encouraged swimmers with a disability. I gave updates at board meetings in Columbus, posted on the board's website, and purchased publicity items to distribute at swim meets. I ordered bookmarks with a photo on one side of an Ohio swimmer with a disability. They included a website for information and my new favorite quote by T.S. Eliot. "Only those who will risk going too far can possibly find out how far one can go."

A high school junior, Beth exchanged emails with another newly injured teenager. She volunteered for fundraisers with the Raptors and the National Honor Society. She tutored elementary students, wrote for the school newspaper, worked on the yearbook, and passed her driving test. She followed in Ben's footsteps and earned a spot on the

Quiz Bowl team. Her specialty? Literature. Mrs. Kizer led the team.

"Beth is one of the best-natured individuals I have ever known," Mrs. Kizer wrote in a reference letter. "I forget many times she is rolling along beside me, rather than walking."

Beth typed lab reports and essays on a standard computer with the keyboard and mouse set to a soft touch. The process evolved. She experimented and settled on three specific fingers to type. She relied the most on her useful left index, the digit she could move a few inches, to touch letters on the keyboard on the left side and center. This same finger also worked her laptop's built-in mouse. The index and pointer on Beth's right hand (with no movement) contracted in an arc and typed on the right side of the keyboard. To hit a key with the right index or pointer, she moved her whole hand to touch a fingertip onto a specific key. When a hand spasmed, she used the other hand and kept going. Her accuracy amazed me but in high school, her peers typed significantly faster. She stubbornly refused extra time for assignments and tests. Against my advice, she took the American College Test (ACT) with no time extension or other accommodations.

Students from the University of Toledo delivered the pool chair that impressively accomplished its purpose. At the YMCA, Beth stayed in her manual chair while I pulled the lift chair on its two small back wheels to a spot on the deck close to the water. She used the toggle switch to adjust the seat to a position slightly below the seat of her manual chair before transferring onto the lift by herself. Next, she pushed the toggle to lower it as far as possible, almost floor level. From there, she used her arms to scoot to the deck and into the water without assistance.

Sadly, we couldn't store the heavy chair at either pool. I could barely lift the device in and out of the car. Instead, we found the perfect home for it in our living room. Beth used the lift to get on and off the floor independently, sometimes stretching out to do her homework while a familiar movie played in the background. John and Beth watched the Austin Powers movies and other comedy favorites and made each other laugh with classic lines.

Thanksgiving weekend, our whole family waited in line at the theater for the second Harry Potter movie, *The Chamber of Secrets.* Beth asked to transfer to one of the padded seats. We lifted her over an armrest to an aisle seat, leaving the empty wheelchair next to her. When a lady tripped on the chair, I moved it right away to a front corner of the theatre where we could keep an eye on it.

Another day, Beth talked me into letting her drive with no one else in the car while she picked up her best friends to see the same movie again. The wheelchair sat in the trunk, out of reach though I made sure to place her cell phone nearby, fully charged. I kept mine close, but she didn't need me until she pulled into the driveway by herself after the movie. John and I allowed this only when one of us stayed home with a car, ready to help if need be. We still worried.

Five months after our Seattle trip, Beth achieved what I thought would be impossible. At the YMCA, she advanced forward on her stomach for the entire 25-yard length of the pool for the first time, her arms working wildly below the surface and advancing at a snail's pace. Her legs dragged behind. She conquered the basic balance of forward motion—without approximating a swim stroke. I expected her to rest at the wall after the 25 yards. Instead, she paused only a moment to take a bigger breath before pushing off and going a little farther.

Holding on to the wall after, she flashed a happy smile my way. Priceless. I returned her smile. All of my worrying and waiting for a plunge into depression had been unnecessary.

Beth pushed ahead toward a greater goal. At swim practices that followed, she focused on increasing the forward distance. *And* tried to add the arm movements of the butterfly in a clumsy, erratic way. Her backstroke had started in a similar way. In the two years since water therapy, the back had settled into a regular rhythm. I admired her tenacity, but mastering the freestyle? Unlikely. I anticipated an impassable physical barrier abruptly stopping her progress.

At the end of practice, Beth leaned her back into a corner, put her hands up on the ledge, and raised her body up as far as she could before being lifted out of the pool. Longer practices resulted in less elevation. A familiar dynamic: complete assistance very (very) slowly becoming partial assistance, with her clear expectation that it would be no assistance in the future. She accepted that damaged muscles would not strengthen nearly as easily or as much as healthy ones. Beth tapped into a well of stubborn teenage persistence, willing to wait weeks and months for small bits of progress.

The logistics of quad swimming evolved. Beth wore her one-piece suit to the pool, only partway to her waist, with loose sweatpants over the suit and a T-shirt on top. In the locker room, I removed the sweatpants and shirt and put the straps of the suit in place. After practice, I pulled sweatpants over the wet suit before we headed home to shower. With improved balance, she asked to try the white plastic shower bench again. It worked with my help, and we gladly gave away the cumbersome metal chair with the rails to friends.

Initially, the butterfly seemed more doable than the

freestyle or breaststroke. Beth raised her head for a breath after two arm strokes of the butterfly as she also did with the backstroke. She competed using the butterfly for the first time at the Turkey Meet in Toledo on Thanksgiving weekend. She loved how it felt to fly (slowly) through the water. She also selected her events for the Ohio Senior Meet in March. With typical courage, she signed up for the 150 Individual Medley (IM) that included strokes she could not yet perform.

Breathing challenged her initial breaststroke attempts. "When I first swam the breaststroke, I went backward," Beth said.

A week before the Senior meet, a Toledo coach suggested dropping the IM. Beth talked him into keeping it. She competed in the butterfly and breaststroke—not pretty— for the first time at the meet in Erlanger, Kentucky. Nine months after Seattle. I lifted her out of the pool while the packed crowd applauded.

Beth and I hadn't known about our hometown's swim club until they attended the same Senior Meet with their coach Peggy. She also coached the high school team. Peggy talked to the Toledo coaches and volunteered to help with some of Beth's solo practices in Tiffin.

At first, we met Peggy at the YMCA pool about once a week as Beth pursued her quest to master all of the strokes. They tackled the intricate details of moving and breathing in the water as a quad.

"Coach Ewald was excited to work with me from the first time I met her," Beth said.

And vice versa.

"It was a new adventure for me," Peggy told a reporter. "I was in the water with anatomy books on the deck, and I would ask her to move certain parts of her body and then I'd try to trace where the nerve ending connected to the muscle. The light bulb went off then because I understood that she didn't have the necessary nerves firing to do a particular movement. So we'd try a different movement to attempt the same goal. It took a lot of trial and error, but she was very willing."

Peggy had a passion for swimming I hadn't seen before. She did not rely on standard drills and techniques for able-bodied swimmers. With Beth, she enthusiastically approached practices with new ideas, willing to try until something clicked. The shared excitement of small successes propelled them forward.

Peggy's focus gradually changed, "from what she (Beth) didn't have to what she did have access to."

I registered Beth for her second USA Swimming Disability Championships, scheduled in early June in Minneapolis. Her improved times at recent meets qualified her for the meet as an S3 as she predicted in Seattle. At the YMCA about twice a week through the spring, I walked the nearby track instead of staying poolside to read. She stayed in the pool about 30 to 40 minutes with breaks.

We drove to Toledo once a week. Beth discovered a new favorite: volunteering at GTAC's WaterWorks to teach safety skills and basic swimming to young children with disabilities. On Saturdays, she planned on WaterWorks after a swim practice. She spoke to the kids about her spinal cord injury before getting in the water with them. First order of business: show them how to roll on their backs to breathe. Exactly like she had been taught at her first water therapy session after her injury. She loved WaterWorks Saturdays, the highlight of her spring.

We lived a few blocks from the high school, and Beth liked the idea of wheeling there instead of driving with me. My first thought: NO! How could it be safe for her to cross alleys and streets in a wheelchair? Beth wanted to try.

On a Sunday, I walked next to her on a trek to the high school. Our driveway stones created the first obstacle. Next, our old neighborhood had broken sidewalks and no curb cuts. We tried a narrow alley instead with bumps, stones, and potholes. And almost zero visibility for cars with large bushes blocking the view.

We crossed Washington Street between parked cars. Drivers approached fast. On the high school grounds, Beth had two choices. A long incline to the front entrance or a harder slope into the parking lot toward the automatic doors. Beth chose to get a ride to and from high school until she graduated.

Overbooking her time shifted from a frequent inclination to an ingrained habit. The Quiz Bowl team finished a winning season, undefeated in the league. Against my advice, again, Beth joined the high school musical, *Hello Dolly*. She wore a headset to manage the stage crew while Maria shined in the lead role. After a show, I chatted with other moms in the lobby without making a quick excuse to leave.

The girls stayed out late at the cast parties after the performances. John and I dropped our strict curfew rule after the car accident. A spinal cord injury changed our perspective with a new awareness of what really mattered and what didn't. John's garden burst into bloom, and I turned toward the sun. I kept busy and distracted with the headache at a lower baseline.

On May 10th of 2003, Beth drove us in her little blue car to the Michigan Wheelchair Games. Three years had passed since her injury and one year since her first swim meet in the same 25-yard pool. She competed in the forward freestyle for the first time. Not a smooth endeavor and quite a bit slower than her backstroke. She dropped 30 seconds off of her 50 back race and 60 seconds off the 100 back, compared to her times 12 months before.

On the drive home, Beth sang and danced in the passenger seat to her favorite John Mayer song. "I am invincible!" Déjà vu. I loved our road trips.

One week later, we attended the Ohio Wheelchair Games. We didn't know it would be our last one. Beth attended a few practices with the Seneca Aquatic Klub (SAK) in Tiffin to get in additional pool time with Peggy. Two weeks after the Ohio games, Beth competed in Bowling Green, Ohio, at her first outdoor meet. She liked being outside and rarely complained about the heat. She claimed to sweat a little, but I never saw it. I monitored her elevated body temperature and mild fever with a forehead gauge.

She accepted my help to wheel over the grass to GTAC's team camp. Her one friend on the team wasn't in sight, and she picked a spot out of the way. SAK swimmers at the same meet included Beth's high school friends, but she hesitated to leave the Toledo team and her first swim coaches.

Beth alternated her arms for the 100-meter backstroke instead of the double-arm technique while the other swimmers in the race swam a 200-meter event. They finished about the same time. Her race results varied more from meet to meet than they did for her able-bodied teammates.

Beth unexpectedly swam her fastest time by far in the 50-meter traditional forward freestyle race. The timing system needed repair, so swim parents with stopwatches stood by the blocks. She touched the wall at one minute and 28 seconds (1:28), still 15 long seconds away from the most difficult American Record in her classification. I suspected the parents with stopwatches of fudging (improving) her time a little.

"I often swim with non-disabled swimmers at 'regular' swim meets," Beth wrote in an 11th grade essay. "Many people are surprised that I compete in swimming since I use a wheelchair, and it has been fun for me to show how people with disabilities can be competitive in sports just as much as others. A swimmer who uses a wheelchair is still an unusual sight at most swim meets."

My schedule needed to align with Beth's since she couldn't drive independently with her wheelchair. I worked at not being a pushy parent and let Beth lead. If she asked to go to the YMCA for a practice, we drove there, but I didn't suggest it. Not happy with her ACT score, she studied practice books before taking the test again. Not my idea. The second ACT improved on her first composite score by a surprising four points. She credited her English teacher Mrs. Kizer for her top score.

Beth set goals on her own, and I supported her unconditionally but not for bragging rights. More than anything else, I needed her to be okay—to be really okay as she claimed the night of the accident. And was it too much to wish the same for myself, for everyone I loved, and for the rest of the world?

With one more year of classes to finish a double degree in physics and English, Ben ran meetings and scheduled open mic slams for the OSU Poetry Club he founded. Always on the go, Maria babysat often, worked at a video store, attended voice lessons, and performed in theater productions. She graduated from high school with honors in May.

We hosted a big graduation party on our backyard deck with John's flowers as a colorful backdrop. Maria chose to attend Tiffin's Heidelberg College to major in education and take advantage of their acclaimed music program. She had intended to be a teacher ever since she toddled into her dad's classroom. Since her sister's injury, Maria had decided to teach children with a disability.

I worried less about disappointments Beth might face, especially after she achieved the impossible and swam forward. Increasingly social and confident, her optimism grew. She fully expected to fall in love, get married, and start a family someday. Like many of her generation, someday would be soon enough. Most of her friends didn't date in high school and easily relegated romance to the future.

At Beth's age, I rode a school bus to the Cleveland Playhouse to see *Romeo and Juliet*. Another day, we watched the Franco Zeffirelli movie version, the most romantic thing I had seen. Ready and willing to make the leap, I longed to be loved intensely and perhaps a bit obsessively—minus the suicide, of course. My generation didn't put off the search for our Romeos and Juliets.

During my junior year at Lorain High School, a senior asked me to prom, and I wasn't impressed with the event. I planned to skip it my senior year and attend a party instead. However, my friend Mary asked her brother John to ask my brother Rick to go to the prom with her. Our parents lived across the street from each other. John suggested a foursome. I agreed reluctantly.

I wore the frilly bridesmaid dress from my sister's wedding with too many ruffles. Between the prom and prom to dawn, we drank spiked punch at my friend's party. I danced with John and when we arrived home, we kissed in my driveway. The next day, instead of the traditional post-prom trip to Cedar Point, I worked at a fundraiser for the Lorain County ARC while John drove back to college to finish the semester.

After my high school graduation, I boarded my first plane for a Norway summer. I won an essay contest that paid for my expenses as an exchange student for USA's

Bicentennial. John and I mailed long, handwritten letters across the sea. By the time I returned to Lorain nine weeks later, our words sealed a lasting connection. He understood me like no one else.

Before Beth's junior year ended, I drove three 17-year-old girls to physics day at Cedar Point in Sandusky. The sprawling amusement park filled with teenagers. Beth and her friends decided to try a few roller coasters. Skipping the long lines, they took their place at the front, joking about the perks of disability. They worked on their physics assignment and bypassed the rides that didn't have enough physical support for Beth.

We watched the Iron Dragon coaster and deemed it safe. Legs would dangle but with a relatively smooth ride. Metal bars held bodies in place securely. However, the Iron Dragon had no elevator and several flights of stairs. I dragged the wheelchair up with Beth facing down, rolling it on the steps for stability. She wrapped her arms around the seat back to stay in place. Two friends each grabbed a metal rod of her chair for back up.

When we arrived at the top, lifting Beth into the tight seat of the ride turned out to be harder than we expected, even with extra help. I suggested we stop and go back to the wheelchair, but she wanted to continue. The fast pace of the assembly line stopped, and people stared. Finally, I stepped back out of the way as the girls zoomed off. Disheartened, I questioned the accuracy of our risk assessment.

In no time at all, the girls flew back to the starting point and stayed put in the car for another round. Beth smiled and waved. I didn't worry as much the second time. I should have stressed more about the narrow steps going down, crowded with teenagers. At one point in the descent, I made the mistake of lifting the chair wheels high off the concrete to try to get around other people. A tilted chair and a tilted Beth made it more precarious. Lucky she didn't fall, we unanimously agreed to avoid stairs altogether the rest of the day.

The heat of the day kept rising. My daughter looked pale and didn't refuse Tylenol to bring her fever down. The girls found cold drinks and air conditioning in a restaurant and arcade. Beth never allowed hot weather to put a glitch in her plans and adventures.

She set up our busiest summer yet and signed up to volunteer at St. Vincent again. She accepted a part-time job in an office and bought tickets for a John Mayer concert. She applied for Ohio's Youth Leadership Forum, a five-day event for teenagers with a disability, and registered for her first (and only) National Junior Disability Championships. Plus swim practices a few times a week and traveling to her second USA Swimming Disability Championships. There would also be something no one anticipated—a midsummer invitation that required an eight-hour flight one way.

A magical summer waited for us.

❧ Chapter 13 ❦
RACING

Beth: I basically swim with my upper body and pull my entire body with my arms. Since my hands can't cup the water, my arms do all the work. It would be something like an able-bodied swimmer with their legs tied together and their hands in fists.

BETH DEBATED ABOUT where to apply to college. All teenagers should have that choice, but the thought of college with quadriplegia triggered more fears. What if she didn't make the best choice? What *was* the best choice?

To start the summer, John drove with Beth and me to the Shriners Hospital in our car instead of traveling in the Shriners van, because we planned on making other stops before returning home. At the hospital, X-rays showed that the progression of Beth's kyphosis and scoliosis had significantly slowed. A doctor told us swimming strengthened back muscles and if the trend continued, she wouldn't need surgery. No fusing the spine with a metal rod. No additional limits to her movement and flexibility with the rod. No risk of more spinal cord damage. I remembered the teenager we met in Green Springs who could walk before fusion surgery left him paralyzed.

The occupational therapist gave Beth a new adapted tool to try, a rocker knife with a knob handle to cut food. A hand surgeon recommended muscle transfer surgery for working thumbs. She politely told the doctor that she could use them without surgery, thank you very much, even though her tenodesis grip hardly compared to controlling each thumb individually. Muscle transfer surgery mandated several weeks of complete dependence. She refused to give up any of her hard-won independence.

The social worker asked about college. Before the accident, we all assumed Beth's college would be in Ohio. After, she decided to major in biology and wrote a list of possible colleges with top biology programs. All out of state.

"The travel I did with swimming opened up the world to me," Beth said.

We finished her appointments at the hospital and drove across town for a brief look at the University of Chicago. The next day, we toured the University of Illinois and met with wheelchair sports staff. The day after that, the University of Michigan impressed us. She also had toured other colleges in the past with her brother and sister including Case Western in Cleveland.

Beth considered Duke in North Carolina and Johns Hopkins in Maryland. With not enough open time for summer visits to both, she asked to see Johns Hopkins before the National Junior Disability Championships in Connecticut.

The first meet of Beth's second swimming summer required a 12-hour drive from Ohio to Minneapolis for her second USA Swimming Disability Championships. Swimming remained complex and challenging, but Beth navigated the car through Chicago on congested highways with ease. Our flight to Seattle a year earlier had been the only time we traveled west of Chicago.

Our hotel sat across the parking lot from the expansive University of Minnesota pool complex. We had never seen one like it. Around the main pool, 50-meters long, a wide deck on three sides opened up on the fourth for a smaller warm down pool and extensive high dive platforms. The ceiling towered about three stories high with spectator seating on the two long sides and clear glass panels on another. Bright. Beautiful.

We met Beth's Toledo coach and teammate at warm ups. The national anthem played as the meet started. An elderly man dived from a high platform where an immense American flag opened behind him. At 16, Beth no longer chose to sit next to me on the deck though she asked me to stay in sight. I understood her developing routine with goggles, swim caps, towels, bathroom breaks, positioning, and showering. I usually sat on the top row of the bleachers for back support against the wall until she signaled me. I got it. Being a teenager with a spinal cord injury created enough problems without adding a clingy mom. I supported her quest for complete independence, yet none of us knew if that would even be possible.

We watched fast races with new records, including the occasional World Record. Beth's expectations soared along with her nerves. As she predicted, her morning times made finals cuts; her previous national meet remained the first and only one where she had not. Even so, sluggish prelims races preceded discouraging finals times. Beth's frustration grew after another slow race on the second morning, and she wheeled into the locker room to wipe tears away. She still advanced to finals and won every race as the only S3 woman at the meet, a fact she did not appreciate. She aimed for swim times at least close to her best ones.

Immediately after the second morning's races, time trials allowed a swimmer to clock an official time in different events. I made a rare request. I asked her coach to sign her up for a time trial in the 200 backstroke.

Three years after her injury, Beth earned her first official Paralympic American Record for the 200-meter backstroke. We both knew it was the easiest S3 record to beat, but I reminded her that only a year earlier, she hadn't been strong enough to swim nonstop for 200 meters. As I anticipated, the success tempered her disappointment with other races.

We tumbled into the predictable schedule of a three day meet for swimmers who qualified for finals. Wake up, warm up, race, cool down, eat, recover, rest, and repeat. Add phone calls to John, Ben, and Maria. The last day of the meet after prelims, we strayed from the routine to visit the Mall of America. To preserve her strength for finals, Beth allowed me to push her wheelchair, a rare occurrence. That evening, we laughed with her coach when she clocked her fastest race of the meet after shopping. Her resolve to work harder magnified.

"Once I realized I was good in the water," she told a reporter, "I trained really hard and put a lot of focus and effort into it because it was this new avenue for me. I hadn't thought I could be an athlete anymore."

Beth set ambitious new goals after Minneapolis. In addition to mastering the forward freestyle, far from being attained, she aimed higher for the ultimate American Record in the 50-meter freestyle, by far the most difficult S3 record to beat.

The next big trip of her second swimming summer took us to Maryland and Connecticut for the first time, with an important, last minute detour. On the open road again in her little blue car, Beth and I took turns driving from northwest Ohio to the East Coast. We turned up the volume on John Mayer or mix CDs and sang along. First stop: Johns Hopkins University in Baltimore.

I pushed Beth up and over a formidable hill on campus, and I couldn't stop myself from stating the obvious. It definitely was impossible with a manual wheelchair. She pointed out an alternative route, much longer, that looked a little easier. We agreed I'd help during her first year of college, but the logistics remained hazy. Our tour guide rambled, and I imagined her wheeling alone on the Johns Hopkins campus. She still refused to consider a power chair or power assist wheels. The odds of Beth letting me push her chair to class, up hills or through snow? Zero to none.

The unusual billboard in Seattle (Quadriplegia at Harvard: A+) had prompted me to look online. I found the young woman pictured on the billboard. Brooke Ellison and her mom wrote a book, *Miracles Happen: One Mother, One Daughter, One Journey.* With an injury like Christopher Reeve, Brooke needed a trach to breathe and could not move her arms. She shared her college dorm room with her mom, and they moved through all of the hours as a team.

Three years after Beth's injury, I thought I might stay in her college dorm the first year though I knew our days as a team were numbered. My youngest daughter never stopped trying to conquer the time-consuming details of self-care as a quad. She worked daily on her loftiest goal, complete independence, with odds not in her favor. Encouraged by small victories, she never gave up.

After Johns Hopkins, we headed to Connecticut for the weeklong Junior National Championships. Hundreds of kids converged from all over the country. Like Beth, many were the only ones with a visible disability in their class or school. At registration, we recognized a few teenagers from the Paralympic meet in Minneapolis two weeks before and another from the Ohio Wheelchair Games. None of Beth's friends from the Raptors could join us.

The first day, many ping-pong tables filled the field house. Beth experimented and found a better way to angle the paddle by tilting her left wrist more. She tested how far she could lean to reach the ball without falling. At her request, I reluctantly removed the two armrests on her wheelchair. She surprised us by winning several games without losing her balance and never put the armrests back on.

The matches ended with a simple meal for everyone in attendance. Caterers stood behind a buffet table and wore clear plastic gloves to set out food. A frustrated mom confronted the servers about the latex gloves they wore. Her son had a latex allergy, more common among kids with a disability than the general population. Beth never had a problem with latex though I agreed that latex-free gloves should be used at a disability event. I also felt sorry for the teenage servers who bore no responsibility for the mistake.

Wheelchairs surrounded the pool at the swim competition. The extremely casual atmosphere contrasted with our recent meets. When Beth raced, I walked alongside her on the deck. I decided to make her laugh. I stayed in her sights and waved my arms in front of me like a coach, the signal to kick harder. She set several new wheelchair sports records. Not the coveted Paralympic American Records.

On a free day, Beth suggested a visit to the Mohegan Sun casino to see the works of art. Wheeling through massive spaces, she realized at one point that we had accidentally entered a restricted area for adults 18 and over. With slot machines nearby, Beth, 17, asked to try the poker slots. I put quarters in the machine and let her tell me which cards to keep. She never touched the slots and helped me lose $30.

I snapped photographs everywhere while Beth collected menus, flyers, and other small things. She bought the perfect summer scrapbook at a shop in the historic bridge district in Mystic, Connecticut. Equally exciting, we bought the fifth Harry Potter book, *The Order of the Phoenix,* to add to her collection, one of the five million copies bought in the first 24 hours. Her happiness was contagious.

We ate lunch at Mystic Pizza, famous for the 1988 cult movie with the same name. I helped her scoot out of her chair to a seat in a booth. Memorabilia decorated every nook and cranny. Beth rated it the best pizza. Ever. She picked out "A Slice of Heaven" T-shirt.

We basked in the sun on the waterfront by Mystic's picturesque harbor on a flawless afternoon. An easy travel buddy, Beth appreciated extraordinary moments. She tilted her face up, closed her eyes, and smiled. I wrapped her in a big bear hug. She reciprocated and softly patted my back; after her injury, I thought that was one of the many things she lost. Knowing how suddenly bad things could happen, I would never take joy for granted again. I embraced the singular moment while a new realization dawned. My guilt? Self-imposed. No one, least of all Beth, blamed me for her injury.

Junior Nationals wrapped up with a dinner and dance in a packed ballroom. A DJ played popular music while hundreds of kids with all kinds of physical disabilities danced standing up, sitting in a wheelchair, or breakdancing on the floor. With no one different and no one the same, they all shined in that snapshot of time. My daughter danced carefree in the middle of it all.

Beth made a last-minute request to spend a day at Harvard in Cambridge before returning home. We drove through New Haven, Connecticut, on the way to Massachusetts. I noticed a sign for another college.

"Would you like to visit Yale?" I asked. A definite, "No." She had no interest in any Ivy League college, with one exception.

"Harvard first got my attention because of the national billboard campaign," Beth said in a scholarship essay, "which suggested an appreciation of the contributions that students with disabilities can make."

Harvard turned out to be more than we expected. A student guide led us through one of the ornate gates into

Harvard Yard, a charming realm. The stately old buildings, statues, and wooded courtyards transported us to a unique world of the past. After the tour, we explored the adjoining Harvard Square. Street musicians performed in a loud and crowded urban setting. The intense humanity of the Square held a charm all its own, with a mix of cultures and languages in every direction. A man in an expensive business suit shared the sidewalk with a homeless man sleeping.

Back in Tiffin in early July, Beth worked part-time in the local Community Action Commission office. She photocopied, filed papers, and answered the phone. She invited Ellen, Jackie, and Lizzy to pose with her for senior pictures with a local photographer. She swam with GTAC about twice a week at an outdoor pool, even when it rained, and volunteered after practice on the neuroscience floor at St. Vincent. She restocked laundry, made beds, filled water pitchers, and brought snacks for patients. With her tenodesis grip, she dropped items a little more often than other volunteers, but fully utilized the wheelchair perk of carrying things hands-free on her lap.

Beth gravitated to the classics between frequent swim practices, her part-time job, and time with friends. She finished *Cancer Ward* by Alexander Solzhenitsyn, a longtime favorite of mine. One passage in particular stayed with me. "It is not our level of prosperity that makes for happiness but the kinship of heart to heart and the way we look at the world. Both attitudes lie within our power, so that a man is happy so long as he chooses to be happy, and none can stop him."

I loved that passage since high school, but a recent thought disturbed the beauty of it. How exactly did clinical depression and body chemistry fit in? I didn't know. One thing I knew for sure: Beth embodied the writer's happiness equation, with perspective adding to meaningful connections. I wanted to be like her someday.

The Youth Leadership Forum of the Ohio Governor's Council on People with Disabilities highlighted Beth's summer. Students with a disability in their junior year of high school had applied to attend as delegates. The five-day event without parents would be a first for Beth and others, with personal care assistants available.

I dropped her off at a posh hotel in Columbus. I kept my phone charged and the gas tank filled, available at a moment's notice. I could hardly wait to pick her up though she sounded happy on the phone. I kept busy by painting a bedroom with John. Maria and I lunched at Taco Bell or shopped between her jobs. I met a friend for breakfast. John and I spent a leisurely day in Findlay. We browsed shops, held hands at a movie, and ordered ginger chicken at our favorite restaurant. Still, I thought of Beth often.

In my darker moments, the uncertainty of her future troubled me. Would her busy life be sidetracked with pressure sores and other health problems? How would an uncaring world treat her as an adult? I easily added worries about the forum to the mix. Would her reluctance to request help lead to frustration?

I was right about asking for help and wrong about her response. Driving home with me to Tiffin, Beth said, "It was the best week of my life!" I smiled, glad to hear it but hoping many others would be even better.

The first night of the forum, she had asked for help to get up on the higher hotel mattress. The other days, she figured out how to do it herself. She set her alarm early and worked to shower and dress completely on her own, allowing for extra minutes to zip zippers and button buttons. Proud that she could. After difficult but independent transfers, she even unbunched her jeans by herself.

Beth shared more details. Introduced to disability issues large and small, she learned about the fight for the Americans with Disabilities Act. The speakers discussed stereotypes and the fact that many people with a disability did not have a job. Advocates talked about limiting Ohio's handicapped parking permits to those who needed them the most. One session explored the ramifications of denied access for everyone with a disability. Information mixed with social events. At a dance, Beth slow-danced with a boy for the first time.

"The staff was great, and there were a number of outstanding speakers," Beth said. "The event had a big impact on my life my first year as a delegate."

The forum anchored her to others with a disability. Beth met delegates, staff, and speakers with epilepsy, cerebral palsy, paraplegia, quadriplegia, dwarfism, learning issues, mental illness, and brain injuries. Others were blind or deaf. She received an invitation to report on the Youth Leadership Forum at the annual meeting of the Ohio Governor's Council on People with Disabilities. She spoke to a large crowd.

"The Ohio forum proved to me that the disability community is widely diverse and vitally important."

Another unexpected invitation led to an eight-hour flight. U.S. Paralympics Swimming invited Beth to attend the Canadian Open SWAD (Swimmers With A Disability) meet in August with the National Team. My daughter accepted before we looked up the location of Edmonton, Alberta. From Tiffin, the trip would cross almost 2,000 miles. We invited Peggy to join us. We packed Beth's brand new passport and her iPod, with a new playlist for meets.

We kept her manual wheelchair until she boarded the plane for her second flight since her injury. I helped her transfer from her wheelchair to an aisle chair on the jet bridge, then grabbed her chair cushion and left her tagged chair with strollers. It lowered the probability of damage, at least a bit. I imagined the chair on top of the luggage pile instead of under it.

We traveled in style when an airline clerk upgraded our economy tickets to first class, our initiation to warm hand towels and extras. A welcome distraction during a long flight, with full meals instead of the snacks offered in the cheaper seats. I helped Beth shift and raise her legs periodically through the eight hours in the air.

When we landed in Alberta, Beth's wheelchair had a bent wheel that made it harder to push. Traveling necessitated frequent repairs, especially replacing worn out wheel bearings. They deteriorated faster than usual after repeated drenchings in locker room showers.

The many countries represented at the Canadian meet created a festive atmosphere. Each team wore national colors and their flag hung near the deck bleachers claimed by each country. The stars and stripes hung from the front of the high spectator seats where I observed along with other U.S. fans. I understood that Beth didn't want to be the only one in a Team USA shirt who sat with her mom. Peggy assisted her on deck. I wore a deck pass to help in the locker room. An unanticipated perk of the pass allowed me to take pictures on deck during medal presentations.

Still somewhat shy, Beth made an effort to meet more her teammates while I talked to other parents. They shared information about grants from the Challenged Athletes Foundation to help with the costs of competing. I also heard about three teenage girls on the U.S. team who had discovered they shared the same birthplace in Russia. They had limb differences and had been adopted by U.S. families in different parts of the country. I listened to many stories, including a young girl with a sudden-onset neuromuscular disorder. She returned home from school one day and collapsed on the floor. Life can change in a moment.

From the stands, I watched Beth laugh at the antics of the teenage boys on the team. One morning, they secretly "borrowed" the Australian team's frog mascot and noisemakers, stoking a friendly rivalry.

Beth met other S3 women from Germany, Norway, Denmark, and Mexico. The women from Mexico and Germany held the top spots in the World Rankings. To race, they left their wheelchairs behind when they stood and walked a step or two to the starting blocks. Their coaches helped them climb on and prepare to dive in. My daughter started the race in the water, often with an ineffectual push off the wall.

With the tough competition, Beth didn't expect to earn a medal for a top three finish. Also unexpected: the swimmer in the next lane stayed in her field of vision, sparking momentum. For the very first time, she experienced how it felt to see and to race a true competitor, to beat her to the finish by less than a second, and to earn a third place international medal.

Waiting for her next race, Beth adjusted her earbuds and turned up the music. She surprised everyone with second place in the 100-meter freestyle race. Right after, officials tagged her for her first drug testing. They worked for the United States Anti-Doping Agency (USADA), the same agency that tested Olympic athletes. Officials stayed close by as a Team USA coach supervised her cool down laps in a separate small pool. From there, Beth participated in her first ceremony for an international medal. Afterward, the USADA officials led the way off the deck while the coach explained the test procedure to her.

In the 100 and 200-meter events, Beth finished ahead of the top-ranked S3 women from Germany and Mexico. She started to think of herself as a distance swimmer. The five S3 women in Alberta, Beth included, swam slower than their previous best times. Health issues like spasms, skin scrapes, minor infections, and low-grade fevers had more of an impact on those with severe disabilities compared to others who did not. Temperature changes also affected quads in a negative way as well as not drinking enough water. The physical stress of traveling and time changes also factored in. That was one of the reasons that teams participating in the Paralympics arrived in the area weeks ahead of the actual event.

Beth rested between the sessions of the three-day meet. No sightseeing in Edmonton, except for the green, hilly view from the airport.

We landed in Detroit with her first international medals, two silver and two bronze. Medals that mattered. The airline lost a sideguard, one of two curved plastic shields to protect clothes from the wheelchair wheels. One small shield cost $100. I bought a replacement and started the long process to be reimbursed from the airline. After Alberta, Beth removed the sideguards before she boarded a plane.

Summer vacation wound down. Peggy tackled the difficult details of the freestyle at the YMCA. She moved in the water with the grace of a seasoned swimmer and often joined Beth in the pool to help with technique. Learning how to swim mimicked the physical therapy process. Beth paid close attention to detailed instructions and understood the goal. Small gains and slow progress did not discourage her. She visualized future success and put the pieces together bit by bit.

Peggy asked Beth to join the Tiffin Columbian High School swim team for her senior year. Initially, I had reservations. I knew the team had a great coach. I wondered if Beth's participation would be mutually beneficial or a token inclusion? A reluctant Athletic Director also needed to be convinced, especially since accessible school buses were rarely available. As a compromise, I drove with my daughter to away meets. Watching more practices, I trusted the coach's instincts on the merits of the high school team.

"Peggy has helped me make all my strokes better," Beth said.

A week after the Canada meet, Beth achieved a milestone much earlier than expected with an official spot on the U.S. Paralympics Swimming National Team. Beth called Ben first with the news since he followed her races and progress. Beth celebrated with Maria, John, and me over frozen yogurt sundaes.

National Team status included team swimsuits and other gear as well as stipends for training costs and specific meets. And a big stack of paperwork. Beth's lung doctors filled out a long form to allow her only asthma medication, a maintenance inhaler. She submitted training logs year-round. Each practice became an official workout including a coach's plan written in a swimming shorthand I never learned. Team status also required reports of her daily whereabouts to facilitate random drug testing through USADA.

In August, I dropped off Beth and Lizzy at a John Mayer concert in Columbus. I easily imagined them singing loudly to the invincible lyrics of "No Such Thing." The girls wore hipster hats bought for the occasion. Beth donned the same canvas hat with gray stripes during the Fishing Has No Boundaries event, a week after Alberta.

We stayed at a hotel with the Toledo team for the fishing weekend. John and I held hands and watched our talented daughters sing in harmony on the karaoke stage. Other weekends, John and I met our good friend, Pat, at a Findlay café for open mic night.

College applications covered our kitchen table before Beth's senior year of high school began. She questioned the need for help during her freshman year and wondered if I could live off-campus instead of in the dorm with her. Separate housing for me for any amount of time would add significant costs on top of her out-of-state tuition, room, and board. High college expenses seemed certain, but John and I decided not to hold her back because of finances. We owned the Tiffin house and planned to borrow off it.

I watched Beth hold a pen awkwardly in her right fist, not hesitating as she wrote her motto on a Challenged Athletes application. ANYTHING IS POSSIBLE. I filed away a note I wrote to myself that said, "Anything is possible, except when it's not." It amazed me how she dismissed all she couldn't do as irrelevant and wholeheartedly believed in the truth of the motto. And it really *was* true but only for her and a small percentage of others with her priceless perspective. Those with and without a disability.

"I think walking is over-rated," Beth said, with a smile.

Unable to stand and not focused on a far-off cure, she continued to defy the usual limits of quad hands. She wouldn't write off any fine-motor tasks she really wanted to do. Her persistence and successes were a tribute to unwavering belief.

My second counselor moved away, and the third nudged me forward. I connected the most to the last one. After nearly three years of weekly sessions in the same small office, I had few tears left. All that time I'd spun in a rut, perseverating on my poor choices the night of Beth's injury — as if I had a replay option.

My new psychologist, a friendly mom, told me the accident could not have happened any other way. She framed it as less of a colossal failure and more of a perfect storm of events. That morning, I woke up very early to set up a refreshment stand for the choir contest. John stayed home to study for his National Board test. The night of the accident, the OSU concert ran longer than expected.

The psychologist's next point hit home. I could not make a good decision (like calling John on the pay phone) because *exhaustion impaired my judgment*. That somehow flipped a switch for me and allowed a measure of forgiveness. I gradually reduced my Zoloft to a lower dose. The headache tightrope remained a precarious and somewhat mysterious balancing act.

At home, Beth gathered summer mementos and made colorful collages with a small paper cutter. She used markers to add descriptions and funny comments on each page, approximating the calligraphy style she learned before her injury. She created a tribute to the magical summer in her first scrapbook.

The last page listed of 15 notable summer firsts including her first American Record, her first passport stamp, her first tuna fish and cucumber sandwich, her first concert without a parent, and her first swim practice in the rain. Beth's very best "first" of the summer? Wheeling in Cambridge, Massachusetts.

"I toured the Harvard campus and just fell in love with it."

❧ Chapter 14 ❧
SURGING

Beth: I don't think it really hit me until I told my friends, and I saw how excited they were for me.

I STOPPED COUNSELING. After all, I was perfectly fine. I finally progressed in the wake of three years of weekly sessions. Guilt no longer dominated my days which felt like a monumental gift. My anxiety and depression stepped down to less of a main event. Still, I couldn't admit I needed help with pain and stress. It looked like it would take a miracle to get my ducks in a row.

I scheduled dentist appointments to fix my second cracked molar, a casualty of teeth clenching despite the biteplate I wore each night. My doctor added a temporary muscle relaxant at bedtime to reduce the clenching. A high dose of Celebrex usually tempered the headache and joint pain and kept me moving.

Beth quietly completed and submitted an early admission application to Harvard in September of her senior year. Only her immediate family and best friends knew she applied.

"I didn't tell everyone since I didn't think I would get in," she said.

If someone asked about college plans, Beth mentioned the University of Michigan or Duke, two of the colleges she planned to apply to after she heard back from Harvard in December.

I appreciated my new rare gift of time since Beth didn't need me at school midday anymore. Never bored, I protected my free hours by not turning on the TV during the day. I personalized three mother's journals, one for each of my kids, with childhood memories and family history. I picked up needlework and writing projects, humming along to classic tunes playing in the background.

I connected with Maria after her jobs, classes, or choir practices, sometimes meeting her for lunch. I called my parents and sent care packages to Ben at OSU. I walked for exercise. I met a friend for brunch most weeks at Bob Evans. When we approached from the parking lot, the waitress saw us coming and had our iced teas ready at a table. Small town perks.

John never suggested I work outside the home in any way. We had enough with his steady income and our frugal ways. Regardless, I convinced myself that I *should* return to a paid job for the school year until Beth started college. She gained more independence and encouraged me, assuming I really wanted to work. She also liked the idea of pushing the limits of her disability more often and not relying on me when she felt rushed or tired.

I debated between a demanding job at better pay and a minimum wage job with less responsibility. With few choices in Tiffin, I decided to support adults with developmental disabilities. A job where I could make a small difference. A local agency offered me the position of group home manager in a nearby town. A familiar job.

A few weeks after my wedding, newly 19, I assumed the role of live-in manager at a new group home in Clyde. John and I moved in before he started his first elementary teaching job. The year was 1977, during the first wave of the exodus from Ohio institutions. The best candidates for community living left first including my four residents.

The transition challenged everyone involved, every day. One notable example: a social worker decided that an elderly man in our home should wear dentures after years with no teeth. After too-many unpleasant dentist appointments, I stood on my head to sell the concept and worked with him morning and night with new dentures. His team added their encouragement at the workshop. The day in 1979 when John and I moved out of the group home, the resident flushed his dentures down the toilet.

A few decades had passed since that first group home job and some Ohio institutions had closed. The exodus slowed to a trickle and included residents with multiple disabilities. I accepted my new manager position on a Friday without visiting the group home first. I could handle most anything for less than a year. Couldn't I?

My job started with a bang. My new boss handed me keys and suggested I meet the residents over the weekend. If the woman on duty asked if she would be my assistant, I should tell her no.

Driving to the home, I passed the pay phone I didn't use the night of the accident as well as the field where my car flipped three times. I knocked on the front door of a run-down, two-story home and entered a dark, depressing living room. I introduced myself to the four residents watching TV and the woman on duty who had been crocheting in a separate room in front of another television. Most jobs didn't allow time for staff hobbies including ones at group homes. I kept quiet and observed. She asked about the assistant position and when I responded, she argued even though she knew it wasn't my decision. She left shortly after with the residents for an outing and hit my parked car with the company van. Presumably by accident.

I worked three 24-hour shifts a week and the residents usually attended a workshop on weekdays. I also drove them to numerous doctor visits and volunteered additional time on other days when Beth attended school. A mess of paperwork needed to be cleaned up in short order for a state inspection, and the house had been neglected to the point of being unhealthy.

The poor condition of the house frustrated me. I loved where I had worked and lived for my first manager job, a lovely old home with beautiful oak molding. My second group home made my skin crawl, dirty and cluttered with evidence of mice. I bleached mold on and in the refrigerator and cleared legions of powdery bugs from overhead lights. I scoured decades of yellow wax off the kitchen floor, cleaned mice droppings out of cupboards, and threw away infested food. My mom and I donated time to replace the wallpaper to brighten the living room.

My hectic paid hours focused on the residents and improving their quality of life. I delivered a pep talk at a staff meeting to enlist their help to raise the bar. Thankfully, the crocheting woman transferred to another home. I aimed for a level of care I would want for someone I loved. With only a few staff and fewer resources, I fell short though I took a small measure of pride in trying.

I recognized the seriousness of my responsibilities, aware of my impact on the day-to-day mental and physical health of the residents. Group home managers doubled as underpaid psychologists, nurses, and nutritionists. I expected the job to be taxing, like my earlier Tiffin Center job, where most of the residents had grown up in an institution without a loving family. The difference at the group home? Working alone most of the time.

I dispensed a complicated litany of pills, my least favorite part of the job—particularly when a volatile resident refused to take his psychotropic medicine. Despite behavior plans I followed, I filled out scores of incident reports. I also slept poorly three nights a week on a day bed. But, it wasn't all bad.

Three of the residents played on a basketball team, and I cheered for them at games with the fourth. Other outings and events could be fun too. Sometimes. In the middle of the night, a genial resident who was deaf occasionally switched on the TV and cranked up the sound. He giggled when a sleepy worker stumbled in and out to turn off the volume. I waited to smile until *after* I turned to walk out of his room.

My body rebelled with less sleep and a full dance card. Managing the group home escalated my headache. The level of pain had gradually increased over a dozen years. How bad would it get? Over-the-counter medications didn't make a dent. Opiates weren't an option. My prescription anti-inflammatory, Celebrex, muted the headache and increased my stroke risk. I read a study about how the brain adapted to frequent pain signals, making it difficult to break the cycle. Obviously.

I made a concerted effort to stay positive at work and at home. I minimized my health issues when someone asked. I hated feeling weak, and I wouldn't be a complainer. I didn't realize that asking for help and complaining were two different things.

I kept up with Beth. She acquired new roles, unafraid, including the top job of news editor of the school newspaper, The Tiffinian. A feature in the paper titled Senior Superlatives reported on a class election that voted her most likely to be President and most likely to be rich.

"I didn't want both, so I gave the rich title away," Beth said, with a laugh.

The votes of her classmates also put her on the Homecoming Court, surprising her. "I was shy in high school," Beth said in an interview. "I had more fun than most, but I wasn't a cool kid."

The night of the Homecoming football game, the court arrived at the stadium in convertibles before lining up to be presented to the crowd. A problem we didn't anticipate handed Beth a rare defeat.

"I wheeled myself everywhere, but my escort wanted to push my chair across the field," she said, while also admitting the difficulty with the bumpy turf. A standoff on the 50-yard line ensued, her escort equally as stubborn as Beth. She reluctantly gave in. "But, I kept my hands on the wheels and pushed myself at the same time!"

When the pageantry ended, Beth sat with her best friends on the cement platform in the stadium's student section to watch the game. Ellen and Lizzy gave her a bouquet of flowers and an adorable present. They made a Build-A-Bear and dressed it up with a fancy dress, homecoming crown, magic wand, and queen banner. They had been sure Beth would win. She didn't and hadn't expected to, yet the bear sweetly reminded her of friends always in your corner.

Beth's wheelchair didn't seem to rule out anything she really wanted to do. At 17, she competed on the Quiz Bowl team and started a dozen college scholarship applications. A Paralympic coach asked Beth to mentor a teenager from Seattle with a new spinal cord injury. The girls exchanged emails about wheelchairs and prom dresses.

"I volunteer for many projects including my National Honor Society's annual food drive. I go to an elementary school once a week as an athlete mentor," Beth wrote. "I love mentoring!"

At the first practice of the high school swim team season, I sat on the YMCA bleachers with a book, just in case Beth needed me. I usually lowered her from the wheelchair to the deck and positioned her swim cap after she tried to do it by herself first. Peggy competently took over the tasks.

Each swimmer carried a net bag with workout gear. In Beth's, the typical flat paddles had been cut to a smaller size to fit her hands, with the flexible tubes adjusted to hold a group of fingers in place. Floating aids strapped on with Velcro. She also utilized a tempo trainer, a battery-operated device the size of a watch face that attached to her ear. It worked like a metronome from music class, clicking out the pace.

I couldn't imagine a better coach than Peggy. She modified the team's workout for Beth with creative variations to avoid too much stress on specific arm and shoulder muscles. She practiced circle turns since she couldn't flip at the wall and push off with her feet like her teammates could. To finish a lap, she approached the wall at the left side of the lane, pushed off the wall with one hand, and completed the half circle to start another lap.

"Walls are bad for me," Beth said. The fewer walls in a race, the faster her times. High school competitions took place in short course pools with 25-yard lengths. A 100-yard race required three circle turns at the walls.

"It pushes her to train with us, and it pushes the other kids because it's taught them that all things are possible," Peggy said.

As always, Beth tried to get out of the pool by herself. With her hands behind her on the low deck, she attempted a few times on her own—almost making it—before being lifted out. She always needed help to get from the deck to her wheelchair and didn't mind when the boys on the team volunteered.

I caught up with her on the way to the locker room, expecting to assist. Beth decided to go it alone for the first time and declined politely. She joined the rest of the girls in the locker room. I waited impatiently in the lobby, wondering if she changed her mind.

Sitting in her wheelchair, Beth lifted a knee with her wrist to raise a foot. The opposite hand guided one side of the sweatpants over the dangling foot before shifting to do the same for the other side. The trick would be placing her feet back on the footrest with the pants bunched up around both ankles. From that position, she used her fists and the one finger she could control to slowly pull the sweats up and over her knees. When the pants finally bunched at her thighs, she rocked from side to side to continue the prolonged fight. Next, she scooted forward and leaned her shoulders on the back of the chair. Anchored, she lifted her bottom up a few inches to pull the sweats up in the back. Inch by inch.

In the meantime, the rest of her team showered, changed, and left the YMCA. I found her in the locker room with the sweatpants mostly on. Beth's first post-practice solution for independence? Put on baggy pants over a wet swimsuit and leave to shower at home. Easier said than done.

For all the other high school evening practices, John or I dropped her off at the entrance of the YMCA, left, and returned later to wait for her after practice. Changing in her wheelchair on her own required extra time at first. She usually wheeled out the YMCA door into a nearly empty parking lot.

Officials with the United States Anti-Doping Agency interrupted a high school practice for one of Beth's random drug tests, her first outside of a national meet. Her teammates were impressed. She sent in another quarterly report for USADA with her location at all times as she would for the next five years as a member of the U.S. Paralympics Swimming National Team. Letters arrived periodically to verify she passed the drug tests. I regularly submitted the extra paperwork and doctor signatures to allow for her one prescription, the inhaler to keep her asthma symptoms at bay. Routine tests with the lung doctor showed small, steady gains in lung capacity.

We rarely made it to the Toledo pool, and Peggy met Beth for an additional one-on-one practice at the YMCA most weeks. They experimented with foot starts, legal for a swimmer with limited hand function. On the deck, Peggy lay stomach down with her head over the water. She reached low to grab Beth's feet and hold them to the starting wall. Repeated trials determined the intricate details of the optimum position to start each stroke. An arm straight or bent, trunk angled or supine, and the mechanics of remaining motionless until the starting buzzer.

I arranged my work hours at the group home to be free for swim meets. The once-a-year USA Swimming Disability Championships evolved in 2003 into Can-Am Paralympic meets twice a year, one in the U.S. and one in Canada. The United States also hosted a special Trials meet every four years before the Paralympics. At a Can-Am meet in Indianapolis in November, Beth earned two American Records in the 100 and 200 freestyle.

"Three years ago, the only way I could swim was with two physical therapists holding me in the water," she wrote in a school essay. "Since then, swimming has become a significant part of my life."

Beth moved up the IPC World Rankings to 10th or better in several events, including the individual medley. The greater the distance, the higher her world ranking. Long races challenged many S3 swimmers. Beth pushed herself farther at each practice.

I booked a hotel and flights for the April Trials meet five months ahead, but we didn't know if Beth would qualify for the 2004 Paralympics. Or if September in Athens would be an option with whatever college she would attend. What we did know: races for women in the S3 classification had been cut to only three events in Greece, the 50 and 100 free and the 50 back. The reason? The small number of S3 swimmers in the world.

"My favorite event is the freestyle," Beth told a reporter, "but fewer people who have (severe) disabilities can do the butterfly and breaststroke, so I'm grateful I can."

The strokes she felt grateful for also wouldn't be an option at the Paralympics for S3 swimmers. Her friends on the National Team with higher-numbered classifications had numerous choices of strokes and distances. The unfair restrictions frustrated me while Beth resigned herself to the news and carried on.

In early December, a long-awaited email changed our course. Decisions about early admission were announced in emails on a specific evening. Beth waited at the computer after school that day. I hovered nearby, hopeful. The house was quiet until . . .

"I got in!" Beth said, squealing with joy.

"What?" I believed her, but I had to read the email too. I hugged her from behind her chair. "Congratulations, sweetie!"

After reading the email a few more times, she lowered herself to the living room floor in her lift chair. Lying on her back, she spread out her arms, closed her eyes, and just beamed. Incredulous, I watched my jubilant daughter. What would happen next? She had planned to send out additional college applications.

"If I don't go to Harvard," Beth told me, "I'll always wonder what might have been." She didn't want to apply anywhere else.

John and I decided to make it happen. Tuition would be $27,448 for the 2004 – 2005 school year. Add room and board plus fees for a total of $39,880. Plus travel costs and my living expenses off-campus in a very high rent area. John and

I intended to borrow money on our home, but four years of Harvard would cost more than it was worth. Beth officially notified Harvard that she would attend and decided on her own to apply for more college scholarships.

Her unexpected acceptance to Harvard launched another shift in the horizon for my family. At first, she chose not to broadcast the news outside of her family and best friends. I asked her why, and she didn't have a clear answer. We respected her choice. Maybe she felt humbled as she processed the big news? I had processing of my own and much to figure out. I would live in Cambridge, Massachusetts during Beth's freshman year. I had mixed feelings. Her acceptance triggered pride and joy but also fear of the unknown and of letting go. Suddenly, endless preparations loomed ahead.

The girls on the high school swim team painted their nails for meets in school colors, blue and gold. For the first time since the accident, Beth painted her nails by herself, not caring that they looked less than perfect. She trusted that more practice would yield better results.

I drove with Beth to an away meet when an accessible bus wasn't available for the team. A flight of steps led down to the pool, and parents watched from a higher level. Beth showed two teammates the best way to bump the wheelchair safely down the stairs.

High school competitions ran like USA Swimming meets though on a much smaller and less formal scale. Everyone stared at the girl in the wheelchair. Beth didn't let it bother her. In the 100-yard butterfly, she finished third, one of three swimmers in the race.

"I was able to score quite a few points in high school," she told a reporter. "My coach put me in the harder events that nobody wanted to do, like the butterfly. Since the top three swimmers scored, as long as I finished I would score points."

After the meet, Beth hurried and left the locker room after the rest of the team. She found herself alone by the pool, so I bumped her up the steps. Peggy and the team apologized a few minutes later in the lobby, but I completely understood. Beth made it easy to forget she used a wheelchair.

John drove her to high school practices on the evenings I worked at the group home. Ohio's winter weather froze the streets and wheelchair wheels. Beth insisted on wearing her favorite red flip-flops to practices. They usually stayed in place with the elastic strap around the back. She plowed her manual chair through light snow.

Responding to questions about her footwear, she replied with a smile that she couldn't feel her feet. If pressed, Beth also mentioned the very short distance from the YMCA entrance to the car and from our garage to the house. Going anywhere else in wintry weather, she wore shoes or boots. With no socks, despite several different kinds I bought for her to try. Beth survived her healthy teenage stubborn streak without frostbite by limiting her time outdoors in the winter.

December blurred with my added responsibilities at the group home. We passed the state inspection with flying colors, only because I worked extra hours. The four men planned with me to host a Christmas party for their family and friends. Beth visited ahead of time to help us make cookies for the event. It made me happy to see how much the residents loved their well-attended party.

I bought college choir CDs from Ben and Maria's holiday concerts and played them continuously when I drove anywhere. At the Christmas party for the Toledo spinal cord injury group, a mom thanked Beth for encouraging her young son to start swimming lessons. His scoliosis stopped progressing, avoiding major surgery. The doctor credited swimming for his stronger back muscles.

At the first home meet of the season for the high school team, Beth swam the 100-yard butterfly in under four minutes. Her time qualified for an American Record. However, it didn't count because the meet had not been sanctioned ahead of time with USA Swimming.

"Beth just keeps improving with every meet," Peggy said. "It's awesome to watch her strokes and racing ability move forward."

A picture in the Tiffin newspaper showed teammates at the end of the lane cheering Beth on as she turned at the wall. Lizzy and Ellen shouted from the bleachers.

"It's fun climbing out of the pool and hearing people clapping for you," Beth said. "It gives you a little boost of confidence."

The annual New Year's Eve bash with Ellen and Lizzy involved more fondue and treats. How easily the 17-year-olds laughed while watching "The Grinch" movie. As though none of them had a harsh disability? Yes. Though we'd all changed since the first months after the accident.

John and I toasted the New Year with gratitude and discussed how Beth's injury had never been a tragedy—for her alone. My disability-related worries still looped through the days. They condensed down to health risks and one big question. What kind of welcome would a young quad receive from a superficial world?

I had bought Beth a Harvard sweatshirt online for a Christmas gift. When she wore it to school in January, her classmates and teachers found out about her college choice *if* they asked. Beth wanted to attend Harvard's admitted students' weekend even though she had already accepted. I agreed and scheduled a meeting at the Harvard disability services office to figure out exactly how it all would work. I had already booked flights to Minneapolis for the U.S. Paralympic Trials in April, so I changed our flights home from Trials to take us directly to Boston for the Harvard event. Beth's senior spring filled up with trips and events.

As the end of the high school swim season approached, Peggy adjusted the details of swim training over weeks to promote fast times at the final meets, called tapering. The girls stopped shaving their legs. Some practices added ankle weights. One evening at the YMCA, Beth wore street clothes and shoes in the water along with the rest of the team. Then, the night before the Sectional Championships, the girls shaved their legs, and the boys on the team chose to shave their heads in solidarity.

Beth felt ready to race at Sectionals and swam the 50 freestyle in a fast 1:13.40, a short course American Record in her classification. Or, it *would* have been. The officials messed up and neglected to turn in the papers to sanction the meet despite Peggy's advance request.

The fastest swimmers at Sectionals advanced to District Championships the following week. Someone with a physical disability had almost no chance of qualifying. Beth and I planned to go to cheer on her teammates, but Peggy told her to bring her swimsuit and goggles.

Districts definitely would be sanctioned, so the rest of Beth's high school team unanimously voted to give her one of their relay slots to allow her to set her first two short course American Records. The girls on the relay team gave up their chance to win because of the substitution.

In the locker room, Beth stressed about their sacrifice. She thought her high school season had ended the week before. It didn't help when an announcement shared the potential records *before* her relay started.

In the 400 freestyle relay, Beth achieved her first two official short course Paralympic S3 American Records, drawing enthusiastic applause from the large crowd. Nevertheless, with the added stress, her time in the 50 freestyle clocked in nine seconds slower than the week before and the 100 freestyle at 17 seconds slower. Beth never asked for recognition, but she smiled when she heard her new records announced at school on Monday morning.

The next health emergency gave us no warning. I woke up in my own bed (not at the group home) on an early March morning and found Beth extremely ill. I drove her directly to the emergency room at St. Vincent in Toledo. I cut time off the hour drive despite the morning rush hour.

An emergency room doctor quickly admitted her to intensive care. After numerous tests, Beth acquired the diagnosis of peritonitis, a dangerous infection. The urologist told us they found extra fluid in the abdomen. A small tear along a previous surgery seam would heal on its own. The nurses also monitored her closely for sepsis, an even more frightening and potentially fatal condition. Sepsis caused the immune system to go awry and spread inflammation that could lead to organ damage, septic shock, and death. Since Beth's injury, sepsis had been added to the list of fatal risks for quads.

I stayed glued to Beth's side in intensive care. I shared her alarm of the persistent fever and significant pain, especially with limited sensation in her trunk. With my sick daughter, I put on a brave face to reassure and comfort, both of us frightened through the first days in intensive care with no improvement. She never asked to look at homework in the hospital, and I never suggested it. I stayed focused on her treatment and care. I walked to the nurse's station when Beth needed something.

To keep things running at the group home, I made quick phone calls in the hallway where I met a dad soothing a baby with a failing heart, a mom entertaining her toddler with a brain tumor, and a grandma weeping about a terminal diagnosis. I didn't share the encounters with Beth. She very gradually felt better and her vitals improved. When I drove her home after a scary week in the hospital, she didn't feel invincible, so John Mayer sang her favorite song by himself from the CD player. We arrived home bone-tired with strong antibiotics. And a new perspective.

No longer a question, Beth and I wholeheartedly agreed that the 700 miles between Tiffin and Harvard was definitely much too far for us to be separated. She decided to live in a dorm her freshman year while I stayed off-campus. We'd be in the same city, but I wouldn't be her personal care assistant. I'd help set up her dorm room and be there for transition support. Fine with me. I couldn't drop her off and return to Ohio.

Beth decided on her own to switch club teams from GTAC to Peggy's Seneca Aquatic Klub. Her friends from the high school team also swam for SAK. They practiced down the street from us, compared to an hour drive to Toledo. The tough part would be telling her first swim coaches at GTAC. They had supported her initial attempts to learn new strokes when it looked impossible to me. She planned to tell them about switching teams at her next practice.

When we left intensive care, the doctor placed no restrictions on swimming. Still recovering a week later, Beth insisted on driving to Toledo with me for a swim practice. After a few laps, she felt nauseous but only asked to get out of the pool to use the restroom. She did not elaborate, complain, or make an excuse. The coach teased and called her a wimp. He honestly didn't know that it was possibly the worst thing to say to a teenage quad, especially one with Beth's sensitivity to appearing weak.

In the locker room, I handed her tissues to wipe her eyes. Seeing her upset, my tears welled up too. She asked me not to mention the insult or her nausea. I urged her to leave with me for home. Instead, she returned to the workout and actually *did* wimp out on breaking the news about changing teams.

At home, I encouraged Beth to make the phone call to GTAC. A talented procrastinator, she decided to put off telling them until *after* the Paralympic Trials meet in April, to give them the credit on the chance she made the Athens Paralympic team. Even if she earned a spot, September in Greece would interfere with Harvard. Should I hope Beth would qualify for the Paralympics? Perhaps not.

❧ Chapter 15 ❧
CHOOSING

Boston Herald (11-15-05): "I had to pick Harvard starting on time or Athens," said Kolbe. Athens loss was Harvard's gain.

MY INITIAL EXPECTATIONS about Beth's injury proved wrong in spite of my experience with disability. I spoke with a lovely friend with multiple sclerosis at a Toledo Raptors fundraiser at the zoo. As we chatted, I remembered our first meeting a few months after the car accident when I compared everyone by their disability, certain that quadriplegia won the worst disability contest. I thought that nothing could be as awful as a complete, or nearly complete, spinal cord injury in the neck.

I stubbornly clung to that misconception, weighing one disability against another. Through the first years, my view gradually shifted until I realized my earlier notion was like a blind person judging a swimsuit contest. Everyone's lives shared the essence of an iceberg, not just quads. What we couldn't see under the surface *always* mattered. One man's heaven could be another's hell—with or without a disability.

Beth volunteered for WaterWorks in Toledo for the second year in a row, helping children with disabilities learn how to swim. At one session, she spoke to a group of preschool kids before getting in the water with them. Blunt questions no longer surprised her. A little boy asked, "How do you sleep in your wheelchair?" He didn't look convinced by her answer.

In early April, she blew out 18 candles on a chocolate cake. Around the kitchen table, Ellen and Lizzy sang happy birthday with John, Maria, and me. I wondered what Beth wished for.

Always skeptical of quad-friendly gadgets, she unwrapped a small present from me and rolled her eyes as only a teenager could. "That's dumb," she said, smiling. "Love you though!"

When I explained the purpose of the curved plastic tool, she agreed with me that opening a soda can with the tool would be better than using her teeth. Regardless, she chose a different solution. Practice more and more, until her hands could do the trick.

Our family calendar looked like a work of art with many notations in different colors. It always included the release dates for new Harry Potter books and movies. Beth and I started a countdown to the third Harry Potter movie, *The Prisoner of Azkaban*. She and her friends grew up with Harry, all encountering new challenges every year.

Beth's last months of high school filled up with senior events. Sadly, we would have to miss the spring wheelchair games in Michigan and Ohio. Her scholarship applications paid off with award presentations in three cities. She kept up with swim training and National Team paperwork.

Beth had a classic case of senioritis, ready to be done with high school. She trained a junior to take over the school newspaper and edited the final issues. She studied for AP exams though Harvard gave no college credits for AP scores. We shopped for a prom dress. Beth picked out a strapless style in light blue chiffon that fell between her knees and ankles, so the fabric wouldn't get caught in the small front wheels. Online, I showed her what seemed like the perfect jeans, made for wheelchair users with a higher back and a lower front. Not interested. Predictably.

My job at the group home taxed my time, always on my mind. Some aspects improved with repetition like complicated medications. The overwhelming responsibility never changed. I anticipated problems though many could not be prevented. I barreled through my 24-hour shifts with a nagging headache I did my best to ignore. On my days off, I often fielded phone calls from my staff and sometimes drove there to help.

I received permission to have a garage sale at the group home with each closet and the basement jammed full of stuff. I cleared out a few mice nests along with tons of junk. The residents helped enthusiastically to earn their own personal money for the possessions they chose to get rid of.

The sale fell on a beautiful spring day, a big success. I enjoyed dropping off the leftovers to Goodwill. The residents were thrilled with their windfall. I documented every penny received and spent as always. With the income from the home's extra stuff, I planned a rare vacation for the residents. The trip to Niagara Falls with two of my staff wouldn't have been possible without the sale. The April day when I found another nest with baby mice in it at the group home, I gladly gave the agency my three-month notice and started the countdown to our Harvard adventure.

Many unanswered questions created anxiety. Where would I live in Cambridge? At the upcoming Paralympic Trials meet in Minneapolis, would Beth make the U.S. team going to Greece? If she did, could she leave Athens early to start her freshman year at Harvard? Would she have to miss freshman orientation? If she did, would it be worth the sacrifice? I needed everything in place to support her as much as possible. Would we be going to Greece in September?

Beth added another stress. She would attend the Paralympic Trials as a member of the Toledo team, yet she had decided to switch to her hometown team. She continued to put off telling GTAC, and coaches from both teams would be at Trials.

I updated my list of Beth's best times and official records. I hoped to add to the list at Trials. Unfortunately, new American Records were not tickets to the 2004 Paralympics for an S3 swimmer in the USA.

Beth and I flew to Minneapolis with the help of a Challenged Athletes grant. John joined us. Airport security glanced in our direction and waved Beth through. On the jet bridge, we followed the cumbersome process to help her to her aisle seat. On the plane, John and I climbed over her to get to the middle and window seats.

At the hotel, Beth twisted nail polish bottles open with her teeth for her pre-meet ritual. Her nails shined in red, white, and blue, fitting choices for her first Trials meet. We arrived at the pool early on the first competition day. John and I watched from the upper level seating, but I also had a deck pass. Through warm ups, driving beats of loud music accented the nervous tension.

Previous meets and records faded to irrelevancy. The only races that counted would take place in the three days of the meet. This fact put the few swimmers with quadriplegia at a disadvantage since they had a higher likelihood of health issues that could impact performance. The first year Beth swam competitively, her times varied widely. Three years later at Trials, stronger and healthier, she raced within a more consistent range.

Beth entered the pool from a side corner and easily dunked under the plastic lane lines to get to her lane. Peggy lay flat on her stomach next to the starting block with her shoulders and head over the pool, reaching down to grab slippery, wet legs. Wired and ready, Beth floated parallel to the lane lines wearing a Toledo swim cap, her feet held to the wall. Patient practice had resulted in the ability to be still for many long seconds before the official start of the race, the timing crucial. Peggy could only release her ankles, no pushing or helping. About 5'8" tall, Beth's foot starts erased about a second off each lap of the backstroke, freestyle, and breaststroke. Vital seconds. For the butterfly, she could get in the best position faster without a foot start.

I held my breath as Beth reset her previous American Records in the backstroke for the 100 and 200 free. Great swims! The 50 free long course, the hardest record to beat, remained far out of reach as her forward freestyle improved incrementally.

Team USA would be in Greece for most of September. Peggy requested a meeting to find out if the Athens Paralympics might be possible for Beth. We learned she could be in Greece for the first part of September and return to the U.S. as college classes started. *If* she made the team, missing the week of freshman orientation at Harvard would be necessary.

The only S3 female at the meet, again, Beth collected 5 national medals. Our flights east would leave before the team announcement ceremony Sunday morning. After finals on Saturday, the team manager called Beth on the phone to invite us to her hotel room. I hurried to keep up as she wheeled down a long hall and knocked on a door hesitantly. The smile that greeted us confirmed good news. Beth earned a spot on the team! She could compete in three races in Greece during her first trip overseas before leaving mid-September to start college classes.

Beth called her swim coaches while John and I shared the news with Ben and Maria. Peggy suggested ice cream to celebrate. She officially initiated the longstanding tradition we observed in cities near and far after every swim meet. Over swirls of chocolate, Beth's enthusiasm overflowed with the promise of adventure as an official Paralympian.

The morning after Beth's exciting Greece news, we arrived at the Minneapolis airport early. John couldn't miss more school, and he flew home to Ohio. Beth and I landed in Boston for Harvard's weekend for admitted students.

Enclosed within a tall wrought iron fence, Harvard Yard housed freshmen dorms, classroom buildings, libraries, grand offices, and the John Harvard statue, all brimming with historical significance. Under a canopy of ancient trees, tourists speaking many languages flocked to the statue, rubbing a buckled shoe for luck.

A world away from our small Ohio town, we found our way to information sessions, welcoming with every detail. Beth soaked it in, excited to be part of it all. I felt out-classed and intimidated by some of the other parents. Not wanting to embarrass Beth, I spent more time with my hair and makeup the next morning.

Outside the gates of the Yard, to the south and east, Harvard Square beckoned with interesting shops and restaurants. People had gathered in the Square since 1630. We bought chocolate treats at Finale. We browsed at Mint Julep, a boutique destined to become Beth's favorite dress shop. The Square embodied fascinating contrasts: a tattooed teenager with many piercings, a veiled tourist with only her eyes showing, an elderly Asian man playing a simple string instrument, a man dressed for a yacht ride, a rich woman in diamonds, and a homeless woman with long dreadlocks.

We met with Harvard's director of disability services. She offered Beth accessible housing in a freshman dorm with a two-bedroom unit, the second one for a personal care assistant. Beth agreed to the plan for her first year and would return to Harvard in the summer to interview prospects for the assistant. Our fair weather visits failed to remind us of the problem of maneuvering a manual wheelchair around campus during winter in the Snowbelt.

Ohio Rehabilitation Services wouldn't help with Beth's tuition because her college was out-of-state. However, our money worries about her college expenses ended unexpectedly. Harvard unveiled a new financial aid initiative to cover all college costs for students from low-income families. John and I each worked full-time, and he had additional income from summer school, all reported on our tax forms. Our combined modest salaries met their criteria for low-income families. The fact that we qualified surprised us. We felt incredibly thankful and fortunate— despite being poor by Harvard's standards.

Beth's excitement grew with speaking engagements in Toledo and Tiffin, plus interviews for two newspapers. She started a Road to Athens journal with her top three goals for Greece on the initial page. "First, swim my best and feel good about races. Second, swim in finals one night. Third, have fun with the U.S. team." Plus her additional goals for the summer: "Number one, stay healthy and fit. Two, improve strength, endurance, and strokes to drop time. Three, have fun with SAK and enjoy the process."

The newspaper articles about Beth defaulted to inspiration, a label she disliked. In her mind, she lived her life the only way she could. In my mind, the word inspiration meant different things, some good and some not so good. At its best, inspiration motivated in positive ways. At its worst, it insulted and exploited. What label would reporters choose if more people with disabilities had a fighting chance, with better support, education, and opportunities?

The Paralympics would be held in September, so school schedules would keep the rest of my family home. I researched expensive overseas flights and hotels as the last month of high school barreled by.

For prom, Beth smiled in cascading chiffon. She tucked the ends of long blue ribbons under her to avoid a tangle in the wheels. Maria styled her sister's hair into a fancy "do" with small, shiny barrettes. Beth and her friends pretended to be ultra-serious models as they posed for silly pictures before the dance.

High school ended in an anticlimactic way, with more important things ahead. At graduation, Beth wheeled up a ramp to a stage at the football stadium and spoke to the crowd as one of four valedictorians in the class of 226 students. Ellen, also a valedictorian, gave a speech about how others change our lives. It reminded me of Beth and "For Good," my favorite song from the musical, *Wicked*.

On a whim, I bought four tickets to see *Wicked* on Broadway later in the summer for Maria, Ellen, Beth, and me. Ellen shared my girls' interest in singing and musicals. I planned a road trip to New York City. None of us had been to The Big Apple.

Family and friends gathered at our home on a beautiful day in mid-June. John and I hosted a party for Ben and Beth, both graduating with honors. Ben earned college degrees in English and physics. I set out Beth's summer scrapbook and high school memorabilia. A binder held many awards and scholarship letters including one for $5,000 from the ChairScholars Foundation, renewable for four years.

Beth's reference letter from Nancy Roberts, the special ed teacher, summed up the last four years. "The mild-mannered, quiet, bright little girl we met as an incoming freshman has grown into an assertive yet humble young woman. Beth is in a wheelchair but is by no means wheelchair bound."

Our third swimming summer began with a task Beth could put off no longer. She talked to the GTAC head coach about her decision to change teams. A stressful call, despite the practicality of swimming with a hometown coach. Peggy coached her individually during one-on-one sessions in addition to regular SAK practices. Beth swam with familiar faces and formed new friendships with Peggy's daughters, both college swimmers who helped with the club team. They sometimes traveled with their mom to watch Paralympic races.

The close-knit, small-town team celebrated with a thrilled Beth after she swam her first mile in one practice: 1,760 yards, over 70 lengths of the 25-yard pool. I watched her finish the feat, marveling at what she accomplished with no leg function or movement.

At a USA Swimming meet in Canton, Ohio, I clapped as Beth reset three American Records and added a brand new one in the 200 Individual Medley. She added "Jump" by Van Halen to her music mix at Peggy's suggestion. At local summer meets, many swimmers wore ear buds and held iPods as they waited to compete. Beth utilized her lap to carry the iPod on top of her towel and goggles. She was the only swimmer at the meet in a wheelchair—but not the only teenager with a disability.

In my support role as Adapted Chairperson for Ohio Swimming, I talked to other swimmers with visual challenges and limb differences. The teenagers with a disability at those USA Swimming meets had no competition, literally. No one else in the same classifications attended. They swam in full heats with able-bodied peers who always touched the ending wall before them. Each of them, my daughter included, raced the clock.

During a SAK practice at the outdoor pool, dark clouds brewed. I waited on the bleachers near the water with the car in the parking lot, certain the approaching storm would trigger Beth's tornado anxiety. Hearing the first distant rumblings, she asked to end the workout. She couldn't get out of the pool and into her wheelchair by herself. Peggy stuck to her club policy and kept the practice running until the siren blared that indicated lightning in the vicinity. It was the only time Beth wasn't happy with her coach. A time she remembered and teased Peggy about later.

Beth and I rushed to the car through driving rain as lightning streaked the sky in the distance. We couldn't get home fast enough. Her trauma abated after she immediately checked the computer and confirmed the absence of tornadoes in Tiffin. I grew up in Ohio with a tornado season every year, and the threat didn't cause anxiety for me. I worried about my job, about the residents and what might happen next. At home, Beth's transition to college dominated my thoughts and living in a strange city by myself in the fall.

Later in June, the Greece buzz abruptly fizzled. A phone call from the head of U.S. Paralympics overruled the earlier decision at Trials. He told Beth that all swimmers must stay the entire month of September in Athens. No exceptions. She handed me the phone at my request, and I attempted to reason with him. When I hung up, we hugged and cried. If only I could make things better, a wish I had made many times before.

The phone call prompted a decision Beth had thought about before. She chose not to wait a full school year to start at Harvard, so she gave up her slot on the Athens team to someone else. The fun preparations ended, replaced with the chore of telling family, friends, and reporters the bad news. We tried to focus on the silver lining. Now she could start at Harvard on time and attend freshman orientation.

Discouraged, Beth followed Peggy's suggestion and set goals for the next four years. The plan included staying on the U.S. National Team, attending at least three Paralympic meets a year, and swimming often on her own at Harvard, following Peggy's workouts. She didn't expect to practice with the Harvard team. In four years, she *did* expect to master the forward freestyle and achieve an out of reach

American Record in the 50 free, the hardest one in the S3 women's classification.

Beth's detailed plan led up to her ultimate goal: the 2008 Paralympics in China as a member of Team USA. The Beijing Paralympics would take place in September, a few months after her graduation from Harvard. She would go on to attend graduate school for medical research or law.

"I've already decided to postpone grad school for a year," Beth told a reporter before she started at Harvard. "Nothing's going to stop me this time. I want to medal in China."

Swim training continued as usual through the nonstop summer. She also decided to try contact lenses for the first time, pleased when she practiced and figured out how to put them in and out on her own. The many small tasks required for independence began to fall in place. At her last appointment with our favorite pediatric rehab doctor, Dr. Miller asked to speak with Beth alone. It made sense. My baby had grown into an adult, with high school behind her and independence ahead.

In Columbus, Beth helped Peggy with an adapted demonstration in and out of the water for Ohio Swimming coaches. From there, we drove across the city to her second Youth Leadership Forum as a staff assistant instead of a delegate. Beth made it her first completely independent trip of five consecutive days. No personal care assistant. No small feat, even with an accessible hotel room.

The day after YLF ended, she slept one night at home before her flight from Cleveland to Washington, DC, to attend her first National Youth Leadership Network (NYLN) conference for youth with a disability.

"It was my first independent flight," Beth wrote. "I'm not sure why, probably just something new and being nervous, but I got teary when Mom left me at security."

At the entrance to the plane, Beth instructed staff on how to lift her to the narrow aisle chair. They waited while she broke her leg spasms on her own. She helped with the many seatbelts and held her arms tucked in as they pushed her to her seat. They stowed her wheelchair with the strollers, minus the cushion and sideguards. When the plane landed, she waited until the rest of the passengers left, reclaimed her wheelchair with help, and met her contact in baggage claim. A van with a lift waited to take her to the conference. I stressed needlessly, again, and breathed easier after her phone call from a nice hotel. Her experience in DC made the stress of the solo flight worthwhile.

"When I represented Ohio at the national conference, I came to understand that the ADA and the work of the early pioneers in disability rights was far from over," Beth said in an essay.

"My generation has grown up since the ADA, so it's easy to take it for granted because we didn't have to fight for it. Learning from the people who *did* have to fight and listening to their stories was empowering."

She signed up for committee work and stayed active with NYLN for the next four years.

In July, Maria prepared for the lead role in *Kiss Me, Kate* at the Ritz Theatre. Opening weekend, we hosted a cookout in our jungle of a backyard. The dramatic transformation from grass to garden featured fast growing poplars, butterfly bushes, a small pond, and colorful blooms of flowers I couldn't begin to identify. A variety of hostas had been gifts from my grandma's farm and my brother's garden. John called the garden his therapy.

I acquired poison ivy easily, a fact that provided me with a convenient excuse to avoid weeding. Even without an excuse, the group home demanded more of my time as I trained a new manager and prepared to leave for Massachusetts with Beth.

The same day as the cookout, we filled up the front row of the theater with our extended family to watch *Kiss Me, Kate*. When the play ended, we jumped up, the first to our feet for the standing ovation. My talented Maria had another weekend of performances and an additional new job as an admission tour guide for Heidelberg. She stayed home while John drove with Beth and me to Massachusetts for his first Harvard visit.

On the highway, another car swerved, and I shrieked. I always apologized for the reflex. The feelings of despair took me back to the night of Beth's injury though the emotions dissipated more quickly than they had earlier.

Arriving in Cambridge, we left the car at a hotel in Fresh Pond and used the MBTA subway, called the "T" for short. At Peggy's suggestion, we met with Stephanie Wriede Morawski, the head coach of the Harvard Women's Swimming and Diving team. We'd read about a deaf swimmer on the Harvard team who graduated in 1996, but we understood a quad had no hope of finishing a race in the top three at any college meet.

Our expectations for the meeting were low. "I needed a pool to swim," Beth said.

The head coach congratulated her on National Team status and mentioned limited lane space during team practices. She also said that team workouts could overtax the upper body of a paralyzed swimmer. All valid concerns. Beth had already acknowledged   that she wouldn't be able to score points on a college team. At that point, we thought the meeting was over.

An unexpected invitation followed when Coach Morawski offered the position of team manager to Beth. As manager, she could practice once a week with the team and swim a second time each week with the team's assistant coach. More than anticipated, Beth happily agreed and planned to practice additional days each week on her own.

At our next stop, Beth and I interviewed prospects for an assistant at the disability services office. A friendly graduate student named Rakhi would share Beth's dorm suite in September. Harvard generously paid for Rakhi's housing and meal plan.

In Harvard Square, talented street performers entertained us. We listened to an older gentleman play an unfamiliar string instrument, and I added money to the Kleenex box he set out for tips. We bought a few books at the Harvard Coop and ended the trip with our first meal at Legal Seafood in Kendall Square.

We ordered our first whole lobster. When it arrived, I shifted the serving plate to point the beady eyes away from me. We also needed help from the server to figure out how to eat it. We shared a Boston cream pie for dessert and posed for pictures by the fish sculpture near the entrance. On the way back to our hotel, Beth showed John how to start the unique chimes in the Kendall Square T station designed by students at the Massachusetts Institute of Technology (MIT). We left metal tubes singing between the trains.

The summer rushed by, and I still needed to find a place to live in the fall. Rundown studio apartments in Cambridge started at $1,400 a month in 2004, so I decided to rent a room instead. I found a rare bargain several blocks from Harvard: one of two bedrooms in a tiny apartment for $600 a month. I'd share the space with a young woman, a church organist from Ohio. Small world.

My last day of work at the group home, I finished painting a small room and hugged the residents goodbye with a promise to visit. What a relief to pass on the responsibility and know I left everything in good order. As I packed for our girls' trip to New York City, I couldn't stop smiling.

We crowded into Beth's car for the eight-hour drive, singing along with popular songs on the radio. After a harrowing drive in Manhattan to the hotel, we left the car in a parking garage and explored on foot and by taxi. By our small town standards, rides in a yellow taxi scared us, an accident waiting to happen. I secretly bought NYC taxi ornaments for the girls for Christmas gifts.

In Central Park, Maria and Ellen lifted Beth into a covered carriage pulled by horses for a ride in the rain. I worried about leaving her wheelchair behind, but it was there when we returned. We enjoyed a ritzy restaurant afterward, the four of us sharing two meals to make it affordable. For dessert, we walked/wheeled toward Serendipity, a popular cafe with a movie of the same name. The steps at the entrance were surmountable but sadly, we didn't have enough time to wait for a table before our show.

Our first Broadway play, *Wicked*, with the original cast, drew us in with exquisite detail in the songs, sets, costumes, and story. Unlike anything we had ever seen before. Wowed, we left the theatre with a "Popular" shirt for Maria and one for Beth with her new motto, "Defying Gravity." On the drive home, we sang *Wicked* songs along with a CD of Idina Menzel and Kristin Chenoweth. I wished we all had the chance to fly.

Late in August, Beth and her close friends met for breakfast on the day Lizzy left for college. They each chose different schools in three states. Her friends wore their HOPE rings. The same one Beth never took off. They hugged and said teary goodbyes in the Burger King parking lot. I'd miss her friends too and their gift of contagious laughter.

Ellen and Lizzy had the same week off for spring break and planned to fly to Boston for their first visit to

Harvard. Beth's ventures continued to impact family and friends in unexpected ways.

Snow White and Cinderella

Beth at Harvard

Foot start with Peggy on deck

Norway

Rio Gold Medal. Published with
permission from the United States
Olympic Committee

Beth and Peggy. Published with
permission from the United States
Olympic Committee

Maria's wedding

BREATHING LESSONS
ஂ Chapter 16 ௸
STRUGGLING

Beth: *College is a time of growth for everyone but for me, it was also a time of learning to be truly independent in a world far away from my Ohio hometown.*

NOTHING IN TIFFIN prepared us for living in Cambridge. Beth's first year at Harvard would be a challenging trial for one of us more than the other.

Beth wasn't the only one saying sad goodbyes to friends and family. We approached our separate adventures the best we could. I anticipated what she would need and made piles along the wall in our dining room. John doubted it would all fit in the car. He was right, but the items at the top of my list made the cut. I put an old backup wheelchair in the car topper along with pliable bags of towels and sheets. I checked my list twice and then three times; a reassuring task on the brink of a college experience out of my control.

We divided the 12-hour drive to Cambridge between us. The packed car made it impossible to use the rearview mirror, so we helped each other with lane changes and merges. We stopped at a hotel in Massachusetts where we slept poorly, buzzed with tense anticipation.

On a sunny September morning, we arrived at the main gate of Harvard Yard and joined the line of vehicles waiting to unload in front of the all-brick freshman dorms. It would be the one and only time we drove our car on the wide concrete walkways of the picturesque Yard. I parked by Thayer dorm and unearthed Beth's wheelchair from the hatchback. She carried what she could on her lap, then talked to one of the dads while I unloaded the rest. His daughter Brittany also moved in.

"My dad, a quadriplegic like Beth, met her before I did," Brittany said. "He came wheeling up to me saying, 'Britt! You'll never believe it! There's another C6-7 quad in your dorm!' He was absolutely impressed."

When Beth introduced me to the dad, he voiced his amazement that she could navigate the campus without a power chair. Our daughters would become good friends.

In Beth's second floor suite, a paper on a bookshelf listed previous occupants since 1886, including Brooke Ellison, the young woman pictured on the "Quadriplegia at Harvard: A+" billboards. She graduated from Harvard in 2000, the same year as our car accident.

The tall windows of the main room overlooked a wide courtyard with lovely old trees. While Beth picked one of the two bedrooms and started to unpack, I moved the car and eventually found a parking place several blocks away. Her roommate Rakhi would arrive the next day, and they would share a common room and a big bathroom with a wheel-in shower. I offered to stay with Beth the first night even though I knew her answer would be no. I supported her independence. I also struggled with letting go. I accepted the uncertainty of whatever my new role would be with her. Living in a strange place on my own and finding a job overwhelmed me.

That evening, I left Beth to move into my new living situation for the next eight months. My head pounded, beating in unison with my heart. What should I expect with the apartment and the person I'd share it with? I had never been on my own without family before, except for one year in a crowded dorm at OSU.

Cambridge looked like a foreign city compared to Tiffin. With no GPS, I followed a printed map. The unfamiliar surroundings stoked my anxiety. I missed a turn and circled unusually narrow one-way streets, former horse and buggy paths. I avoided poorly parked cars, heavy traffic, assertive walkers, and too many bikes. I wedged the car into a tight space on Ellsworth Avenue, wishing for a fraction of Beth's courage.

I took a deep breath and carried my duffel bag up crumbling concrete steps to the dirty front door of a shabby building. My roommate Janet greeted me with a residential parking permit for Beth's car. Without it, parking cost a fortune.

Janet led me through the entryway to a dilapidated apartment. The slanted wood floor creaked loudly as I crossed the tiny living room. Wall registers rattled and clanked. The kitchen consisted of a sliver of space with a metal shelving unit for food instead of cupboards.

I placed my duffel on the worn wood floor of my small, empty, dark bedroom with no ceiling light. The cheap mattress and frame I ordered online would be delivered the next day, so Janet's couch would be my bed the first night. Another map led me to Target to buy food, bedding, and an inexpensive lamp. I missed a turn on the way back and inadvertently explored the curving streets of Somerville. My sense of direction failed me, and my eyes welled up. In the dark, I searched for the few street names I recognized.

When I finally arrived back at Janet's, I put oatmeal, cereal, canned soup, peanut butter, whole wheat bread, bananas, and apples on the top metal shelf in the kitchen. The fridge door held my yogurt and milk. I felt out of place and missed John. That night, I tossed and turned on the couch until the sun rose. Too much on my mind.

The morning after move-in day, our second day in Cambridge, I carried Target bags with Cheez-its and laundry soap to Beth's dorm, a brisk 12-minute walk away. At Harvard's computer center, she bought her first Apple computer with the student discount. On Massachusetts Avenue, called "Mass Ave" by locals, she picked out a futon chair that converted into a single mattress for the suite's common room.

Beth decided on her own to test herself and handle all aspects of personal care by herself, even after her roommate moved in. Consequently, Rakhi's job description changed from personal care assistant (PCA) to simply a wonderful friend. Independence with a nearly complete C6-7 spinal cord injury required exceptional patience and significantly more time.

"I tried to see how far I could go, and I continually tried to do more on my own," Beth told a reporter. "It took a little over four years. The doctors told me they had never seen anyone with my type of injury become completely independent."

My main goal in Cambridge? To be available for any kind of transition support. To make sure Beth was okay. We agreed I'd have a lot of free time. I worried about where to apply for a job and maybe more than one.

Beth asked me to go with her the first time she swam at Harvard's Blodgett pool, located south of the main campus over the Charles River. She didn't know what obstacles she might encounter. We walked through the Square to get to the pool, almost a mile away from her dorm.

The sidewalks over the Charles River on the Anderson Memorial Bridge had high, steep curb cuts, impossible in any kind of wheelchair. Beth pointed out that she could wheel in the street even though aggressive drivers filled the narrow lanes and sped over crosswalks. She could also avoid the bridge by calling ahead for an accessible shuttle to drop her off in front of the pool. From the sidewalk to the building entrance: a significant downward slope. Heavy doors to open. Crowded lanes during open swim. A pool chair lift temporarily out of service.

As always, Beth attempted to put on her swim cap. She could get it mostly on but when it bunched at the top, she pulled it off and handed it to me. I lowered her from the wheelchair to the pool deck and set her mesh equipment bag next to her goggles and printed workout from Peggy. I watched her swim from the stands. She stopped to put on hand paddles or a tempo trainer or to move for another swimmer in the lane. Sharing a lane with a stranger challenged her, and she finished the workout early after about 40 minutes. The corners of the pool included a much higher side, so she couldn't get herself out the usual way. Instead, she put her back to the side edge of the pool and lifted herself out of the water to the deck after several tries.

I checked with Beth, and she reluctantly agreed for me to ask one of the lifeguards to lift her knees while I lifted her upper body to her wheelchair. In the shower, no bench meant showering in her chair (minus the cushion and backpack), not a good thing for wheel bearings. Changing clothes in her wheelchair created the biggest obstacle.

Beth had mastered sliding on sweatpants over a wet suit, but she would have classes right after swim practice some days. I sat nearby as she pulled off the wet suit inch by inch, dried off, and tackled underwear and jeans. She let me help when the jeans bunched up under her, and she needed to give her arms a break. When we left the building, the slope back up to the sidewalk was difficult. She could wheel it slowly but that day she let me help with a hand on one of the push handles. On the bridge back to the Square, I insisted on helping with the high curb cuts to stay on the sidewalk.

At Bertucci's in the square, I ordered pasta and Beth chose a margherita pizza. She talked about the pool, happy that swimming at Blodgett was *doable on her own*. I returned her smile, grateful for her extraordinary perspective.

Through my eyes, everything in Cambridge challenged both of us. After lunch, we stopped at the freshmen mail center to pick up a box and to check out her mailbox. Out of her reach, she was reassigned a lower one. I put the mailbox key on a new, rigid plastic key holder along with her dorm room key.

Later that second day in Massachusetts, I answered an ad from a student who needed a part-time PCA. I decided my main job would have less responsibility than a group home job, and I dropped off my resume at the Harvard Coop bookstore, one of my favorite places in the Square. The pay also would be less but would cover my living expenses. With a flip phone and no computer, I didn't have internet access. I dropped by the Harvard Information Center in the Holyoke Center Arcade to check my email on one of their free computers.

The third day, a young woman in a motorized scooter interviewed me briefly. First thing on the fourth day, I started the PCA job. I drove to an upper-class dorm at the Quadrangle (called the Quad) north of the main campus. Driving instead of walking turned out to be a terrible idea. Parking required circling streets around my destination for a long time to find an open spot. My new job involved memorizing the steps of a complicated morning routine. I also met the same student in the early afternoon on the main campus.

My fifth day in Cambridge, I left the car parked by my apartment. During inclement weather, the parking situation switched from unlikely to impossible. For that reason, I walked almost everywhere regardless of the forecast, including the half hour each way to the Quad in the morning. I stopped back at the Harvard Coop employment office to remind the director about my application and management experience.

The sixth day, the bookstore called for an interview and on the seventh, I filled out employment papers. It was a co-op that paid rebates to students which had prompted the official common name, the Coop. I started full-time from 2 to 10 p.m. in textbooks after a quick training. My back ached from standing at the cash register. Homesick, I began the habit of calling John after work on the 30-minute walk back to my apartment.

With my two jobs, I rarely saw my roommate. The little time that I spent at the dingy apartment during the day, I usually stayed in my bedroom with the door closed and read books from the public library.

I connected with Beth often during orientation week, shopping with her in the Square or dropping off things she needed. She met me at the dorm entrance to let me in. From there, we rode the elevator to her second-floor suite. She thanked me for setting up her dorm room but didn't give me a dorm key. And, I wouldn't ask for one. Independence mattered.

Orientation wrapped up with tradition. Freshmen watched *Love Story* with added audience participation, the last movie filmed on the Harvard campus in 1970. News quickly spread among freshmen about "Thefacebook," a website exclusively for Harvard students initiated only months before. Beth joined her peers to ride the beginning wave of social networking before Facebook expanded into a public forum.

Freshmen dined together in a stunning wood cathedral with stained glass windows. The chamber resembled the dining hall in the Harry Potter movies. The main entrance had many steps, so Beth wheeled the extra distance to the back entrance of Annenberg Hall to the elevator. She set a tray on her lap and could reach most of what she wanted. The friendly ladies at the dining hall offered to assist though Beth rarely asked for or accepted help.

The 1,500 freshmen met new friends at meals though entering alone and deciding where to sit could be intimidating. Beth preferred to snack in her room until Rakhi encouraged her to go to Annenberg more often. When they dined there together, Rakhi led the way to sit with other students; she also decided on her own to identify herself as a freshman. Rakhi was a first-year Harvard student, yes, but in graduate school.

The proctor on Beth's floor hosted a party to watch a debate before the upcoming presidential election. Harvard hired college graduates to live in the freshman dorms and gave them more responsibilities. Part of a unique support system.

I assumed I would do—*should* do—Beth's laundry, especially during the challenging transition. I needed to make one small aspect of her days easier. She categorically refused. At home, she couldn't get close to the washer and dryer with her wheelchair and had never done laundry. In the dorm, she could reach the side-by-side appliances. Still, I attempted to change her mind. I could do it faster. She'd have more free time. I even offered to take her clothes to a laundromat, in case she didn't want me to use the dorm laundry room. That wasn't it. I suggested she ask Rakhi. Nope. Next, I offered to pay for the laundry service on campus. Never happened. Instead, I explained how to sort clothes. I don't think she was listening.

Beth drew a line in the sand with laundry. However, doing it herself was never a priority until she put on her last pair of clean underwear. She bought extra underwear at the Gap in the Square to put the task off longer.

She slowly dragged a big, overstuffed mesh bag full of dirty clothes across the floor, down the hall, and into the elevator. Laundry soap and a baggie of quarters sat on her lap. Like many college students, she learned the hard way that whites don't stay white if you wash them in hot water with dark colors. She carried clean laundry back up to her room on her lap. Most of it found a home on an extra chair in her bedroom instead of the dresser drawers. A small price to pay for independence.

Months before Beth moved into the dorm, she'd planned to volunteer through Harvard's Phillips Brooks House. She chose to work in a program for children with disabilities at an inner city Boston school. She volunteered in a special education classroom on Friday afternoons and took turns with other Harvard students to plan and purchase materials for activities. Unconcerned about getting to the big city, Beth soon discovered the unpredictability of old elevators on the T subway. Other Friday volunteers carried her in her wheelchair on steps and escalators.

At the Coop, I stood at a cash register in the textbook department as students lined up to the far back wall. Eight of us, all new employees, rang up large bills at eight cash registers. Beth and Rakhi waited in line one evening. On my day off, I returned to textbooks with Beth and bought a heavy stack of new books including several thick novels for a Charles Dickens freshman seminar, her favorite class.

The first weeks, my legs and arms ached. Disconnected and sad, I missed John, Ben, and Maria. I was happy for Beth and the adventure of Harvard, but I could see that she struggled too.

Beth's first semester required more reading than was humanly possible for anyone needing sleep. She wanted to read every word, an impossible task. Like other freshmen, she doubted she belonged at Harvard. College swamped her, and she needed extra time to take care of herself, by herself. Swim training also required extended blocks of time.

She called the shuttle operator to schedule rides to and from Blodgett pool. From her dorm, she wheeled a long stretch across Harvard Yard to get to the shuttle that dropped her off at the sidewalk above the pool. She learned to weave back and forth down the hill to the entrance, to cut her speed and maintain control. With the pool lift fixed, she used it to get in and out of the pool on her own. On days with no class after practice, she put on sweatpants instead of her usual jeans but without a wet suit underneath. And getting back up the hill to the street? Always a slow challenge, particularly with wet pavement. On lucky days, another student going the same way gave her a boost.

As fall began, Beth practiced once a week as team manager with the Harvard Women's Swimming and Diving team (HWSD), plus a supervised practice with the assistant coach another day. Beth planned additional pool time on her own with workouts from Peggy. At first, she compromised with three practices a week instead of five, to free time for a heavy homework load.

The HWSD swimmers made Beth feel welcome. At one practice, the coach asked her strong college swimmers to complete laps without using their legs. It was surprisingly difficult for even one length. And harder still, using fists instead of open hands that cupped the water. Beth swam hour and a half practices with modified drills and breaks at the walls, with gradually increasing upper body strength. She thought of the frequent muscle soreness in her arms and shoulders as a reward for a good workout the day before.

After about a month, Coach Morawski asked Beth to swim with the team twice a week (up from once a week), plus two one-on-one practices with the assistant coach. With lane space an issue during team practices, Beth learned to stay to one side in the lane, shared with a teammate who passed her often.

In Blodgett's public locker room, Beth removed her seat cushion and backpack before showering in her wheelchair after practices. I offered to buy a plastic shower chair for the locker room. Instead, she decided to ask the coach for one but put it off, always reluctant to ask for anything special.

When the wheel bearings needed to be replaced, the smaller front wheels stopped moving freely, catching and sticking. I drove her wheelchair regularly to a repair shop in the next town to the west, Belmont, where they replaced the expensive bearings. Beth's hurdles with removing a wet swimsuit, showering, and dressing in her chair gradually became slightly easier.

One weekday evening, Beth joined the HWSD team and one of the coaches on an excursion to a Boston club to support two teammates in a burrito-eating contest. She heard a joke with an element of truth. The main reason they swam on a college team? To eat anything they wanted!

The T stop closest to the club had no elevator, meaning Beth stayed on the subway and rode past it to the next stop, then backtracked several blocks. Two swimmers walked the extra distance with her. At the club, Harvard football players carried her up a flight of steps. The two girls in the contest earned second place at the end of a late evening. On the way back, Beth joined the group at the closest, inaccessible T stop and again, the football players carried her on the steps. Stretched thin, she joined the other swimmers only hours later for an early morning practice, commiserating over their exhaustion and sharing plans for naps.

Beth and seven other freshmen accompanied their professor, a Dickens expert, to the catacombs of the rare book library to look at signed first editions of Dickens' books. The depths of Harvard's libraries had not been exaggerated.

The autumn months turned into a strange and lonely time for me. Every morning, I woke up early in a cramped apartment and made oatmeal. I hiked the half hour to my PCA job, rain or shine. I memorized the routine and my role in it. I tried to avoid impatient reminders from the student if I paused too long.

The young woman I assisted had significantly more physical function than Beth. The older student could stand, take a step, and use her hands well yet required a PCA four times a day. Twice for me and twice for her live-in PCA. One morning, I carefully shared with her how she could get on and off the toilet by herself—with practice, of course. My suggestion was not appreciated, and I never said anything more.

I wasn't trying to make less work for myself. It genuinely made me sad to see the necessity of scheduling personal care assistance four times a day, especially when I was sure that once a day assistance in the morning would be enough. I couldn't understand why she wouldn't even try, especially since she already had me and another PCA to help her practice safely.

After my morning job, I had about four hours free. Anything Beth needed was my priority. I helped her pick up boxes in the mailroom. I took her wheelchair to get the bearings replaced while she used an old backup chair. I bought snacks for her or groceries for me and carried my dirty clothes to a laundromat. (She still wouldn't let me do her laundry.) Most days, I stayed in Harvard Square between jobs. I drank tea, read books, and wrote stories for children, alone with my constant tension headache. Nothing made it completely go away and many things aggravated it. I aimed to keep it at a lower level and avoid pain spikes.

In the early afternoon, I helped my morning student at a public restroom on campus before starting second shift at The Coop at 2 p.m. The crowds in the textbook department thinned out as the semester progressed, so my hours dropped to seven a day, five days a week. I stocked shelves and sent emails about ordered books. One evening, I recognized Wallace Shawn who played Vizzini in the classic, *The Princess Bride*. The movie had played more than a few times during popcorn parties at our Tiffin home. I also chatted with actress Sharon Stone. Coop employees often shared frequent celebrity sightings.

During my break, I sat outside in nice weather to eat my peanut butter sandwich, people watching and listening to talented street musicians. I eavesdropped on tourist conversations and made a game out of guessing the languages they spoke. The game carried over to my work hours at the Coop, where I sometimes asked customers what country they lived in.

At 9 p.m., I joined the line waiting to punch out before I trekked past Beth's dorm to my apartment, a half hour walk. After talking to John on my walk home, I sometimes called Ben, Maria, Beth, or my parents. I carried pepper spray and a whistle. Alone on dark Cambridge streets, I felt surprisingly safe with plenty of people all around.

Each night, I poured a bowl of cereal or heated up a can of soup before showering and sleeping, with the notable exception of Friday evenings. To usher in the weekend, I stopped at CVS after work to buy a pint of Ben and Jerry's frozen yogurt, either Half Baked or Cherry Garcia. A difficult decision. I always had good intentions of not eating it all at once.

I transferred to the Coop clothing department from textbooks. Many I worked with had more than one college degree, underemployed. That set the stage for interesting philosophy and political debates while we folded and refolded endless Harvard sweatshirts for big displays. I had friends at the Coop but no close friends.

Everyone Beth and I met had a story. Harvard students stood out in one way or another in addition to strong academics. With the Massachusetts Institute of Technology (MIT) down the street, a freshman joke claimed that MIT students were smart but Harvard students were interesting.

Cambridge was nothing if not interesting. I grew up near Cleveland in Lorain, the International City. Many cultures had settled in Lorain along with some of my ancestors, drawn by the jobs at the steel mill and shipyards. Cambridge beat Lorain in diversity, hands down. My co-workers hailed from India, Germany, Iran, Russia, Kenya, Ireland, Puerto Rico, Jamaica, and more. For the first time in my life, I numbered among the distinct minority as a white American.

One morning, I walked back to my apartment from my job in the Quad, picked up the car, and drove to the grocery store and laundromat before my shift at the Coop. Running short on time, I parked on the outskirts of Harvard Square. When my shift ended at 9 p.m., the car was gone. I blamed the misleading parking signs and called the police to find out where it had been towed. Not recognizing the address, I walked to the taxi line on Mass Ave.

My taxi driver weaved through many dark streets as the fare ticked up to over $25. At the lot, I also paid the towing charge and received a hefty parking ticket. Finally, behind the wheel in Beth's blue car, I looked at a city map to figure out how to get back. I found the lot within walking distance of the Square to the northeast. Or a brief drive. I knew parking tickets translated to big bucks for the city of Cambridge, but I hadn't realized the boon for taxi drivers as well when they chose to drive a longer way to the tow lot.

Through the disability services office, I accepted a third part-time job as a scribe for a Harvard senior with cerebral palsy. I typed while he spoke for a practice session, then the real thing for his essay tests and final exams. My typed words appeared on a large wall screen for the student to read. The young man impressed me, and I learned about different subjects as I typed. Sadly, it was only a few hours each semester. The job paid more per hour than my other two combined, and I liked it the best.

In the news, Christopher Reeve's death hit me unexpectedly hard. A pressure sore on his back became infected, and strong antibiotics no longer worked for him after nine years of frequent health issues with a high spinal cord injury. John and I carried the Reeve Foundation's Superman tags and supported the nonprofit's research. The message of hope on the tags said, "Go Forward." We mourned Reeve's passing, a grim reminder of the risks of quadriplegia. I bought more antibiotic cream to treat the leg and foot abrasions Beth acquired from swimming.

Many community festivals in Harvard Square attracted overflowing crowds that spilled into and closed the streets. The HONK! Parade during Oktoberfest drew me in, unlike anything I had seen. Think Dr. Seuss with brass horns, stilts, unicycles, and bikes! The event attracted costumed brass bands from around the country and the world.

Not long after, I worked at the Coop during the Head of the Charles Regatta, the world's largest two-day rowing event. With too many bodies in Harvard Square on a normal day, the regatta tipped the crowd to a crazy level and swamped the stores. At the end of my shift, exhausted, I gladly left the colossal mess of clothes behind. It required several days to restock and put the displays back in order.

On October 27th, Boston's Red Sox won the World Series for the first time in 86 years. Students replaced the pumpkin on the head of the John Harvard statue with a Red Sox stocking cap and scarf. In Harvard Square, students and locals mixed for a party. Beth braved the crowd for a short while as people danced on the roof of the Harvard T stop. She returned to her dorm to study while the loud celebration continued. John teased and called Beth a lucky charm since she moved to the area before the win.

Maria and Ben traveled to Boston for the first time with John for Thanksgiving weekend and our holiday dinner at Legal Seafood. How wonderful to all be together again! We watched *The Lion King* on tour from Broadway. A work of genius in every way, from the set to the costumes. And of course, we also had to watch the fourth Harry Potter movie *The Goblet of Fire* before we hugged goodbye too soon.

After the Boston trip, Maria shared a big life-changing decision with us. A college sophomore, she planned to graduate early from Heidelberg and when she did, she would move to the Boston area to teach. We supported her decision though it made me sad to think of both my girls in Massachusetts in the future, more than 700 miles away from John and me in Tiffin. I wasn't ready to let them go.

I understood the draw of the Cambridge area. I had never been in another city as vibrant. A place that charmed with old-world history and diverse humanity, all the while assaulting the senses with too many emergency vehicles, taxis, cars, and bikes. It was a place that also isolated and challenged me in ways I never expected.

✌ Chapter 17 ✌
STORMING

Beth: *It changes everything but then again, I don't think it really does change much.*

THE WINTER OF 2004-2005 set records for New England, and not in a good way. The frigid months also brought unwelcome lessons for Beth and me. In Ohio, I never walked long distances outdoors in winter, so I rarely bothered with a scarf, hat, or gloves. In Massachusetts, I bundled in layers for my early morning walks to the Quad. When new snow fell overnight, it transformed the landscape to something clean and bright, at least for a little while. I appreciated the beauty of Cambridge even with dirty piles the plows left behind. The towers and steeples of timeworn buildings shimmered with dustings of snow.

After her injury, Beth had limited her winter wheeling from buildings to a nearby car and vice versa. In contrast, Harvard required extensive wheeling where even a light snow made pushing her chair difficult. With no vehicles allowed in the Yard, Beth lived in the freshman dorm farthest away from the closest shuttle stop in Harvard Square. Health insurance usually paid for a motorized wheelchair for quads, and I encouraged her to order one for bad weather. Or special wheels with motors to fit her manual chair. She refused. Rakhi and I offered to push her to class or to the shuttle stop. Stubborn, Beth told us she'd ask only if the snow rose too high for her to wheel through.

We learned the hard way how even a small amount of snow and ice could be dangerous for a quad in a manual chair. One bitter day in early December, Beth rode the shuttle from the pool to the bus drop-off in Harvard Square. From there, she wheeled across the Yard to her dorm. The six-minute walk (wheel) doubled to 12 with light snow on the ground. Despite wearing wheelchair gloves, she ended up with white, numb, and hurting fingers.

It signaled a serious problem whenever Beth had pain in her trunk, arms, or hands, all areas with less than normal sensation. I pushed her to the student medical center where a doctor treated mild frostbite in her fingers and suggested better gloves. Not an easy solution for a quad. Beth preferred gloves with open individual digits to get a better grip on the chair's big wheels. They exposed her fingers to the cold and required a considerable amount of time to put on. Regular snow gloves or mittens soaked up moisture from the wheel rims. Bulky gloves that kept her hands completely warm and dry interfered with wheeling. I purchased new pairs of each kind anyway.

After my morning job at the Quad, I headed to Harvard Square, a canvas bag always on my shoulder with a writing project and a book. Bright holiday music surrounded pedestrians and sometimes competed with a street performer braving the cold. Glitter and garlands hung over the streets while store windows beckoned with cozy scenes of home and hearth. Christmas in the city.

The Coop competed with the Square with lavish decorations and elaborate displays in every department. My second shift usually passed quickly between standing at a cash register and folding endless sweatshirts. I walked home in the dark. The significant number of pedestrians on the sidewalks late at night continued to amaze me.

In my sparse little bedroom, I opened my sewing bag and stitched lace on wings of felt peace doves to give to work friends. On my day off, Beth and I sang along with the performers at the annual Christmas Revels at Harvard's

Sanders Theatre, a beautiful rounded space with a dome ceiling made of natural wood.

First semester classes finished for Beth, with finals to be held after a two-week reading period in January. She packed several textbooks and novels before we drove home to Ohio for the holiday break. John Mayer and others sang to us from the music mixes Beth made. Notably missing on the drive was her N'Sync Christmas CD. In Tiffin, we played it on repeat. We watched favorite holiday movies with Maria. John suggested a dinner date. My best gift? Ben home from Columbus and all of us together.

I accepted my invitation to a Christmas party at the group home where I had worked. I hugged the residents, not surprised that nothing had changed. I left later with relief and no regrets.

At my mom and dad's farmhouse in Vermilion, the old Henning homestead, a tall live tree with mostly handmade ornaments lit up the high ceilings and long windows of the parlor as it had every December for well over a hundred years. Ben, Maria, and Beth gathered in front of the tree with their four cousins for the traditional holiday photo. I stood in the same spot many years earlier with my brother, sister, and cousins. At my in-laws in Lorain, John pretended to steal presents from his sister, Jean, to make her smile. She counted down the days until her January birthday.

Beth rang in the New Year as she had for the last five years, with her best friends, Ellen and Lizzy. They watched the new *Elf* movie and shared college stories. They made more plans for their first visit to see Beth at Harvard in the spring. I loved how the girls continued their New Year's Eve tradition of fondue, movies, and laughter.

A few days into January, Beth and I started the drive back to Massachusetts. John stressed over the snowstorm in our path. I didn't worry about weather, but I respected it.

Especially after I hit an ice patch on Rt. 90 through Buffalo and spun full circle across three lanes. I shrieked and steered out of it, suddenly winded. With no cars near us, I stopped for a moment and breathed deep to counter the tidal wave of panic and sorrow, complete with memories of the accident that injured Beth. Lucky for us, few cars braved the weather. By the time we made it to Cambridge, the cars multiplied as usual.

Beth studied for finals and swam with the team for three practices a week at Blodgett, her new favorite pool, with two more practices each week with the assistant coach. She called me one morning, exhilarated. Coach Morawski asked her to race at a Harvard home meet for the first time. Beth ordered the team T-shirt for parents with her name on the back, and we celebrated with Finale desserts in the Square. At her dorm, she showed me new gifts with a big smile: the HWSD team swim cap with a warm up jacket and pants.

At the early January home meet, I sat in one of the red seats in the section for parents, right above where the team congregated on deck. I proudly wore my shirt, but it wasn't about me. I was thrilled for Beth. I also met friendly parents, understandably surprised to see me in their section and a girl in a wheelchair with the team. They no doubt questioned their daughters after the meet.

A full crowd gathered in the upper stands. Beth joined a procession led by the Harvard team captains, chanting in unison all the way. The young women gathered in a circle to wrap up the cheers before warming up on deck. I never thought I would see my daughter with a college swim team.

Wearing a coveted Harvard swim cap, Beth wheeled by herself to the far corner of the huge pool and used the chair lift independently to get into the water. She swam under the plastic lane lines easily, no longer a test as it was at her first wheelchair games.

Beth pushed off the wall with her hands to begin the 200 free race while others dove off the starting blocks. I watched the clock and jotted down the numbers whenever she touched the wall. I sat forward in my seat, my excitement growing with each lap. The other girls finished the race, and I held my breath as she swam the last lap by herself. I wished John, Maria, and Ben could have been there.

Beth's first race at Blodgett pool set a new short course S3 Paralympic American Record in the 200 free—and in each of the official distances along the way, the 50 and 100. Three new records in one race! The announcer shared the news with the crowd, and the young women on the Harvard team cheered the loudest. And not for the last time.

Beth and I missed the party of the year for John's sister Jean in Lorain. We called on the phone to sing her happy birthday. Jean chimed in with her signature off-key vibrato and left us smiling. The day of Beth's last final exam, a classmate helped through rising snow to and from the test. The snowfall shifted to a winter storm, burying sidewalks and cars.

The worst of the blizzard hit on a Sunday. The amount of snow reminded me of Ohio's 1978 blizzard. John and I had camped out with the four men at the group home in the basement, the warmest place in the house until the furnace stopped working. A National Guard truck drove us to a shelter with heat. Not my most pleasant memory.

In Cambridge in 2005, unearthing Beth's car wasn't possible. Besides, there was nowhere for the car to go. Ellsworth Avenue had endless drifts much too high to drive through.

Everything closed, including the Coop, but I needed to scribe for a final exam. When I couldn't reach anyone by phone, I decided to walk to the Quad for the test, scheduled at the same dorm where the student with cerebral palsy lived. I also wanted to check on my snowbound daughter.

I layered my clothes and added an extra pair of socks. The first person in my apartment building to try to leave, I worked for several minutes to free the frozen front door. Next, I fought with the icy snowdrift forming a barricade on the porch side. I could barely squeeze out. The porch floor, steps, and sidewalks disappeared in an ocean of white.

Frigid blasts blew my breath away. I waded through thigh-high drifts on Ellsworth to Broadway. An attempt had been made to clear the bigger street, making my ankle boots briefly useful. I walked in the road around abandoned cars even though I couldn't begin to hear a vehicle approaching with the wind. The few cars on the ice-covered street drove slowly.

I advanced less than a block and turned around, ready to give up, when a lady in a van offered me a ride. She headed north on Mass Ave and told me she had never picked up anyone before. A first for me, too.

The friendly lady drove slowly up Mass Ave for over a mile. With barely one driving lane and no option to pull over, she stopped the van in the street to drop me off two blocks from the Quad, saving the day. Surrounded by rolling hills of snow, I trudged down the middle of a closed side street the rest of the way, numb and battered by the gale.

Only one other pedestrian braved the blizzard on a street usually teeming with students and residents. We could hardly even make eye contact, bundled to the max and looking down to cut the wind attacking our faces. I had never been so happy to reach and enter a building. In the warm room where I listened to the student and typed his words, snow and ice melted in a puddle under my feet.

After the final, I dreaded the walk ahead. On my way to Beth's dorm, I stopped at the only business open, the Starbucks at the corner of Mass Ave and Shepard Street. A kind soul had shoveled a narrow trench from the door to the street. The snow on each side reached almost to my chest.

I sipped a hot chai tea and carried a latte for Beth for several blocks to Thayer. I climbed high snow hills on the ramp to the entrance. I called ahead, and she met me at the door to let me in. Her latte chilled by the time I arrived. Noah, her floor proctor, had already arranged to bring her meals from the dining hall. Beth's biggest frustration with the blizzard? The interruption in pool time for her swim training. Instead, she focused on the exercise routine Peggy wrote on laminated cards, using stretch bands that strapped to her hands and heavy exercise balls.

I couldn't talk to John or anyone on my walk home from the dorm in the strangely empty street. Besides the loud, angry wind, I focused my attention to lean forward and stay upright on the ice all around me. I slipped to the ground once. My extra layers of clothes lessened the impact, but the gale made it hard to get back up. The stinging cold ached, bone deep. Finally arriving at my apartment, I fought with the front door and high drifts again. I grabbed clean clothes and peeled off frozen ones in the shower before turning on hot water. I wondered how long it would take to feel warm. I looked at my phone after I made a boiling cup of tea and wrapped up in the comforter on the bed.

I missed several calls from family. I called John first, my best friend. The separation hurt. He had already talked to Beth, and I calmed his concerns about me in the blizzard. It felt natural for me to play down the challenges of the day. In the past, John and I had joked about my tendency to minimize and his to exaggerate. After the phone call, I realized how my desire to not worry loved ones often trumped my need to share unpleasant experiences. I made notes on the subject for a future writing project. A better writer than speaker, I always expressed myself more clearly on paper.

Drifting snow continued to block the dorm ramp after the blizzard winds died down despite frequent clearing by maintenance staff. No kind of wheelchair could get through, and I stopped to see Beth each day before or after my Coop shift, often carrying a bag of Cheez-its and fresh fruit. The sidewalks stayed impassable for days afterward, so I joined the many pedestrians walking in the streets close to cars. Compared to walking in the gale force of the blizzard, trekking to the Quad and Beth's dorm in bitter temperatures on icy roads seemed doable.

I pushed Beth's wheelchair to and from the shuttle stop to resume swim practices, with snow still drifting across cleared sidewalks. The shuttle drivers helped her up and down the icy hill at the entrance to the pool in the aftermath of the blizzard.

Besides snow, Harvard presented other access issues. With massive historic buildings, wheelchair entrances often involved out-of-the-way back doors. Some required prior arrangements for keys, key cards, or lifts.

An unanticipated obstacle ruined a cold morning. While Rakhi volunteered in India, the only elevator in Thayer broke down. Beth couldn't find help to get down the steps in time for the shuttle to the pool. Frustrated, she called her coach for the first time about missing a team practice. The fixed elevator remained unreliable.

Harvard's maintenance director gave Beth his cell number and put a repair team on call. He explained that a new elevator required gutting the historical building. Not an option. Replacement parts for the ancient elevator had to be specially made.

Beth hated to ask for assistance. Still, she loathed missing classes or a swim practice more. She placed the phone numbers for the maintenance director and floor proctor on speed dial. They usually responded quickly. Noah hadn't gone to bed yet early one morning when he and the director carried Beth down two flights of dorm steps at 5:45 a.m. for swim practice.

I helped with the steps whenever I could. The day arrived when the elevator could no longer be fixed temporarily. The director offered to put Beth up in a nice hotel close to campus. She chose to stay put and arranged for help to get down and up the steps.

The dorm elevator added ongoing stress. A relatively new elevator at the back of Annenberg came to a stop partway to the dining hall with only Beth inside. One of the servers heard her and stayed close by, talking to her for about 30 minutes until the elevator moved again.

Over the weeklong semester break at the end of January, Beth and I boarded a crowded bus to New York City to see the Broadway musical, *Rent*. At the accessible entryway to the theatre, we waited to be seated near the actors' entrance. Recognizing one, Beth was star-struck when he greeted her with a smile and a hello. Drew Lachay from the boy band 98 Degrees played the role of Mark.

The opening song introduced us to the compelling concept of measuring our lives in love through all 525,600 minutes in a year. I loved "One Song Glory" about the heart-wrenching desire to create one pure, true thing to contribute to the world. Since childhood, I dreamed of writing stories no one else could tell, perhaps ones with the gift of helping the reader in some small way.

After the show, we planned to taxi back to our hotel. Beth wore unlined boots with no socks and a dress that bared her knees. Theater patrons quickly filled the taxis in the frigid night. Taxi drivers also tended to avoid people in wheelchairs, and Uber didn't exist yet. We ended up walking a mile to the hotel, stopping every few blocks at an open business to warm up. She let me push her chair to protect her hands.

Beth's roommate returned from India and pushed her to class after new snow fell. Rakhi shared sad stories about her volunteer work with children who had become orphans in the late December earthquake and tsunami. The tragedy killed more than 230,000 people in 14 countries. Living in Cambridge, a truly international city, I felt more connected to a big world than I had in Tiffin.

About three weeks after the blizzard, Beth's car still sat encased in snow and ice up to the windows. Snowplows clearing the street piled up extra snow on one side. A parking announcement from the city of Cambridge incited panic. Officials would begin to ticket cars that had not been moved since the storm.

The next morning, crowds of people attempted to free their cars all over town. I tried my best with Beth's car using a small shovel, with little progress a half hour later. I paid two teenagers to help who had chipped ice away from the wheels of another car. Spring couldn't arrive soon enough.

A new semester packed Beth's days with classes, volunteering, swimming, ongoing assignments, and a heap of books. Her first semester grades, all B's and A's, calmed her fears of not belonging at Harvard. She didn't stress about breaking her all-A streak from high school. College life challenged her physically and mentally with the daily basics, so she prioritized her time and avoided social activities. With early morning swim practices and late-night studying, she took advantage of breaks between classes for power naps.

Beth worked to take care of herself through her toughest winter. The continuous scrapes on her legs and feet from the pool walls healed slowly. She placed waterproof bandages on the worst ones. When a cold surfaced, she treated it seriously to avoid chest congestion and pneumonia. She followed her lung doctor's advice with decongestants, extra water, nose spray, and more sleep.

Swim training maximized the impaired lung capacity caused by her injury but when she caught a cold, she still had a small, weak cough. She discontinued the last of her asthma medicine, the maintenance inhaler, with no return of symptoms. She appreciated being medication-free except for a round of antibiotics now and then. A rare thing for a quad. It supported my theory that being healthy overall could minimize the number and severity of infections.

The 2004–2005 college season ended with HWSD as the undefeated Ivy League Champions. Team practices stopped for the rest of the school year, but Beth focused on her four-year plan and continued to practice religiously. She grounded herself at Blodgett pool.

A surprising event highlighted our spring. Relatively few athletes with any kind of physical disability competed on college teams, and an even smaller number had quadriplegia. Beth hoped to continue as manager of the swim team the next year with the privilege of practicing with members a few times a week. Instead, Coach Morawski asked her to be an official member on the roster of the HWSD varsity team starting her sophomore year. The invitation was a gift she hadn't expected—serendipity in its purest form. All the more treasured because she would be the first on the team with a visible disability. The first wheelchair user. The first quad.

"As a swimmer with a disability going into a Division 1 school," Beth told a reporter. "I didn't know how I would be welcomed because I am not going to be able to score points."

"We were not sure how it was going to work," Coach Morawski said in a *NCAA Champions* magazine article. "Everyone is absolutely impressed by her."

Elated, Beth said, "I had no idea Harvard would accept someone with a fairly severe physical disability on the team."

Only my youngest could refer to quadriplegia as *fairly* severe.

As tulips bloomed randomly in Harvard Yard, I talked to Beth on the phone about every other day, and we met each week for lunch. We'd split a turkey sandwich and two small chocolate desserts at our favorite spot, Finale. After, we stopped at the Brattle Square Florist where I bought a few of her favorite sunflowers for a vase on her desk.

Rakhi surprised Beth with a small birthday party at Finale and a beautiful chocolate cake. Soon after, Ellen and Lizzy visited with Lizzy's mom, Deb. The girls camped out in the dorm room, and Deb stayed with me in my apartment. The next day, we watched Beth practice at Blodgett before exploring Boston. We walked the Freedom Trail to the Holocaust Memorial and headed to the Prudential Center to watch the sun set.

We rode the elevator past the Skywalk viewing level and stopped at the Top of the Hub restaurant on the 52nd floor. Glass walls offered a beautiful panoramic view. On a budget, we sat at a table in the bar instead of the expensive restaurant. Underage, the girls drank sodas, and we all shared a plate of cookies. Lizzy pointed out landmarks and neighborhoods in all directions even though she had never been to Boston before.

In late April, Beth and I flew to Michigan for GTAC's Second Annual Disability Open. She planned to officially get back on the U.S. Paralympics Swimming National Team since she had temporarily lost that status by declining her spot for the Greece Paralympics.

"I heard stories from the other swimmers," she said, "but I don't have any regrets. I knew I'd have more chances."

Beth happily reunited with Peggy and other friends on the pool deck. Her fan club watched; my parents, John, Ben, and his girlfriend all traveled from Ohio to join me in the upper stands. Maria had to work that weekend. Everyone in our family showed interest in Beth's swimming, but Ben shared the understanding of intricate details of classification, competitors, rankings, and records with Beth and me. I fervently hoped Beth would regain National Team status but not to be pushy or to brag. I simply wanted whatever was important to her.

Wearing a Harvard swim cap, Beth swam the 50 butterfly in record time, then we heard an announcement about her disqualification. International Paralympic Committee rules required air space between the elbow and the water for the butterfly which she could do but not every stroke. In the 100 freestyle, she touched the wall just tenths of a second under the needed qualifying time for the National Team and reset her American Record. Beth beamed when she saw the time on the scoreboard then waved at us in the stands while we hooted and hollered. Despite the chilly day, the post-meet tradition of ice cream carried on at a Dairy Queen, ending with goodbye hugs with Peggy and the rest of Beth's fan club. I hugged John longer. I wished he could return to Massachusetts with me. We both had school years to finish in different states.

All of the freshmen living in Harvard Yard would move the next school year to one of the upper-class houses. Beth signed up for the housing lottery with two friends. No personal care assistant. The lottery worked a little differently for Beth. The only accessible options were in the Quadrangle, the farthest housing from the main part of the campus. She would live in a dorm with multiple elevators. Newer elevators. Her dorm suite would have an accessible bathroom. A dining hall in the same building added another advantage.

I would no longer be needed in Massachusetts when Beth started her second year of college. Proud, I fully appreciated her improbable accomplishment of independence as a quad—but not the 700-mile separation approaching in the fall.

The spring sunshine brightened my view. I ran low on Zoloft with no refills, so I gradually discontinued the anti-depressant and packed for a long weekend abroad.

Beth and I headed to Logan airport in May for her first overseas trip, a month after the Michigan meet. She had accepted her invitation to the inaugural Paralympic World Cup in Manchester, England. British Paralympics paid the travel expenses with funds from their national lottery for all of the athletes and coaches attending from around the world.

Peggy and I flew to Manchester on our own dimes though she started the process to become a U.S. Paralympics coach. I had been to the London area of England during my Norway summer as an exchange student. We explored Manchester's stunning town square and massive historic buildings.

Beth's hotel bed for the World Cup was too high for her to transfer independently. She asked a teammate to remove her twin mattress and prop it along a wall. She slept on the hard box springs to avoid asking for help to get into bed.

The large pool complex held teams and spectators from every corner of the world. Beth didn't request a personal care assistant for the trip because she didn't require one, but I missed being with her in the hotel, the locker room, and on deck. Like others on the USA team, even those with better-working hands and arms, Beth squeezed in and out of a new tight leg suit with help from team coaches who called themselves "hiney hikers."

It felt strange for Peggy and me to be spectators in the upper stands instead of in the middle of things on deck. She couldn't sit still and often watched the meet standing up. Beth raced the 100 freestyle in a mixed heat with swimmers in higher classifications. She reset her American Record in the event by swimming her fastest stroke, the back, during freestyle races.

For Beth's big race, the 50-meter backstroke, Peggy and I watched S3 swimmers wheel or walk to the starting blocks while the announcer introduced them to the overflowing crowd. A range of disability showed, including cerebral palsy, spinal cord injury, and limb differences. In a perfect world, all had identical functional abilities. Beth held the ranking of eighth in the world in the 50 back. She took her place in a full heat of S3 swimmers for the first time. A rare race with true competitors.

During backstroke races, Beth could see women to her immediate right or left if they swam at a similar speed. The race started, and she could see one swimmer moving with her. I stood up and cheered as she picked up her pace and raced the competitor. The two touched the wall at exactly the same time to earn and share an unexpected third place bronze medal.

After the race, officials "tagged" Beth for random drug testing. They followed her to the cool down pool and then to the staging area to be presented with her medal. Kiko, a friendly U.S. Paralympics coach, stayed with her and other teammates being tested while the rest of the team returned to the hotel.

At first, I thought Beth's last race moved her up to third in the IPC World Rankings for that event since she earned a bronze medal. However, other swimmers in the race did not hit their best times so some of their earlier, faster times still counted in the current ranking time period. Beth moved up to sixth in the world in the 50 backstroke and seventh in both the 50 and 100 freestyle.

The last evening at England's World Cup, Team USA celebrated the meet with a pub dinner of fish, chips, and mushy peas. Beth's food tastes broadened, leaving behind her childhood staple of macaroni and cheese for late night pad Thai with tofu on Mass Ave, spinach salads in the dining hall, and sushi in Harvard Square.

Back home, Peggy shared her thoughts. "It's quite an accomplishment to see Beth take her swimming to such a high level in such a short period of time and know that she is still improving. This was the first international meet for Beth to swim in a whole heat of like disability classifications from all over the world. To place third and earn a Bronze medal is just incredible. There is a big horizon ahead for Beth."

❧ Chapter 18 ❦
BELONGING

Beth: *I couldn't imagine a better college experience, and a large part of that was being a member of the Harvard Women's Swimming and Diving team.*

LIKE MOST OF the world, my first assumptions about paralysis focused on the wealth of experiences denied by quadriplegia. Soon after the accident, I thought that might include things like being head over heels in love, being an integral part of a college sports team, and traveling far and wide. Or the opportunity to make a contribution toward a better world. Beth proved me wrong, over and over again. I'm glad she did.

I typically wasn't an excessive worrier. The crippling anxiety I experienced after Beth's spinal cord injury had been triggered by guilt and deadly health risks. When I lived near Harvard, I worried only a little about all my children and general things like finding meaningful work and a loving partner. Maria and Ben had significant others, and my youngest felt no rush on that issue. She had a very full plate. Both of my girls were appalled that I had married one week before my 19th birthday. Much too young in their minds. We had no way of knowing that Beth's first steady boyfriend lived across Harvard Yard in another freshman dorm or how they wouldn't meet until years later.

Late in the school year, my mood plummeted quickly after I gradually discontinued Zoloft. I banked on my body adjusting over time. It did—but not in the direction I hoped. At the same time, my roommate Janet left for Ohio to be married which meant I needed to move out of the apartment before she returned from her honeymoon. I arranged to sleep on a sofa bed in a Coop friend's apartment near the Quad.

The school year would end one month ahead when I would drive home to Ohio with Beth.

On my moving day, I woke up to an alarming new low, exacerbated by a piercing, throbbing headache and a flare of intense fibromyalgia. Unfortunately, the maximum dose of Celebrex couldn't reach that level of pain. Deep depression stung, mentally and physically. Every small thing seemed much too difficult. I forced myself to go through the motions for my morning personal care assistant job, barely saying a word and wiping tears away discreetly. After, I trudged through the 30-minute walk from the Quad to my apartment on auto drive.

I passed through the tiny apartment for the last time to take the garbage out, my steps creaking on the uneven floor. Janet had bought my bed, and I left her my lamp and the bedding. When I pushed my key under Janet's door, I carried my duffel, the same one I moved in with eight months earlier. I placed it in the trunk of the car.

I had the day off from the Coop and planned to move into my temporary housing that evening. I stood at a corner, overwhelmed by sadness and the simple choice of which street to cross. And, the idea of moving to a friend's apartment where I'd never been before. The sunny day colored in despair, carrying me back to my old guilt and regret. I couldn't stop crying. I felt weak and worthless.

Frustrated and embarrassed, I decided not to reach out to John or anyone. I didn't have anywhere to go, no bed to curl up on. I rode the T into Boston with the plan of hiding in a movie theater while I regained control. Instead, I paced in the expanse of the Boston Common, trying to calm down enough to call my friend Bonnie. I told her I'd move in the next day instead of that evening. I walked aimlessly not caring how I looked. Far from home, I didn't know anyone in Boston. Even in tears, I certainly wasn't the strangest sight in the Common on that or any other day.

Five years had passed since Beth's spinal cord injury. I knew I had so much to be thankful for. I usually could focus on gratitude and had no reason to feel despair. But there it was, unbidden and unwelcome.

The depths of this sudden new depression frightened me. Small choices became daunting and paralyzing. I thought about Beth not needing me in Cambridge for the next school year. The idea of her at Harvard and me in Ohio triggered old fears of health risks. How could I be in another state? I realized that I needed her more than she needed me. Intellectually, I understood that was a good thing but not emotionally. And what about pneumonia? What if a car hit her when she crossed the congested streets? What if she picked up a superbug virus from her chair wheels, and antibiotics failed?

With worst-case scenarios swarming in my head, I rode the T back to Harvard Square and hurried to Beth's car. I drove to Fresh Pond in western Cambridge to one of the cheapest hotels in the area, still expensive at $80 a night.

In my hotel room, I couldn't stop crying through desolate sleepless hours. With a searing headache, I thought about going to a hospital, but I wanted to hide this from my family. I picked up the phone to call John and stopped, determined not to worry him.

Exhausted, I dozed in the early morning hours. It was a day off from the PCA job, thankfully. I called off work at the Coop and stayed in the hotel room with the television and lights off until checkout time. I couldn't justify another expensive hotel night but after I checked out, I didn't know where to go. My friend Bonnie worked second shift, and I couldn't move in to her apartment until 9:30 p.m. I refused to cry on Beth's shoulder.

In the light of day, I admitted the big roles that body chemistry and pain played in my depression, more than not getting my ducks in a row. Thoroughly humbled and deeply shaken, I called my Ohio doctor's office for a new Zoloft prescription. I braced myself for painful days until the medicine started to help again. Depression felt like a punishment for God knows what. I avoided people as much as I could.

Too restless and weepy to sit or read or write, I wandered through the afternoon and evening. I was no longer in denial about the depression my doctor diagnosed 24 years ago—and stuck with a Zoloft dependency or maybe an addiction. When John called, I shared the skeleton outline of my withdrawal problem with an emphasis on solving the problem and starting back on the medicine. I loved his unconditional support and tried to make peace with the fact that I needed medicine to function. I looked forward to life without debilitating sadness.

I rewarded myself for not spending another night in a hotel by purchasing a new Life is Good shirt with a peace sign. The company's philanthropy resonated with me, and also their motto. "Life is not perfect. Life is not easy. Life is Good." Amen.

My last days as a PCA and Harvard Coop employee ended with easy goodbyes. I loaded the car in two trips with Beth's backup wheelchair, single futon, lift chair, floor lamp, refrigerator/microwave unit, and more. I labeled the items and pushed my limits by moving the items by myself to the basement storage room at the upper-class house where she would live in the fall. Everything hurt the next day.

I scribed for the student with cerebral palsy for the last time as Beth finished her final exams and swam her last practice at Blodgett until September. We watched colorful dragon boats race on the Charles River before I packed the car for the drive to Ohio.

I couldn't wait to be back home for the summer and planned to appreciate every minute. Not the coming school year but the one after that, John and I would have an empty nest with Beth at Harvard, Ben in Columbus, and Maria graduating early and moving to Boston. I understood that my kids needed to find their own way in life, but I would miss them. Feeling sorry for myself sparked a radical idea: moving to Massachusetts if John retired in two years after 30 years of teaching in Ohio. Maybe.

Summer vacation officially started with an additional drive to Chicago for the wedding of Rakhi's brother. The five hours seemed easy after the trek from Boston. I looked forward to our road trips in Beth's blue car with CDs and sing alongs.

At the wedding, I wore a long blue dress with a tunic top to a beautiful ceremony. Beth danced at the evening garba in a short sequined top that bared her midriff above a matching ankle-length skirt, a gift made in India from Rakhi's parents. When we learned that a bare midriff means the wearer is looking for love, everyone laughed.

Back in Tiffin, Beth reunited with Ellen and Lizzy not knowing it would be one of their last summers together. Maria gave her little sister a special gift, a beautiful sunflower quilt. She had sewed the wall hanging for a college class on women's traditions. Last spring, John attended Maria's emotional presentation at Heidelberg when the students spoke about their quilts. I wished I could've heard her talk about Beth's favorite flower and the passion for life they shared. I also had missed Heidelberg choir concerts and solos but not anymore.

Swim practices with SAK filled Beth's calendar for her fourth swimming summer. Peggy showed us an underwater video from the previous summer with sloppy strokes. A recent one with smoother movements reinforced Beth's belief that she could master the forward freestyle. At the outdoor pool, two teammates lifted her in and out as they had for high school practices. One morning, they carried her out to the diving board—under protest. Her attempt to enter the water gracefully ended in a belly flop though she didn't lose any sleep over her lack of diving skills.

Ben missed our biggest family trip to Scandinavia for his job in Columbus. My second mom Anne-Lisé invited us to stay with her for two weeks. The rugged beauty of the fjords had not diminished since I had been an exchange student 28 years before. Something *had* changed, though. I loved Anne-Lisé, but her driving on mountain roads scared us. John sat in front with her, and our daughters told him not to close his eyes. He had an important job, to watch the road and alert the driver about frequent close calls.

We stayed several days at Anne-Lisé's rustic summer cottage in Tjome. For breakfast, she served tubes of caviar and chunks of cheese with heavy bread and wide crackers. I passed on the caviar. My girls decided to swim in the Oslo fjord, a short distance from the cottage through the woods. Big rocks met the water with no beach. I positioned Beth's chair the best I could and lowered her to the rocks. The cold water (64ºF) nixed their plans to swim. Instead, I shot a photo of them in shallow water and complied with Beth's request to return to her wheelchair. At least, I tried. Maria and I slipped on wet rocks. Beth burst out laughing. Then, all three of us couldn't stop. When we tried again, we fell again. And a third time. Laughing and lifting never worked. Finally, Maria and I accomplished the task after settling down and planting our feet in a less slippery spot. We teased Beth, blaming her for our bruises.

We snapped pictures to add to our scrapbook at the Worlds End (Verdens Ende), a desolate spot on the water with many small, bare rock islands. The islands reminded me of stepping stones for a giant heading into the strait of Skaggerak and the North Sea. The Worlds End looked exactly the same as when I first visited.

Oslo made lasting impressions. The new Nobel Peace Center topped my list as well as Vigelandsparken, a lovely sculpture park built on a stunning scale and depicting the stages of life. As a teenager in 1976 at the same park, I sat next to the U.S. Ambassador at a formal ceremony to celebrate the U.S. Bicentennial. After he spoke, I stood at the microphone in my stars and stripes top and skirt. I read my prepared speech, and a man presented me with flowers from Anne-Lisé.

Years later, Anne-Lisé and I toured the Edvard Munch art museum together for the second time, along with her granddaughter and most of my family. At an Oslo pub with fresh flowers on our table, my teenage daughters ordered long island iced teas, their first legal drinks.

In Denmark, we drove with Anne-Lisé past cows grazing on small strips of grass next to narrow rivers. We visited Gretha and her daughter, Belinda. When I first met them in 1976, Belinda had adorable blonde pigtails. We toured the sights in beautiful Aalborg and spent lovely relaxed evenings in Vorupar on the coast. We carried Beth into small bathrooms where her wheelchair wouldn't fit. One evening, Gretha treated us to dinner at a fancy restaurant on a turbulent North Sea beach. Our server and friends teased John and me about ordering water instead of alcohol—a social sin in Scandinavia.

Back in Oslo, an airline called with unwelcome news. They rescheduled our flight back a day, and we lost a day of sightseeing. We said heartfelt thank yous and sad goodbyes with Anne-Lisé. Our layover in Paris turned into a fiasco.

First, the staff acted like they had never seen a wheelchair. We waited for a strange cubicle on wheels that rose high in the air to the back door of the airplane. The four of us reluctantly entered the cubicle which carried us a long way to a terminal.

Second, we learned our flight to Detroit had been delayed to the next day, and the airline wouldn't pay for a hotel. Third, we picked up our luggage and waited for Beth's manual wheelchair to be returned to us. And waited longer. At the customer service desk, rude airline staff nonchalantly told us they couldn't locate her wheelchair. No big deal. How could a wheelchair be lost? We moved Beth to a regular molded plastic chair since her back hurt in the airline wheelchair, but she still wasn't comfortable. John kept asking the desk staff to check again until they finally made a phone call. Or, pretended to. Tired and hungry, we were not happy campers. Two long hours passed before they found the wheelchair.

We boarded a crowded airport shuttle to a hotel. On the way, the driver pulled over for an unscheduled stop just to smoke a cigarette while the rest of us had to stay on the shuttle, packed in like sardines. The hotel charged outrageous prices. We overpaid for a tiny room with one bed, and two of us slept on the floor. When we arrived in Detroit, we brought with us a new appreciation for U.S. airports.

Back home, Beth bought the new Harry Potter book, *The Half-Blood Prince*. I started reading it about a week later after Beth and Maria both finished it. During a family trip to Columbus to see Ben, we watched *Murderball*, a documentary about the remarkable U.S. Paralympics quad rugby team that competed in Athens, Greece. An aggressive sport with frequent injuries, rugby caught Beth's interest when a friend had invited her to use his special rugby wheelchair at a Columbus practice. Ben volunteered to go with her and pick her up off the floor when she got knocked out of the chair. I loved to hear them laugh.

Peggy vetoed Beth's plans to participate in the rugby practice and also the sit skiing she wanted to try. Peggy reminded her that a broken leg or arm would derail her freestyle and Beijing goals. Beth technically could swim with a broken bone, with no cast, but increased spasms slowed her down.

"Peggy is immensely caring," Beth said, "very driven, and she thrived on the challenge of coaching me in a new way."

In late July, I flew with Beth and Peggy to Oregon for a rare national meet at an outdoor pool. Swimming under the hot sun meant the few with quadriplegia contended with fevers.

Despite a rising body temperature, Beth earned American Records in the 200 free and 50 back. She would've added another in the 150 Individual Medley (IM) except for an uneven touch at the ending wall—a disqualification. Beth's right hand bent into a fist more than the left, so Peggy started the paperwork for an IPC exception.

In Portland, no other S3 women competed. Other swimmers in Beth's races quickly moved ahead and out of sight at the start. After a race, a local reporter asked about her decision to give up her spot for the Athens Paralympics.

"I'm definitely not going to miss out on China," Beth said, "and have put myself on a three-year training schedule to qualify."

Between swim sessions, we drove the Columbia River Scenic Highway to picturesque waterfalls, with Mount

Hood in the distance. Beth and I recalled the view of Mount Rainier where her swimming journey started. We wondered where we would be if we hadn't gone to Seattle, where Beth set big swimming goals and where we saw the unusual billboard, "Quadriplegia at Harvard: A+."

As Beth's second year of college began, I helped her move into Pforzheimer House in the Quad (Quadrangle) where she'd live for the next three school years. The irony of a quad living in the Quad did not escape us. My trek to the basement storage room to uncover her belongings proved dangerous. A few months before, I could reach everything in the room. Since then, students packed the entire room to the ceiling. I climbed shaky heaps and shifted furniture. A student helped me grab the heavy lift chair off the floor and over more piles. Lucky, I recovered Beth's things undamaged.

In her second-floor dorm room, I hung Maria's sunflower quilt on the wall from an old-fashioned picture rail molding. I stocked Beth's mini fridge and bought boxes of Cheez-its. She shared a three bedroom, one bath suite with two quiet friends, both future doctors. They studied most of the time, like she did.

I slept on her futon for two nights until a sad drive transported me away from Beth. I should've been grateful she no longer needed me close, but the separation hurt. It wouldn't be fun for me to live in Cambridge another school year, work three jobs, and share a dingy apartment with a stranger. Even so, I wished I could be in both places.

With no assistant or mom down the street, Beth selected biology as her major, a concentration in Harvard-speak, and spent part of her days in the science labs with ongoing physical challenges with equipment. She usually chose to wheel the mile to and from her labs and classes. She led NYLN conference calls in addition to mentoring. She continued to make time for the Kids with Special Needs Achievement Program (KSNAP). Beth's friend Brittany also volunteered, and they rode the subway into Boston on Fridays.

"I directed a volunteer program that mentored students in special education classrooms in Boston Public," Beth said in an application. She also expanded the program to two schools. "We visited classrooms every Friday and took the students on field trips."

Beth's first year on the roster of the Harvard Women's Swimming and Diving team, she depended on the early morning shuttle to get to swim practice with over two miles between her dorm and the pool. She operated the pool's chair lift independently to get in and out of the water. She entered the locked varsity locker room by pressing numbers on a keypad. Easy, compared to handling the heavy doors of the building. Her secret sis left signs and little gifts at her assigned locker. One morning, Beth had a new adhesive hook near her locker for her towel since she couldn't reach the high hooks. She no longer had to leave her towel at the bottom of her locker. Strong team bonds formed a community that depended on each other.

"I made amazing friendships," Beth said.

She joined the rest of the team for scheduled workouts in the weight room. She knew what to do, using Peggy's personalized workout as a guide. Beth figured out how to hold traditional weights with uncooperative hands, along with heavy balls and stretch cords. The team often swam after the weight room. Nothing if not persistent, she put on and positioned her swim cap by herself after four years of trying and failing to achieve the task.

Beth's days filled up more than mine. I bridged the miles between Cambridge and Tiffin with phone calls, emails, and care packages. I also tried to help from a distance, to free up at least a little of her time for more important things.

I made travel plans for upcoming Paralympic swim meets. I responded to requests for details for newspaper articles and updated her resume for a reporter. I started a Challenged Athletes travel grant application, and she finished it with her goals and the essay. I ordered wheel bearings. When she needed a new bag for the back of her chair, I researched options, emailed her the best ones, and bought the one she selected.

Beth took over repairs for her wheelchair, scheduling a service to come to her dorm only after the intermittent catching of one wheel progressed to a consistent and frustrating obstacle. Her dirty laundry piled up until she couldn't find clean clothes to wear. Her priorities filled her days: swim training, classes, homework, volunteering, mentoring—and sleep.

Grateful to be home, I reconnected with the rest of my family. John and I visited Ben in Columbus. John taught 3rd graders while Maria attended Heidelberg College, worked at a video store, led college tours, and babysat. She sang in the college choir and show choir. She had a double major in elementary education and special ed. She wasn't home much except to sleep though we found times to meet at Taco Bell to catch up over burritos and sodas.

I loved my suddenly wide-open life, but I also felt the need to get a job to help with finances even though John never pushed me to work outside the home. I had few options in our small town, with little opportunity without a college degree. Any minimum wage job limited me to low income. I considered working at the Tiffin Center again, a state job and my highest wage option. However, John might retire after the next school year, and we might relocate. It didn't seem fair to the residents to purposely work at the center for a short time. Plus, I would have to start over again in direct care in the most difficult module.

I chose a job that offered more flexibility than the Tiffin Center. I decided to bite the bullet and manage another group home for the same agency I worked for in the past. At group homes, the turnovers in staffing were even more frequent. Before accepting the job, I toured the Tiffin home, a modern duplex in good condition and a big improvement over the previous house I managed. I said yes. I wished later that I had said no.

My first day as manager, I trained to administer meals to a resident with a feeding tube, followed by me training other staff. I liked the four men who lived at the home and knew two of them from when I worked at the institution. I worked 24-hour shifts, 3 p.m. to 3 p.m., often three in a row. It simplified staffing the overnight hours but tested me, mentally and physically. Sleeping well at the group home rarely happened. I scrambled to get up to speed on preferences, goals, routines, behavior plans, scheduling, outings, medications, paperwork, meal planning, grocery shopping, and new state requirements. On my days off, I was on call.

The day-to-day responsibility for the health and welfare of four men was daunting. The men attended the county workshop for adults with developmental disabilities on weekdays. Ideally, that time would be for administrative planning and paperwork. Instead, since the residents had multiple health issues, weekdays often included taking one of them to a doctor's appointment. I tackled complicated medication regimens as well as ordering refills, scheduling appointments, and checking the daily documentation for each shift for every small thing. I often drove to the group home on my days off for at least a few hours to keep up.

My agency's new quality control supervisor visited one weekday morning after the men boarded the workshop bus; she had been the manager before me of the same home. She pointed out missing papers in the resident binders which I was aware of. I regret not being more assertive. I wish I'd spoken up and showed her my long to-do list that included the missing items. Papers *she* neglected to obtain as the previous manager. Instead, I stewed.

Next, my agency's director made a counter-productive decision about a resident's behavior plan by caving in to pressure from the resident's sibling. I typed up evidence to support a better approach, to avoid dependence on a walker he didn't need. I met with the director to plead the resident's case to no avail.

Later that day, the same resident threw a tantrum near midnight. Following the new behavior plan, I had to encourage him to use the walker by his bed on the way to the bathroom. He didn't need one. The ill-advised plan guaranteed more acting out, increased dependency, and needless frustration all around. When his persistent yelling finally ended, I poked my head into the other bedrooms to reassure and quietly tell the other residents everything was okay. Good intentions, bad outcome.

The youngest resident, nonverbal, had a compulsive personality. He thought my intrusion meant it was time to get up. He jumped out of bed and started his morning routine. My attempts to explain and redirect irritated him. He insisted on changing clothes and sat at the kitchen table in the dark. I tried to reason with him. Agitated, he tried to tip over the table and would have succeeded, except the home had an unusually huge and heavy one.

When he calmed down, I brought him a bowl of his favorite cereal with milk. He finished eating and sat in his rocking chair in the living room, still angry. I kept him company while I wrote out the required incident reports. Each one needed to be copied and faxed to three people.

The thought of Beth in Massachusetts depressed me even though I knew she could handle living independently with her disability. I missed her. We had been a team.

My sadness amplified the normal day-to-day stress of my job. With elevated headache pain, I had trouble sleeping at the group home. I barreled through more weeks with unpaid overtime hours. Often on the verge of tears, I talked to John and let him convince me the stress of the manager job wasn't worth the money. Looking back, I could have ridden it out.

Staffing group homes over the holidays always created a challenge. Instead of quitting my manager job in November before Thanksgiving and Christmas, I decided to be considerate of the residents and other staff by leaving early in the New Year, almost three months away. I turned in my notice, relieved to see the end in sight and focused on setting things in order for the next manager.

I talked to Beth on the phone after she finished a 2,400-yard workout in one practice. Almost a mile and a half, 96 lengths in the 25-yard pool. Swimming that distance had not been possible a year before. As college competitions began, Beth would compete at all home meets at Blodgett pool as an official member of the Harvard Women's Swimming and Diving (HWSD) team. Always too busy, she didn't ask to travel with the team to away-meets and valued the extra time at her dorm.

I wished I could've been there for the first home meet of the season in mid-November. Beth dropped 15 seconds in the 100 free compared to her first Harvard meet 10 months before! And, reset two of her short course American Records.

"She's probably one of the easiest people to coach in the sense that she always has a smile on her face, she's got a great positive attitude, and she's willing to try anything," Coach Morawski said in *The Harvard Gazette.* "And she just kept getting faster and faster."

"For her to make that commitment to coach me and this year I'm on the roster, is really important," Beth said. "It's been great. I love it!"

She received team swimsuits, caps, warm ups, and best of all, her favorite comfortable, heavy sweatpants the team called "dhas" (pronounced d-haas) because of the DHA imprint, the Department of Harvard Athletics.

One of the few perks of being a group home manager was setting the weekly schedule. I set up my work hours to join Beth for a long weekend in early December. She made her way to Boston's Logan airport on her own. She traveled with a duffel on her lap and a full backpack on her wheelchair handles and rode in an accessible taxi to the airport. She stayed in her manual wheelchair until the plane boarded, and she moved to the small aisle chair to access her seat. She kept her duffel and backpack with her on the plane to avoid baggage claim later. The last passenger to deboard, she stayed on the plane until someone brought an aisle chair to carry her to her own wheelchair.

I flew out of Detroit and met Beth at the Minneapolis/St. Paul International Airport. How wonderful to reconnect with her after being separated for the first time. I drove a rental car to our familiar hotel across from the university pool complex.

I had a good sense of direction. Ever since I grew up a few blocks from Lake Erie in Lorain, Ohio, I could usually find north, to the water, from different places around the state. However, my lake sense, my true north, didn't work in other regions.

I stuck to a routine to navigate around a strange city for swim trips. I had a cell phone but no smart phone or GPS.

With my printed maps to navigate around a new city, I started to gain my bearings by the time the swim meet ended. In Minneapolis, I could relax, knowing where to go from previous swim meets.

The beautiful pool at the University of Minnesota bumped down to second on Beth's list of favorite pools after Harvard's Blodgett. She achieved an unexpected milestone at the winter meet: a PanAmerican Record in the 100-meter backstroke. She also added a brand new American Record in the 150 IM (backstroke, breast, and free) and reached an incredible fourth place in the IPC World Rankings in the 200 freestyle!

I wished the 200 free could be an official S3 event. We hoped the 2008 Beijing Paralympics would include at least one long event in her classification. Beth set and reset American Records on the Harvard Women's Swim Team and the U.S. Paralympics National Team, working toward the perfect freestyle, the ultimate 50-meter freestyle record, and Beijing.

I said goodbye to everyone at the group home in early January and gratefully turned in my keys. I gave myself the gift of time to live in the moment, connect with others, and take better care of myself. I aimed for the lower headache level I had before the manager job.

A few weeks later, I accepted an invitation to a birthday party at the group home. Glad to see the residents again, I appreciated having no responsibility for their lives. Not long after, the resident at the group home with the feeding tube passed away, and I attended his funeral. I cried during his sister's eulogy as she described his joyful greeting when she visited him, something I had the privilege to witness.

I kept in touch with Beth from Ohio while she finished her first official season with the HWSD

team. Harvard was famous for extraordinary professional
connections. Beth found that to be true, but she appreciated
other associations as well. The college's shuttle bus drivers
pitched in to surprise her with a bouquet of flowers for her
20th birthday in April. Even at 6 a.m. on the way to the pool,
Beth conversed pleasantly with the drivers and always
thanked them. She became friends with the bus dispatcher
Bonnie who also used a wheelchair. At the dispatcher's
request, Beth spoke at two Boston schools. Bonnie attended
HWSD home meets with her young daughters, and the girls
asked Beth to autograph their meet programs.

In the spring, she missed a week of college classes to
fly to Antwerp, Belgium with the U.S. Paralympics National
Team. She earned four first-place finishes. Her hometown
coach traveled with the team as a new U.S. Paralympics
coach.

"Coach Peggy has helped me get better with almost
every meet," Beth told a reporter in our hometown. "She's
been with me every step of the way."

When a riot broke out in Antwerp, the coaches rushed
to gather up the sightseeing swimmers. All were fine. Some
even found inexpensive treasures in the diamond capital of
the world. My daughter purchased a gift for Maria, a ring
with a small diamond, similar to the HOPE ring. Beth had
worn her HOPE ring every day since her injury. Exactly like
the one her best friends owned, the rings continued to be a
meaningful reminder of the love of good friends.

During John's spring break, we drove 12 hours from
Tiffin to Cambridge, taking Route 90 most of the way. A
decade earlier, the one-hour drive from Tiffin to Vermilion
seemed long. Not anymore.

I bought tickets for our first Red Sox game at Fenway
Park with John and Beth. We lined up by the field to meet
some of the players. Many lingered to talk to the smiling

college student in a wheelchair with the navy blue Red Sox cap.

The stadium had old-fashioned charm with the brightly-painted homerun fence, the green monster. All the seats in the stadium sold, so many others paid to stand to watch the game. The enthusiastic, rowdy crowd reacted to every play, something I'd never seen before. It was my first experience with the city's intense sports fans but not my last. Bostonians took their professional sports teams seriously, a fact encouraged by many winning teams.

We weren't prepared for the cold wind, so I signed up for a credit card to get a free Red Sox blanket. I wrapped it around my daughter's shoulders (and later cancelled the card).

John's break coincided with Parent's Week. We visited Beth's class on Ethics, Biotechnology, and the Future of Human Nature. The guest speaker that day was Dr. James Watson, the former head of the Human Genome Project, who discovered the structure of DNA with Dr. Francis Crick. His affinity for eugenics created a controversial discussion with the class.

Dr. Watson encouraged the students to have many children. Beth chimed in the class debate on the potential of stem cells and the controversy over discarded embryos. She supported research even though she never focused on a cure for her disability. An upcoming vote in Congress heated up the debate across the country over federal funding for stem cell research. We didn't know that Beth would be in the middle of it.

❧ Chapter 19 ❧
CONNECTING

Beth: *I spent my summer in DC where I fell in love with the excitement on the Hill and the chance to make policy that makes a difference.*

A MAGAZINE QUOTED Beth as saying, "I think that limits are self-imposed. I don't believe there are limits."

A reader complained, calling it a lie for people with disabilities. Were the limits of blindness self-imposed? Or the limits of a cut spinal cord?

In any case, Beth did not lie. In her world, the quote had always been true. She found everything meaningful in her life in what she *could* do. What she couldn't? Dismissed as insignificant.

As Beth wheeled forward, she paid attention to opportunities. Many of them were fortunate accidents of one kind or another. Through NYLN, she learned about a Congressional Intern Grant through the American Association of People with Disabilities (AAPD) and the Mitsubishi Electric America Foundation. The grant covered the huge expense of summer housing in Washington, DC. She submitted the grant application and also applied to congressional offices for an intern position.

"I was accepted into Senator John Kerry's office first, so I jumped on that," Beth said. "I was so excited because I respect him."

As the summer began, I shopped with her for dress clothes and a professional-looking bag for the back of her wheelchair. I helped Beth move into an accessible dorm at George Washington University (GWU). The AAPD interns shared dorm suites on the same floor. Beth toured museums and monuments with her two roommates. She connected with the other interns as well as the hustle of big city life.

"It was a life-changing experience. The disability community is so active in DC."

The Metro subway, newer than Boston's T, carried Beth to Capitol Hill on weekdays. She reluctantly conceded to the occasional push from strangers as she wheeled up the hill, past the Supreme Court building, and on to the Senate offices, especially on wet sidewalks. She worked on disability and health care issues at a desk right next to the Senator's friendly office manager Mary.

"We had installed handicapped door openers, and she never used them," Mary said. "She has an unbelievable attitude and is sweet as can be. Nothing will stop her."

The internship coincided with Beth's fifth swimming summer. She still trained year-round on the U.S. Paralympic National Swim Team. She frequented a crowded YMCA pool in DC after work.

One evening on the way back to the GWU dorm in pouring rain by herself, Beth bypassed the subway elevator she needed because of a too-friendly homeless man. She wheeled several more blocks in the storm to the next Metro stop.

Washington, DC, was unfamiliar to Beth during her first extended stay as a summer intern. One day, she wheeled through an unfamiliar part of the city to meet a friend for dinner. Approaching an overpass by herself, armed only with her gift for minimizing obstacles, Beth increased her speed. She made it halfway up the hill to an even steeper incline. With no tilt guards to prevent the wheelchair from tipping backward, she leaned forward, turned the big wheels toward the road at a 90° angle and stopped. She wore wheelchair gloves with her fingers exposed for a better grip.

If she reversed her course to go back down the hill, she'd burn her fingers on the wheels trying to slow her speed and might lose control of the wheelchair. Going up the hill the rest of the way wasn't a good option, especially without a "running" start.

The overpass had two lanes of traffic in each direction, with no parking lane, bike path, or extra space for a car to pull over. Beth decided to go back down the hill and find a subway stop, when a young man stopped his car right in the lane next to her. He put on his flashers, jumped out, and quickly pushed her up the hill. She realized he was deaf when she thanked him. After dinner, she avoided the overpass by taking the Metro home.

I drove eight hours with John and Maria from Ohio to Washington, DC, to visit Beth over the July 4th weekend. I bought tickets for a play at the Kennedy Center for the first time. My girls and I enjoyed the musical, *Little Women*. For the July 4th parade, we congregated by a curb on Constitution Avenue in blistering heat. Beth and I took a break in air conditioning at the Smithsonian American History Museum nearby. Many ethnic groups danced in vibrant costumes. Notably missing? The county fair royalty, tractors, and other farm equipment in Tiffin parades.

Senator Kerry's office manager arranged for Beth to sit next to him at the intern luncheon. Meeting him for the first time, my daughter asked him about the upcoming Senate vote to allow federal funding for new stem cell lines.

"I asked him if I could be on the (Senate) floor with him," Beth told a Boston reporter. "I hope that as the Senators are voting, they can see a face that reminds them of what they're actually voting for."

"As a person in the disability community, I've met so many people whose main goal is just to get better, and stem cell research is their one opportunity to find a cure."

When Beth told me on the phone about her big ask, I realized that the shy, quiet girl she'd been before her injury had been left behind for good. Senator Kerry not only agreed to her request, he decided to include Beth in his stem cell speech. He requested and received special permission for "privileges of the floor" for her to join him in the Senate on July 18th.

"If you ever need to be reminded of why it's morally right to lift the ban on stem cell research, just listen to Beth," Senator Kerry said in *The Boston Globe*. "She's more eloquent on this subject than any lobbyist or member of Congress."

Beth's day on the Senate floor included conversations with Senator Ted Kennedy and others. She hoped to meet Hillary Clinton, but the Senator kept busy on her phone. When Senator Kerry spoke at the podium to his colleagues, he introduced Beth and shared her story. He said she served as a "silent, powerful reminder of what is at stake here." He also signed the paper copy of his speech for her to keep. Newspapers covered Beth's story in Boston, Toledo, Tiffin, and Washington, DC. John collected them all.

"As her Dad, I'm just intensely proud of her," John said in *The Toledo Blade*. "She's a courageous young lady. How many 20-year-olds spent the day on the floor of the U.S. Senate tracking an issue that's so important to them?"

The Boston Globe printed my quote. "She's not someone who is focused on the cure. She's very much living her life today. We're all hoping that stem cell research will offer her more options in the future but in the meantime, she's making the most of everything she has."

The Senate passed the stem cell bill with the support of the Democrats, Nancy Reagan, and many other Republicans. Regardless, President George W. Bush vetoed it the next day, benching the issue for three years until the next president ended the federal limits on stem cell research.

Research undoubtedly paved the way for significant improvements in treating many conditions. However, a complete cure for the unlucky quads (like Beth) with cut spinal cords in the neck *and* old injuries? Not likely in my lifetime. We followed Laraine's advice to not be the first in line for a cure. We knew several people who paid a fortune for stem cell treatments in other countries with little or no results. I thought it best that Beth's heart wasn't set on walking again. Even so, I hoped stem cells would make her life easier one day.

At weekend parties in the GWU dorm with the other grant interns, Beth's new friend Haley introduced her to beer pong. Letting go of the last remnants of her shyness, Beth accepted her first dates.

Washington, DC, became her favorite big city. Beth's next few years would probably revolve around big cities, where it was easier to not have a car. At her request, I sold her car to a friend from the Toledo Raptors who needed the hand controls. I cherished our fun memories in that little blue car.

Over a long August weekend, John and I met Beth at the San Antonio airport for our first trip to Texas. Oppressive heat welcomed us. I bothered Beth with temperature checks and wondered who had the idea for a swim meet in Texas in August. Between prelims and finals of the U.S. Paralympics meet, I left a trail of sweat through the River Walk and the Alamo, monitoring Beth's temperature often. John's camera captured butterflies on bright flowers, thriving in the stifling heat.

Beth and the other National Team swimmers learned about lactate testing, an important element of competitive swimming. Lactate increased in arm and leg muscles during races, a potential problem if the athlete had another event in the same session. A quick poke for a drop of blood right after her first race revealed Beth's lactate level. After she warmed down with leisurely laps, a coach tested her blood again. If her lactate level needed to be lower, she swam slowly for a longer time. Through this process, repeated after other races, they determined the optimum warm down for each swimmer so that muscles would be at peak performance for the next race.

Beth's swim times in San Antonio earned her a place on the World Championship team going to South Africa. Unwilling to miss a month of college, she gave up her slot immediately to allow someone else to go in her place. We knew the Beijing Paralympics would not be declined. Her IPC World Rankings rose to fourth and fifth with the 100 and 200 freestyle.

Back at Harvard for the start of Beth's junior year, I carried her futon chair and other items up from the basement storage room. I set up her dorm room before I drove back to Tiffin. She changed her concentration from biology to health care policy with the goal of attending law school. Beth told a reporter about her DC summer and why she changed her major.

"I really fell in love with the policy side of things. After the internship, there was an opening in Senator Kerry's Boston office to work specifically on disability issues with one of his staffers. They invited me to do that. So throughout my entire school year, I worked in his Boston office. It's completely different because it's much more focused on his constituents. But I really loved that because you get to talk to people on an individual basis."

Beth rode the T by herself from Harvard Square to the Senator's office near the Massachusetts State House. One day a week, sometimes two. She stayed on the subway and passed the T stop closest to the Senator's office to avoid a steep hill. She planned for extra time to wheel the additional distance back to the office. She also signed up for text alerts to get advance notice when the T elevators broke down.

"When I answered phone calls, I recognized a desperation in their voices as they reached out to their Senator who was all too often their last hope in solving their issues," Beth said. "It was rewarding to resolve specific disability-related complaints, but some we could not help."

She stayed in touch with Mary in the DC office and joined the Senator and staff for events, including a campaign rally at the Perkins School for the Blind in Watertown for Deval Patrick, soon-to-be Governor of Massachusetts.

Coffee, Beth's new habit, stoked long days of classes and homework, swim practice and meets, plus volunteering for KSNAP and Senator Kerry. Her friend Brittany also recruited her to help develop a new website to share individual experiences with paralysis.

Beth's new major allowed her to create and follow an individualized program. She selected classes relating to health care, a wide field of study including economics, regulations, inequalities, public opinion, politics, quality control, and buzzwords like adverse selection and moral hazard. She took advantage of an opportunity to take courses at two of Harvard's graduate schools.

"I explored health care policy and disability issues with courses at Harvard's Kennedy School and Law School," Beth said. They were her favorite classes.

Maria stuck to her plan to relocate to Boston. She hustled with a heavy class load to finish the degree requirements for her double major in three and a half years. Before long, two of our three children would be in Massachusetts. John agreed with me that we could live there too. He knew how much I wanted to be near our kids.

John started his 30th year of teaching in Tiffin, his last before retiring in Ohio. We planned to sell our house in the spring and move in the summer. He decided he'd teach for a few more years in the Boston area because of the much higher cost of living there.

I accepted an activities job at Tiffin's upscale Elmwood nursing home. Almost 30 years earlier, 19 and newly married, I worked as the first manager of Elmwood's first group home in the nearby town of Clyde.

I worked five days a week on the Alzheimer's unit, learning more than I wanted to know about the disease. On the best days, we sang songs, told stories, made crafts, played games, walked together, and laughed. On the worst days, a sweet woman died in her bed, and alarms blared when residents unable to walk thought they could. Or someone fell. Or a medical emergency required an ambulance. Sirens always reminded me of the night of my car accident.

Beth swam six times a week during her junior year and rode the bus at 6 a.m. with her teammates who lived in the Quad. She often arrived at Blodgett in sweatpants, with a swimsuit underneath that she'd pulled on before getting out of bed. The team stretched together on deck before getting in the water. Skipping regular practices? Not an option. When the rest of the team swam doubles, a second practice on the same day, Beth stayed with one.

Coaches added a snorkel to the modified swim paddles and floats in Beth's equipment bag. The snorkel eliminated the breathing challenges of her forward strokes. Practices lasted about 90 minutes, and she typically swam a hundred laps of 25 yards each. However, during peak times in her training cycles, workouts hit two hours and 3,000 yards, almost two miles. An impossible task for most of us.

Assistant coach Becca worked with Beth on a variety of drills, alternating strokes and incorporating interval training. Becca exchanged emails and coordinated training cycles with Peggy. Beth appreciated all of her supportive coaches and her team.

"My undergrad was devoted to swimming and health policy," she wrote. "It was a struggle sometimes to be independent and keep up with the work, but I grew a lot during that time. I learned how to make new friends, to manage my disability, and to advocate for myself, not to mention becoming a much stronger swimmer with HWSD. I like to joke that I spend more time in the pool than I do in class. I love this pool!"

The locker room had a new plastic shower chair that Beth finally requested. From a sitting position in her wheelchair, taking off a wet swimsuit in the locker room required patience. I suggested suits one size bigger, but she preferred them tight. Resolve and repetition gradually made dressing in her wheelchair easier, from button down sweaters to the zipper on her skinny jeans.

Often the last to leave the varsity locker room after a practice, with her hair wet, she wheeled up the hill at the entrance to the sidewalk on North Harvard Street. If she had a class after practice, she wheeled over the bridge toward the Square instead of taking the shuttle. On frigid days, the hair below her hat freeze-dried. The curb cuts on the bridge had steep inclines, impossible in any kind of wheelchair. Unwilling to ask for help from one of the endless pedestrians, Beth wheeled in the street alongside the curb instead, sharing a lane with aggressive drivers.

Across the river, Beth often stopped at Dunkin' Donuts for a soy latte and a whole grain bagel with blueberry cream cheese. Peet's Coffee also was a favorite a little farther down the street. One morning at the Kennedy School of Government, she rode the elevator with Madeleine Albright, the first woman Secretary of State.

Beth's largest class, Justice, attracted hundreds of students to Sanders, my favorite theatre. Dr. Michael Sandel led lively discussions on all aspects of justice that kept students engaged—and the public as well. Harvard aired Justice online for free.

The college competition season approached. One of Beth's friends on the U.S. Paralympics National Team also swam on the Yale team and successfully fought to compete at all meets, home and away. In contrast, Beth appreciated the time she gained by not traveling with the team.

"The trips sounded exciting, but staying back gave me more time for school work and volunteer activities," Beth said.

She sent swim workouts to the National Team manager and reported her whereabouts to the United States Anti-Doping Agency. Little to no social activities. Yet.

One November morning, Beth stopped at the dining hall for coffee on the way to a HWSD home meet. The cup slipped, and scalding liquid spilled on her left thigh. She felt discomfort but when she removed her leggings at Blodgett, she didn't expect to see the small red hole in her thigh. Her coaches discussed the emergency room and asked a dermatologist friend in the stands to look at it. The doctor, a former college swimmer, cleaned and covered the third-degree burn, emphasizing the need to prevent infection. Wide scarring when it healed would be unavoidable. It surprised me that the dermatologist gave permission for Beth to compete at the meet.

I heard about the burn the same day but not the severity. She neglected to disclose all the details. She left out the part about the burn exposing the bone. I assumed it wasn't serious since the doctor and coaches allowed her to swim. She didn't want me to worry. Nevertheless, I was alarmed when I saw the burn a few weeks later.

Skin problems healed slowly for quads, and infections? Dangerous. We revisited the issue of drink holders. Rejected in the past, Beth gave in. I attached her first one to the front frame of her wheelchair. I also nagged her to stop procrastinating on another medical issue. Beth's kyphosis (bowing) caused a skin abrasion in one spot where her backbone rubbed on the rigid wheelchair back. She eventually made time for a seating clinic appointment, and a ridiculously long insurance process finally resulted in a new chair back with a gel cushion.

Her right elbow swelled and hurt for the first time. Initially, her doctor and the team's athletic trainers recommended compression wraps and anti-inflammatory meds. She never stopped swimming and felt healthy and stronger than ever, except for the elbow.

In mid-December, Maria packed a suitcase for her flight to Boston after her last day of student teaching in Tiffin. She had applied for teaching jobs and followed up with direct calls to ask for an interview. Her assertiveness, a skill I struggled with, landed her an interview in Cambridge. She flew by herself for the first time into Logan airport.

Maria slept on a futon in Beth's dorm room and rode the T by herself to the interview. She tapped into her passion for teaching children with disabilities. After, the sisters met for dinner at Bertucci's in the Square before they flew home together. A few days later, Maria accepted the job as a lead teacher in the Cambridge Public Schools' Special Start program for preschoolers with a disability. The position would begin in a few weeks, in early January. I was proud and excited—and also sad she would be leaving home.

Maria had decided to be a teacher at a young age. At her first library story hour with no parents, the librarian told me how she found her way onto the storyteller's lap. At home, her little sister was her student. Maria also loved to help in John's classroom during summer school. She declared that we would all live together forever in our Tiffin home, happy-ever-after.

More than a decade later, Maria planned her move to Boston while John and I prepared to sell our home of 22 years. Our last Christmas living in Ohio embraced nostalgia. We watched *The Princess Bride* with popcorn. We played N'Sync Christmas music while we wrapped presents. Ben visited, and we laughed at old videos the girls called "baby tapes." One of our favorites showed Ben, 5, pulling his little sisters on a blanket around the dining room table over and over. A giggle fest. The video captured a perfect silly afternoon. At the Vermilion farmhouse, we connected with extended family and met new babies.

Beth rang in the New Year with Lizzy and Ellen for the last time, a replay of fondue and favorite movies, including *Elf* and *The Grinch.* Still laughing so easily. I admired the young women they'd become.

We prepared for another 12-hour trek. I drove with both girls in Maria's Ford Focus from Tiffin to Cambridge. No hatchback or chair topper. We stuffed the small car to the hilt with Maria's belongings—plus a wheelchair. Beth sat cramped in the back seat for the all-day drive. We planned to get her out of the car to wheel around or move the contents to give her a different position, but Beth shifted on her own and chose to stay put to get to her dorm faster. We drove directly to Pforzheimer House, where Maria and I camped out in Beth's suite that night. In the morning, a real estate agent showed apartments to Maria and me, less than a week before she'd start her new job.

After viewing several places, Maria decided to rent the second floor of a house near Davis Square in Somerville to avoid the even higher rent in Cambridge. She could move in the next morning. Next, we shopped for a bed. Maria picked one to be delivered the next afternoon.

Maria and I slept in Beth's dorm room one more night. Bright and early the next day, we unloaded the contents of her car into the empty apartment. Maria brought her shopping list for a Target run. We made it back in time for the bed to be delivered.

The box springs wouldn't fit up the narrow, winding stairway to her apartment. The young delivery guys tried another way. One precariously balanced on the front porch steps and pushed the box springs straight up to the other who leaned over the second-floor balcony. Success. I stayed two more days before flying back to Ohio and treasured the time. I admired Maria's bravery in moving to an unfamiliar big city with her sister, the only person she knew.

Back to work, I engaged the residents at the nursing home and tried to brighten the moment, the hour, the day. In Lorain on a weekend, John and I sang happy birthday to his sister, Jean, one of the last songs she'd sing when her Alzheimer's progressed. Another day, Maria called me on the way to the emergency room at Mt. Auburn Hospital in Cambridge. Beth, suddenly sick with strong nausea, headache, and fever, had asked her sister to take her to the hospital.

I worried about sepsis. The leading causes of death for quads were pneumonia, septicemia (blood poisoning caused by sepsis), and suicide.

The emergency room staff identified an infection and waited for other test results. After a few miserable hours, Maria lost her patience with the staff. An ambulance carried Beth to a Boston hospital while Maria followed in her car. An attentive doctor understood quadriplegia. He ran more tests. By morning, Beth's fever dropped, and he ruled out peritonitis and sepsis. He released her with strong antibiotics and instructions to return to the hospital if anything worsened. I was already on Rt. 90 in Pennsylvania en route to Cambridge.

Beth's severe symptoms lessened by the time I arrived. I brought her chicken soup from Au Bon Pain and helped as much as I could for a few days. I encouraged her to slow down though she quickly returned to her full schedule.

Big changes approached. At home, I divided a lifetime of photographs into four piles, one for each of our kids and one for John and me. I threw away old albums and put the photographs in labeled boxes of memories. Our ordinary lives had detoured to less traveled roads—with more on the horizon.

❧ Chapter 20 ☙
LEADING

Beth: *Rio was an absolutely amazing experience.*

MY EFFORTS TO anticipate and avoid problems failed during a Paralympic meet in Canada. I met Beth at the Montreal airport. She wasn't a fan of flying but that didn't stop her from getting on planes. She surprised people by traveling alone with a duffel bag on her lap and a big HWSD pack on the back of her chair.

I had no rental car reservation. The subway had been recommended, and it worked—if you could climb flights of steps. We decided on taxis instead. On the last morning, we rode through a heavy March snowfall to the swim meet.

One of Beth's big wheels flattened during prelims, a first in seven years of air-filled tires. After her injury, I worried about many things, but a flat tire had been completely off my radar. Overly optimistic, we hoped a new inner tube in an odd size could be easily found at a local bike shop. On a Sunday. During a snowstorm.

I left to save the day while Beth rested in our hotel room. I planned to pick her up with an inflated wheel in my hand before the last finals session. I hailed a taxi carrying the flat wheel and a list of bike shops; thankfully, Montreal had several. A friendly driver headed for the nearest one while I called others. Phone recordings said some were open though no one answered.

Beth called me in a panic when I left the third bike shop with the flat tire. She learned it was a big deal to miss a finals race at a championship meet, with paperwork required in advance. Time ticked away, and drivers acted as though they'd never seen snow before. Plows blocked roads and piled snow on parked cars.

Miraculously, the fourth bike shop had the right size inner tube. By the time they fixed the wheel, and I arrived back to the hotel, finals had already begun. The taxi driver waited while I ran up to our room with the wheel and flew back down with Beth who wore her swimsuit under sweats. Peggy called us from the pool. We *might* make it in time for her first race. A traffic jam tested our patience and dampened the beauty of the white wonderland.

Finally, I paid the driver way too much, and we rushed to the pool deck where Peggy waved frantically. Right next to a starting block, Peggy and I stripped Beth's coat and sweats off in seconds and literally dropped her in the lane. Another quick moment, and the race began. Her hastily donned goggles came off and floated in the water behind her. We laughed about it later, but it wasn't funny at the time.

In hindsight, we should've borrowed a wheelchair from another swimmer for Beth to get to finals with Peggy. Friends on the team with prosthetic legs sometimes traveled with wheelchairs. I bought a set of foam-filled tires the next day, the only kind she's used since.

Beth's times in Montreal qualified for the Parapan American Games in Rio de Janeiro to be held in August. Saving money for the probable trip to China, I decided not to fly to Brazil, especially since Peggy would travel on the U.S. team.

One April morning in pouring rain, Beth met her co-workers from John Kerry's office in the town of Hopkinton. The Senator arrived, greeted Beth by name, and led the way to the start of the Boston Marathon wheelchair race, moving cones out of the way for her. John Kerry's daughter shared her umbrella with Beth. The Boston staff asked her to work in the Senator's office for another school year. Beth reluctantly declined to open up a little breathing room as a senior.

In Tiffin, I worked most days at the nursing home while John taught his last months in Ohio. We mapped out our move to the East Coast. Our furniture cost too much to transport, so we made plans to sell it. John created signs for a big garage sale. We evaluated every item large and small to keep, sell, or donate. I tossed most of the stuff accumulated over 30 years into garage sale boxes. We planned to move in a few carloads.

We kept family treasures, including my Grandma Barnes' fancy fruit bowl with etchings on clear crystal. As a child, I sat at her kitchen table near the bowl and a plate of molasses raisin cookies. My grandma put ice cubes in my glass of milk, a habit I thought peculiar. From her kitchen, I had a clear view of a small room with tables full of blooms, a collage of color. I loved the lavenders, creams, pinks, and blues. Some solid, some variegated, some fancy with ruffles. In a clear glass jar, green stems with roots floated in water, a nursery for baby plants. The room full of African violets captivated me, a soft-spoken child who dunked cookies in iced milk.

I had bought three Amish cedar chests and filled them with childhood keepsakes, one for each of my kids. Maria had hers in Massachusetts. John and I drove another to Ben in Columbus. He worked as a supervisor for ADP and planned for graduate school. The chest reminded him of gerbil bedding because of the cedar scent. To simplify his upcoming move to graduate school, Ben gave away the chest to his cousin in Columbus but kept most of the contents.

Situated near Beth and Maria, Newton topped the list of best small cities in New England. John applied there and to a few other school systems in the area. Two schools called him for interviews that he scheduled during his April school vacation.

To start spring break, we drove to Somerville and dropped off a carload of boxes and Beth's cedar chest to store at Maria's apartment. We visited the girls between their busy work and school schedules.

John and I relied on our new GPS to find the Newton school for his first interview. I dropped him off and waited for his phone call at Not Your Average Joe's, my new favorite restaurant. John felt good about his interview. Like Maria, his passion for teaching showed.

John accepted a second grade position in Newton to start in the fall. With crazy home prices in the Boston area, we viewed many apartments to rent. Our house payment in Ohio had been $475 a month including property tax and insurance. In 2007 near Boston, the rent for a nice two-bedroom apartment started at $1,900 a month, plus utilities. Slightly higher salaries did not begin to make up the difference though it would be worth it to be closer to Maria and Beth. We paid a deposit on an apartment in Watertown Square with a July move-in date.

At his request, John's friends hosted a modest happy hour for his retirement instead of a big traditional party. Gifts included an intricate scrapbook with personal messages from co-workers. The last day of school, he brought home a box of mechanical gadgets and science toys that he used to entertain his students. We teased John about being a talented comedian—for second graders.

The two-story Tiffin home we bought in 1984 for $39,000 appraised 23 years later at $105,000. In the midst of the housing crisis, home sales had slowed nationally and even more in Tiffin because of factory closings. We listed the house for $99,000. On a lucky day, a young couple requested a second showing of our home. We told them we would accept an offer of $90,000, and the home where we raised our children sold. An early closing date forced us to rent a Tiffin apartment for two months.

Beth's second trip to the Paralympic World Cup in England fell conveniently during reading period, Harvard's open study time before finals. I stayed home. Peggy flew to Manchester as a Team USA coach. Aware of Beth's earlier solution for the high bed at the same hotel, Peggy placed the box springs along the wall and left the mattress to sleep on.

I turned in my notice at the nursing home and sold our second work car. We left our old house and garden walkways on an emotional day. So many memories. I wish I had kept the seeds of the flowers we called 4 o'clocks. They thrived in the dirt of a front window well. Over decades, the colors blended into one-of-a-kind blooms.

At a tiny apartment across town, John and I carried a double mattress to the bedroom floor and a single bed on a metal frame for Beth in the living room. The only other furnishings: a TV, card table, and two matching chairs. And important things, like my African violets.

Beth's sixth swimming summer began with my drive east to pick her up at Harvard and bring her to Tiffin for the last time. She swam with SAK and Peggy at the outdoor pool and on her own at the YMCA. She researched her senior thesis. Always reading, Beth checked off more books on her top one hundred classics list. We both read Jane Austen books and watched movie renditions, always rating the books higher. She completed her Harry Potter collection with the seventh and last, *The Deathly Hallows*. The first 24 hours of sales set a new record with 11 million copies sold. She waited in a long line with Ellen and Lizzy to see the fifth Harry Potter movie, *The Order of the Phoenix*. A dinner in Sandusky with Laraine ended in a teary farewell, perhaps for the last time.

Beth reviewed graduate school applications and made notes for admission essays. "I have met many people with disabilities who are limited by inadequate health services. This stark reality has shifted my focus from a childhood desire to be a doctor to fighting for disability rights."

At the CAN-AM Championships in Vancouver, Beth excelled in the 200 free. Distance events tapped into her ever-increasing stamina and allowed her to find the best rhythm. They also translated to her top spots in the World Rankings and high odds of earning medals.

The IPC announced that the 100 free event for S3 women at the Beijing Paralympics would be dropped, leaving only two events, the 50 free and 50 back. One length of a long course pool, both sprints. Not one distance event. Eliminating all except two short S3 events for Beijing would carry forward by precedent to the next Paralympics, where they might be cut again. At least 90 percent of all Paralympic swimmers carried classifications with higher numbers than Beth. They had opportunities to qualify in many events in a range of distances and strokes.

Firmly closing the door on distance events, Peggy and the Harvard coaches shifted the focus of Beth's workouts. They eliminated circle turn practice and added more sprint sets. She wouldn't race again in the butterfly, breaststroke, individual medley, or 200-meter events. I suggested she reset her first slow American Records, including the 200 back. She also could easily claim more records in other strokes and distances. Beth chose not to reset slow records or swim other events just to get her name in the records more often.

Her forward freestyle progressed to surpass the speed of her double-arm backstroke, making the 50 free her best chance for a medal. And placing her higher in the World Rankings. She aimed for the 50-meter freestyle American

Record, the most difficult in her classification. Beth shared her newest goal: a small tattoo on her leg when she made the Beijing team.

I shared our new Massachusetts address with family and friends. The wrong address. In mid-July, our new apartment waiting, John and I drove to Massachusetts. Beth chose to stay in the Tiffin apartment by herself for less than a week to continue training. I would return to Ohio in five days. She spent time with Ellen and Lizzy. Peggy drove her to and from swim practices.

When John and I arrived at Watertown Square in a heavy car, the wrong apartment waited for us. The leasing staff apologized for their mistake and significantly dropped the rent at another, nicer complex owned by the same company. Instead of unloading the car in Watertown Square, we drove a little farther to the next suburb, Waltham. We chose an apartment with big windows at the top of Bear Hill, where chipmunks played on the balcony. The downside? It extended John's commute to work a little, and our rent would jump to the usual higher rate, over $2,000 a month, after a year. In the meantime, we could live in an upscale, sunny, spacious apartment. We called Macy's to change the delivery address for our new mattresses. We unloaded the car and called family to correct our address.

John picked out our first flat screen TV, and we set out on a mission to find the perfect sofa. We also stocked up on groceries for our empty kitchen. The second day, we perused more sofas from Dedham to Natick to Burlington. The third day, we bought the sofa we had seen the first day, a wine-colored reclining sectional. It would move with us three times.

I left John in Waltham without a car but with Maria not far away. I drove back to Ohio by myself, singing with CDs most of the way. In Tiffin, Beth and I folded clothes at a laundromat and packed for her training camp in Colorado and the Brazil games after. Sad to end their long Tiffin history, Beth said goodbye to Ellen and Lizzy. I'd miss her friends too.

I dropped Beth and Peggy off at the Detroit airport. Then I sold the beds, emptied the apartment, loaded the car, and gave away the rest. I headed east, excited for the new beginning. I replayed my favorite Joshua Radin song, "Everything'll Be Alright."

Wherever we lived, John made it my home. When I arrived in Waltham, our apartment only had a sofa, a TV on the floor, and two mattresses. I unpacked my grandma's etched crystal bowl for the kitchen counter and added fresh fruit. My African violets survived the car ride and found new windows to love.

John and I searched for simple, sparse furnishings in many stores. Maria and I checked sales and clearance racks for good deals as always. John teased about metal shelving units in all the rooms and made do with just one in the garage. I coordinated the shower curtains with the towels in two bathrooms, something I'd never done before. We displayed family pictures everywhere. Our furniture matched for the first time, and I got a kick out of shopping for kitchen towels with a red theme. I found some with brightly-colored poppies, complimenting a set of red bowls with white polka dots.

Medication kept the lid on my depression but failed to stop the headache. The pain level cycled as always, with my heartbeat sometimes throbbing in my head. The base level had continued to increase very gradually since the onset.

I walked Bear Hill for exercise and helped John get his classroom ready. He reviewed the curriculum, all new to him. He also scheduled the teaching tests Massachusetts required despite his National Board Certification and 30 years of experience. I debated about when to apply for a job. John suggested I postpone job applications until after Beijing, a year away.

Beth called from the team camp at the Olympic Training Center to share news. Her friend on the Harvard men's team, Geoff, swam on Team USA at Brazil's PanAmerican Games, held right before her Parapan American Games in the exact same venues. He emailed with details of the beautiful brand new aquatic center and athlete village in Rio de Janeiro.

Held once every four years, the Parapan American Games hosted 1,150 athletes from 25 countries in 2007. Peggy led the U.S. Paralympics Swimming Team as head coach for the first time. The team of 14 swimmers voted Beth Co-Captain. Julie O'Neill, promoted to the top spot in U.S. Paralympics, told a Tiffin reporter, "Beth just has a great personality. She's dedicated, intelligent. She's got all these pieces, and she's one of the athletes we look to for leadership."

"She's an incredibly positive person," Peggy added, "and it rubs off on people she comes in contact with."

When the team landed in Rio de Janiero, security hurried them from the plane to the terminal because of gang shootings across the runways. They arrived early to train and get over jet lag. Peggy led team-building activities, a few repeated from Beth's high school and SAK teams. In the pool, Beth grabbed the ankles of a swimmer ahead of her as they raced a lap. The team played water polo in the deep end while Beth bobbed and treaded water. They also raced with funny strokes. I followed the trip in email newsletters with photos from U.S. Paralympics. They included quotes from the athletes, including Beth.

"I am really excited about being here, and I am very honored to serve as the captain for the women's team. It is a great learning experience for all of us."

The aquatic center, built to hold about 8,000 people, attracted capacity crowds. It was Beth's first competition in front of an enormous and enthusiastic audience. She chose the forward freestyle during free races instead of the backstroke of most of her competitors. In both the 100 and 200 free, she earned silver medals.

Beth swam the 50 free in prelims with a time five seconds slower than usual after a freak injury. She dislocated her big toe falling into the pool. She felt less discomfort than I would have in the same situation but pain nonetheless. Beth's body quickly reacted with strong leg spasms that dragged her speed down during the race. Right after, the team doctor for the USA manipulated the toe back in place. She returned to the pool that evening for finals to earn a bronze medal in the same event.

Another day, Beth's 50 back ended unexpectedly. In a close race, she touched the wall before all of the rest, including the swimmer from Mexico who held the IPC World Record for the event. I wish I had been there.

During the medal ceremony, Beth wheeled on a ramp to the tallest stand. Wearing gold around her neck and holding beautiful flowers, she rode a wave of emotion and patriotism as the USA national anthem played loudly—for her.

"Hearing our national anthem while on the podium is something I will never forget," Beth said. "It made it extra special to be the one to win the 54th medal (the team's goal)."

Spectators treated the swimmers like celebrities, cheering loudly when Beth gave her flower bouquet to a local girl in the stands.

"Totally felt like rock stars," Beth told *The Harvard Gazette*. "Everyone wanted our autographs and pictures. We got mobbed by young children. It was wonderful."

After Brazil, Beth flew into Boston, our Ohio days over. She helped me complete her new bedroom with a blue duvet cover and throw pillows. Before her senior year of college began, I often drove her to Blodgett for workouts, about a half hour drive from our apartment in northwest Waltham. Maria joined Beth at the Bear Hill pool to sunbathe with books and to swim.

John's change in jobs left us with a one-month gap in our health insurance. He bought coverage through his Ohio retirement at a reasonable cost. Against his advice, I decided to go without health insurance through August to save us several hundred dollars. As luck would have it, I couldn't stop coughing with a persistent chest cold. I should've gone to the doctor. Instead, I waited another week until my new insurance started. Bad idea.

❧ Chapter 21 ❧
REACHING

Beth: *Becoming independent. That is my greatest achievement.*

BETH'S HARVARD COACH requested that she meet a little girl with a physical disability from a local club team. They swam together twice. Beth dabbled a little in coaching and talked to the girl and her mom over dinner in the Square. A Paralympic swimmer in Michigan also asked Beth to mentor a teenage girl with a new spinal cord injury. Ongoing friendships included her first mentee from Seattle who visited Harvard for a college visit almost four years after they began to exchange emails. They met face-to-face for the first time and caught up over lunch. Beth's web of connections never stopped growing.

I learned new lessons. My lung capacity diminished with a full-blown, miserable, and intense pneumonia. For the first time, I experienced the anxiety triggered by not breathing easily. Antibiotics had no effect the first two weeks, so a lung doctor added steroids, inhalers, and a different antibiotic. I felt a little better by the end of September, in time for visitors. Still coughing, I assumed that a month of antibiotics had eliminated the possibility of being contagious.

My parents arrived with my niece Meghan and her husband Phil. He engineered Beth's lift chair on the team of UT students. We walked part of Boston's Freedom Trail and rode a trolley. When others boarded a boat for a harbor cruise, I shared ice cream with my dad at Legal Seafood.

Maria and Beth visited us at the Waltham apartment for jovial family dinners. After the visit, my dad contracted pneumonia, probably from me. He spent a rough week in a

Lorain hospital, and I felt awful about it. My pneumonia completely cleared three months later. The extended coughing elevated my neck and head pain.

My new doctor sent me to chronic pain classes at the Benson-Henry Institute for Mind Body Medicine founded by Dr. Herbert Benson, the cardiologist who wrote *The Relaxation Response.*

I drove east on Rt. 9 to Roxbury, a suburb of Boston. A nurse led the classes, teaching us about the science of meditation and how those who meditated regularly experienced significant health benefits. My diverse classmates experienced a wide range of medical problems. The nurse encouraged us to accept pain, the same concept that angered me when I first heard it in Ohio. Since then, I had found no cure, and I understood that resisting pain did nothing good.

Dr. Benson visited a class and spoke about pain as a benign thing separate from our identities, to enable us to drain its power. To prevent pain from diminishing our experience of life. To make it an inescapable reality more than an obstacle. To make peace with multiple causes of pain, some clear and some not. I completed homework and daily meditation practice.

At our last class, we shared unanimous results. All of us improved, including me, though our actual pain levels stayed the same. What? Across the board, our minute by minute and hour by hour *responses* to pain improved, enabling us to cope better day to day. The class also helped me gain perspective as I met others with debilitating pain. It could always be worse.

My doctor referred me to a specialist when the headache spiked, and my left arm prickled and hurt. I made an appointment with a physiatrist, a specialist in muscles and rehabilitation. Dr. Ariana Vora at Wellesley's Spaulding office diagnosed my headache as cervicogenic, pain referred to the head from the cervical spine or soft tissues (or both) within the neck. Complicated by displaced jaw joints, fibromyalgia, and advanced arthritis. A body scan revealed my unusually high level of arthritis literally everywhere. My neck, left elbow, right knee, and hands bothered me most— 49 years old, going on 90.

Dr. Vora ordered physical and occupational therapy to focus on my neck muscles in constant spasm. At one session, a patient complained loudly about over-the-counter medicine that completely eliminated her wrist pain because she hated taking pills. Whining about the absence of pain? I'd be happy if mine dropped from constant to sporadic. My physical therapist with daily headaches rolled her eyes at me in solidarity. I also tried acupuncture, facet joint injections, and Botox shots. I drove to a Brookline shop to talk to an elderly Chinese man. He listened to the heartbeat in my wrist and sold me bitter, exotic herbs. Once.

Daily exercise, meditating, and holistic approaches tamped down the headache to a lower base level. I appreciated my evolution of sorts: to be able to make time for me and not feel guilty about it. I valued myself more. I no longer thought of myself as weak and flawed for not getting those ducks in a row. We all lived in the same messy pond.

I finally absorbed the idea of taking care of myself first which allowed me to give to others in a better way. I started a gratitude journal and made extra efforts to connect with friends and family. I tried not to anticipate or worry about the next headache flare. I had no need to hide negative feelings from my husband and few to share.

For the first time, I told John about my breakdown at the end of my year in Cambridge. He wished I had reached out for help then, and I did too. We felt in tune and closer than ever.

One fall morning, Beth wheeled across the pool deck, and the Harvard men's coach led his team in applause for her Rio medals. She swam six days a week in and out of the HWSD season. Coaches planned her training cycles to build up to her most important swim meet to date, the Paralympic Trials in April.

Occasionally, I met Beth in the Blodgett lobby, helped her over the alarmingly-inaccessible bridge to Harvard Square, and bought us brunch, our favorite meal of the day. I encouraged her to use the bus after practice more often. She didn't.

Maria taught five preschoolers with multiple disabilities in the Cambridge Public Schools. She started the class with two full-time teacher's aides, one with a master's degree. In the Boston area, many adults with multiple degrees settled for underemployment to obtain health insurance.

A student with complex medical needs moved away from the sanctuary city of Cambridge to Boston with her mom, an illegal immigrant. I worried with Maria about their deportation to a country with subpar children's services. I volunteered in her classroom a few times and helped with field trips. Her enthusiasm and compassion created a safe space for the children who progressed at a surprising pace.

Maria created and followed an extensive schedule in 15-minute increments to allow her and her aides to maximize instructional time. She had high expectations and energy. I remember thinking that the residents at my old jobs would benefit from Maria's level of passion. Sadly, staff tended to have low expectations at too many institutions and group homes.

I watched Maria work enthusiastically with a boy speaking his first words. Later, she sat quietly on the floor, blocking the only exit out of a padded play space where a little girl threw a major tantrum. The child tried to get Maria's attention in negative ways. My daughter ignored the screaming. I thought, "She'll be a great mom someday."

During a musical performance for parents, all the children, nonverbal and otherwise, played a role. I sat on the stage next to a girl's tiny wheelchair and held a toggle switch for her to push. The switch played a recorded phrase. The boy learning to speak wore a butterfly costume. He flapped his wings and bounced to the microphone at regular intervals to cheerfully yell, "Chomp!" A word he couldn't say a few months before. The audience loved it. I did too.

Ben applied to several graduate schools across the country for a master's program in literature. He decided to go wherever he received the most financial aid. With acceptances in hand, Brandeis University won in Waltham, Massachusetts. All three of my kids would live close to us for the next school year. I bought another Life is Good shirt from a shop in Newport, Rhode Island, where John and I traveled for a day trip. The landscape from the cliff walk brought the fjords of Norway to mind, a fusion of rippling water and majestic rock, oblivious to the passage of time.

Beth's senior year at Harvard created a mosaic of color squares on her computer's calendar. Orange for classes, red for assignment deadlines, yellow for disability work, blue for swim workouts, purple for fun, and green for everything else, including volunteering and swim meets. She made a concerted effort to increase the purple blocks on her calendar. She participated in more Harvard activities, most for the first time, including the annual '80s Dance, '90s Dance, A Cappella Concert, and Comedy Show. She also cheered for her friend Brittany during a rugby game.

"Brittany got me out of my shell during my senior year," Beth said. "Before then, I hardly ever went out socially."

Early one weekend morning after the T stopped running, Beth, Brittany, and three friends hailed a taxi in Boston. The driver said only four of them could ride at one time. Brittany creatively insisted Beth needed to sit on someone's lap because of her disability. The driver kept his thoughts to himself as all five girls rode in the taxi to Harvard.

"I carried her into a few restaurants and bars," Brittany said. "We refused to let inaccessibility stop us. Inadvertently, we ended up getting a lot of people talking about why accessibility isn't more consistent and reliable."

With a full load of classes, Beth prioritized her homework, kept up on writing assignments, and saved books to read later. She no longer tried to read every word. Graduate school applications required chunks of time. She applied to four law schools and a doctorate program at Harvard's School of Public Health.

For her third season on the HWSD roster, Beth added new pump-up songs to her swim meet mix, including "Stronger" by Kanye West. I smiled when she sang along to the chorus. Maybe challenges really did make us stronger. During team practices, she typically swam a mile. In October, a doctor tried to drain her inflamed right elbow. He found no fluid, just swollen tissue.

Coach Becca worked with Beth during one-on-one sessions at Blodgett as well as team practices. "I never heard her complain," the coach said in *The Harvard Crimson*.

John and I looked forward to all of the HWSD home meets her senior year and often sat with Maria in the red seats. At a November meet, with Harvard dominating the point count, three teammates wore flippers in a relay with Beth substituted as the fourth. Other swimmers clustered at the end of the lane to cheer her on. She cut a whopping 10 seconds off her previous short course American Record in the

50 back, set at a HWSD meet only a year before. An article in the *NCAA Champion* magazine described how Beth, "added another level of excitement to home crowds at Blodgett Pool, especially when records were at stake."

In early December, Coach Morawski traveled to Maryland for her first Paralympic meet where Beth introduced her to Peggy. Beth stressed about involving both in races. Peggy anticipated her concern and stepped back. Senator Kerry's office manager Mary watched Beth race one evening from the stands and joined us for dinner after finals.

Swimmers on the men's team honored Beth and the other seven seniors on her team with bouquets of flowers at the last home meet. Afterward, John, Maria, Beth, and I ordered pad Thai and big bowls of vegetable noodle soup at a Vietnamese restaurant in Harvard Square. The following weekend, I drove Beth to Yale in Connecticut to compete at the last away meet of the season. She laughed and clapped when the freshman swimmers on her team danced and sang, "We're All in This Together," from *High School Musical*. Beth finished her Harvard career with six Paralympic American Records set at Blodgett pool in the free, back, and butterfly.

"No matter what team we raced against," Beth told a reporter, "people always came up to me and congratulated me. It was kind of strange sometimes, but I guess it's great for them to see someone with a disability compete on a college varsity team."

At Beth's last HWSD banquet, the team donned gorgeous fresh-flower leis, gifts from a senior from Hawaii. The Coaches Award for attitude and contributions to the team surprised Beth. In return, she presented a gold medal to Coach Morawski in gratitude.

The head coach framed the gold with a written tribute. The medal found a new home in the hallway leading to Beth's favorite pool among pictures of Harvard's best. Though she would have more to add to her legacy.

"She's an inspiration to many," Coach Morawski said.

"The most amazing thing about Beth is though we classify her as someone who's disabled," Coach Becca told a reporter, "she's just someone who shows the people around her how able she is."

When the college swim season ended, Beth immediately plunged into a new training cycle. She worked with her Harvard coaches to prepare for the Paralympic Trials in April. Other Harvard teammates trained for the USA Olympic Trials or the Olympic Trials in their home countries.

At the end of February, Beth woke up one morning with a high fever and congestion. A chest x-ray showed a small pocket of pneumonia in the lower right lobe, not as severe as her first pneumonia. She insisted on trying antibiotics first before considering a hospital stay. I couldn't convince her to minimize her swim training for more than a few days. She gradually felt better despite a relentless senior year and pool schedule.

Beth and I flew together to Minneapolis the first weekend in April. At the Trials meet, she would probably earn a spot on the Beijing team. Even so, nothing was guaranteed. Everything hinged on how fast she swam in the next three days.

We welcomed Coach Becca to her first Paralympic meet. She met Peggy after emailing back and forth about training goals and workouts for almost two years. Beth laser-focused on swimming fast. No shopping at the Mall of America in the afternoon as she did at her first Minneapolis meet five years before. From the upper tier seats, I wrote to-do lists with end of college details and watched races.

A young girl from the United States in her early teens swam as an S3, newly classified. She didn't make finals cuts, like many at their first national meet. Judging from her expression, she saw the possibilities as Beth had six years before. No one had any way of knowing the new swimmer would be reclassified to S2 and S1 in the future, caught in the vague criteria of the low-numbered classifications. However, I had no doubt she'd be at the next Paralympic meet, getting faster and making more new friends.

The morning after Trials, the ceremony to announce the Beijing Paralympics team filled the pool lobby. They called out names randomly, not alphabetically. The swimmer or coach moved through the crowd to be congratulated at the front. Each received a red, white, and blue hockey jersey with USA on the front and their last name sewn on the back in large letters. As the number at the front grew, I questioned my expectations. Beth glanced my way, and I responded with an encouraging smile. Then Peggy stood at the front with the team. Hearing my daughter's name a minute later, we shared a wave of relief and elation.

Beth put on her hockey jersey with Kolbe in big letters on the back. As cameras flashed, she never stopped smiling, basking in the achievement of her four-year goal. To share the good news, I talked to John in Waltham while Beth called Coach Becca who had left the day before. Faithful to our tradition, we outlined Beijing plans with Peggy over scoops of chocolate ice cream.

"Beth's talents lie in her ability to set goals, both short and long term, overcome obstacles, and accomplish those goals while consistently maintaining a positive and fun attitude," Peggy wrote for a reference.

I flew with Beth over Boston Harbor into Logan airport. John picked us up, and we dropped our daughter off at her dorm with only weeks left in her last semester. The next goal? Her first tattoo. Since she couldn't swim for a few days after the inking, she'd planned the timing perfectly, immediately after a big meet and right before her next training cycle. It would be the last time two days passed without a long pool workout until after Beijing.

The day after the team announcement in Minneapolis, I held Beth's leg down firmly at a tattoo parlor in Harvard Square. Her leg protested the needle and bounced with involuntary spasms. She chose a two-inch design on her upper left thigh of the new U.S. Paralympics symbol of a bold blue star with three waving lines of color below. The star turned out flawless despite a moving leg. A clear and bright reminder of success. We shared Beijing details with Maria over dinner at Bertucci's in the Square.

Both of Beth's elbows swelled for the first time as she started her most intense training cycle with a focus on the forward freestyle, consistently faster than the backstroke after six years of practice. A doctor prescribed a strong anti-inflammatory at a high dose. Hit with a piercing, unrelenting headache, Beth called the doctor. He ordered an MRI for the same day. I drove her to the test, relieved I lived close instead of in Ohio. I'd never seen her in that much pain before. Fortunately, the test results came back normal, and her symptoms gradually disappeared when she stopped the prescription.

Unwelcome news arrived with the updated IPC World Rankings. Three S3 competitors from Asia, all teenagers, entered the rankings for the first time. All in the top five. All with brand new classifications. It was a very rare situation. Beginning S3 swimmers usually entered the rankings in the double digits. There appeared to be two possible explanations: the swimmers had trained and *not* competed for years or they had more physical function than other S3s, a classification fail. Either way, the new swimmers bumped Beth down the women's rankings list from seventh place to 10th in the 50 free and from eighth place down to 11th in the 50 back.

Four years previously, Beth set a realistic goal to medal in Beijing, particularly in the 100 free. She placed third at the World Cup repeatedly and earned four medals, including gold, at the Parapan American Games in Rio. Even with the S3 events cut to two sprint races in Beijing, earning a medal at the Paralympics had been attainable—until three new crazy-fast beginning swimmers suddenly grabbed top spots in the World Rankings. Beth's chances of medaling immediately dropped from possible to impossible. Yet, there was no turning back. I struggled to let go of the disappointment. Beth and Peggy accepted the news and carried on. The new modified and unspoken goal? To make finals (top eight in prelims) in at least one event and hit the difficult time in the 50 freestyle to earn a new S3 American Record.

Beth's senior thesis deadline approached. Long to-do lists on her laptop overwhelmed, but she met deadlines. Barely. Afternoon power naps kept her going into the night, but she still looked exhausted. Swimming workouts reached new heights of intensity.

Working at a frantic pace, Beth stayed up too late while I learned how to relax for the first time. I meditated most days, trying different methods and a variety of prompts. Visualizing the headache as an evaporating dark cloud didn't help. The traditional body scan became my go-to meditation even though the 30 minutes highlighted the specific ache in each body part. Usually, the aches combined into a general feeling of malaise.

Never bored, I left the TV off during the day and always had plenty to do. I often played music in the background, from musicals to classic rock. If I finished routine tasks, I tinkered at writing or picked up my sewing bag. Grateful for the year off from work (outside the home), I walked down and up Bear Hill and focused on eating better.

Beth officially presented her senior thesis, titled Framing Disability: A content analysis on media agenda-setting of disability issues in a political context. She earned high honors for analyzing how often specific disability issues appeared in newspaper articles in a presidential election year.

An important decision needed to be made. Beth heard back from the graduate schools. With acceptance letters from three law schools and Harvard's Ph.D. program at the School of Public Health, she narrowed down the decision to Georgetown Law in Washington, DC, or Stanford Law in California. The idea of going to graduate school in an unfamiliar place appealed to Beth since she expected to work in DC after law school. She selected Stanford without visiting the campus, with no open weekends prior to the decision deadline. She wasn't concerned. A great school, great weather, and great outdoor pools. How could she go wrong? As planned four years before with Peggy, Beth accepted at Stanford Law, then promptly and officially deferred law school for one year. Nothing would interfere with her month in Beijing.

Beth's happy news about Stanford coincided with bad news for John. The first-year teachers in Newton received pink slips. Their contracts would not be renewed because of major budget cuts. We couldn't believe it. He had National Board Certification, stellar evaluations, and 31 years of teaching experience, but only Newton seniority mattered. I updated his resume and helped him apply for teaching jobs while he finished the school year. He interviewed in Waltham and South Boston.

At the end of April, I met Beth at the new pub under Harvard's Annenberg Hall. A packed crowd gathered to launch SPINALpedia, the new disability project Brittany co-founded with Josh Basile. The Braddigan band performed at the event. Beth spoke to the crowd along with two other quads, including Brittany's dad.

"My goal was to create a support resource that uses the power of people's experiences to motivate people with new injuries to adapt their lives," Brittany said. The band's lead singer, Brad Corrigan, added, "As a musician, I love stories that are real, and there's nothing more real than someone sitting in a wheelchair, saying that there's always hope."

During the concert, a stranger tripped and accidentally knocked Beth's chair over backward. I moved across the room to help, not worried. She had tucked her head safely forward as she fell, chin to chest. Brittany pushed everyone out of the way, including me, before lifting Beth off the floor and back into the wheelchair. Apparently, this had happened before, and Brittany managed the situation to deter anyone inexperienced or drunk from helping. Beth teased her, and Brittany apologized to me, but there was no need. Why would I object to someone looking out for my daughter? With SPINALpedia successfully launched, the website followed with video clips sharing individual experiences with paralysis.

The day after the concert, John drove Beth and me to the airport for a last-minute weekend trip to Florida. Dr. Hugo Keim, President of ChairScholars, asked Beth to speak to a large crowd of kids with disabilities and their families at the annual festival near Tampa. Dr. Keim and his wife Alicia shared with us how ChairScholars expanded to include scholarships for young people with disabilities in Florida and across the country. The festival would be the perfect opportunity to thank them in person for Beth's most generous college scholarship.

Under an immense white tent at the April festival, I talked to remarkable parents and thought of John. More social than me, he often said that everyone has a story. Beth wheeled up the ramp to face the crowd and talked about being open to opportunities and going for the gold, in sports and in life. She encouraged the kids to enjoy the perks of using a wheelchair, like how push handles are great for holding bags. And favorite shoes that last forever.

After her speech, some asked for an autograph. It turned into a teaching moment when another mom noticed her unusual grip on the pen. Others crowded around as Beth showed them how she held and wrote with a standard pen.

Beth's overseas travels during her years at Harvard concluded with her third trip to England's World Cup in May and another 50 back bronze medal—in the absence of the three brand new S3 swimmers. Would they skip the Paralympics? Not likely.

Back at Harvard, Beth planned her last Friday activity for kids with disabilities and said goodbye to the students and a new KSNAP director she'd trained. With no minutes to spare, swimming six days a week, she worried about finishing papers and studying for finals. And before long, glorious freedom.

Graduation encompassed a whole week of senior festivities, including a fancy champagne breakfast on tables covered with white linen. At a luncheon to recognize seniors in the health policy program, I watched Beth wheel forward to speak to the group. My quiet and shy teenager had bloomed into a confident and articulate young woman. We celebrated her second Peter Wilson award, $7,500 for graduate school, at Bertucci's.

My parents drove from Ohio to join us for the pageantry of the Harvard commencement. Professors in colorful robes with banners led the parade into Harvard Yard. The Class of 2008 followed. Students from Harvard's 10 graduate schools identified their specialties with creative additions to their graduation robes and hats.

We witnessed the perfect ending to Beth's years as a Harvard student. J.K. Rowling, author of the Harry Potter series, spoke at the 357th Commencement. During her speech, John received a phone call offering him a teaching job in Waltham.

I listened to Rowling's rags to riches speech and remembered the evenings in rehab when Beth and I read Harry Potter books aloud to each other. It was a lovely reprieve from overwhelming days. If only I'd known then where she would graduate from college. And what would follow.

RACING FORWARD
❧ Chapter 22 ❧
COMPETING

Beth: *Thanks to four years of HWSD training, I know I am ready to take on my international competition in Beijing! It truly is an honor to represent the United States at the Paralympics and to be part of such an incredible team. Go USA!*

BETH'S SEVENTH AND LAST swimming summer, she lived with John and me in Waltham during the first weeks. I drove her to and from summer workouts at Blodgett in Cambridge, a half hour drive each way. The days revolved around swim training, notched up to a new magnitude. Her right elbow flared again. The bursitis would improve with rest although that wouldn't happen anytime soon. She relied on icepacks and Motrin.

I drove Beth to my favorite physiatrist, Dr. Ariana Vora, who stopped the constant muscle spasms and pain in her arm with a few acupuncture needles. The same doctor would later do the same for the spasms in my neck.

Beth focused on eating healthy, exercising, and lifting weights in addition to swim workouts six days a week. A few days, she practiced twice. I dropped off Beth at the airport for a flight to British Columbia for the last Paralympic meet before Beijing. When she returned to Massachusetts, Harvard coaches asked Beth to share her story at their summer swim camp.

John and I moved across town to avoid a $400 a month rent increase at Bear Hill. Beth helped me pack and unpack boxes. I also found Ben an apartment in Waltham close to Brandeis University. He drove from Columbus, Ohio, and rented a one-bedroom apartment on Moody Street, famous for restaurants and shops from many cultures. All five of us gathered for a family cookout before Beth left for the Paralympics.

On August 17th, Beth and the world watched Michael Phelps win his eighth gold medal in the Water Cube. She wrote, "Watching the amazing Olympic swimmers shatter record after record in The Cube has been incredibly exciting, especially knowing that I'll be there soon!"

Beth's last swim practice with Coach Morawski and Becca at Blodgett ended with hugs and tears. I dropped her off at Logan airport on August 19th for a flight to Colorado Springs and the Olympic Training Center, where the rest of the Beijing swim delegation gathered. She acquired a big duffel bag full of team gear and started her "Swimming to Beijing" blog.

A training camp at a military base in Okinawa, Japan, allowed Team USA swimmers to recover from jet lag and avoid the air pollution in Beijing. Beth soaked up the sunshine one day on a pristine beach by the South China Sea. The team staff shared updates and great photos through an email newsletter. Beth could take pictures with her basic phone, but I hoped the disposable cameras I bought would take better photos. The cameras stayed buried and untouched in her bag.

On September 2nd, the U.S. Paralympics Swimming Team relocated to Beijing's Athlete Village among lush gardens, part of the mammoth Olympics complex. About 44,000 helpful volunteers kept everything running smoothly for over 4,200 Paralympics athletes from 148 countries. Beth shared a room with an impressive young veteran, the first woman to lose a limb in the Iraq War. Their housing unit consisted of three bedrooms, two bathrooms, and one common room. A sign on the door identified the unit as the nail salon for Team USA and the best for prosthetics. Prosthetic feet sported nails in the prerequisite red, white, and blue.

Team USA swimmers would compete in the latest body and leg suits that added a little buoyancy; the same new suits contributed to the unusually high number of World Records at the Olympics just weeks before. Beth wore the Fastskin LZR Racer and the Blueseventy, severely tight leg suits. Coaches helped swimmers squeeze into them. The team tested the suits during a practice in Beijing's Water Cube.

"I'm excited to race in The Cube," Beth said. "I feel faster than I ever have before."

I arrived in Beijing on September 5th after a 13-hour flight with the goal of meeting my friend Linda at the airport. We both had daughters on Team USA. I also needed to find Matt, a swim coach from Michigan and a friend of Linda and her daughter. Matt lived in Beijing and offered to let Linda and me stay in his apartment for the first week while his roommate traveled. For the second week, we had a reservation at the Continental Grand hotel within walking distance of the Water Cube.

I'd been in a few overseas airports before. Even so, Beijing's airport thoroughly confused me. I eventually discovered that Linda's flight should have already arrived at a different terminal. I frantically waited for a slow bus to take me there, feeling lost and late. With no international cell phone and not knowing Matt's address, I had no way to find them if we didn't connect at the airport. Could I find them at the other terminal?

The worst-case scenario would require me to find a hotel for the first week. That seemed doable, so I breathed a little easier. I found out later all the hotels were full.

Luck was on my side. Linda's flight had been delayed. I finally arrived in the correct place and asked where arriving passengers entered the expansive terminal. I held my first of many conversations with language barriers with friendly Chinese volunteers.

I had no idea what Matt looked like, but there weren't many young American men waiting by the arrivals. My relief when I found him felt tangible, a wave of gratitude. He reminded me of Ben as we chatted during the wait for Linda. Matt told me about his job teaching English in Beijing. When Linda arrived, we traveled by taxi to his apartment. On the way, he pointed out lush flowers lining all the main roads. The week before the Olympics, blooming plants suddenly appeared in a colossal landscaping effort.

Matt lived in a tiny two-bedroom apartment on a high floor in a run-down residential building. When I stood in the middle of the bathroom, I could touch all four walls, use the toilet, and take a shower. The water from the showerhead drenched everything in the room and fell into a drain by the toilet. Low water pressure contributed to a sewer smell, and we kept the bathroom door closed. I didn't mind the less-than-luxurious accommodations. Matt shared the rare gift of seeing the real Beijing.

Our first morning in China, Linda and I walked to the local police station to fill out forms and register for the specific days we'd stay in the residential district. Pleasant elderly residents gathered outside on the sidewalk with young children and exercised to start the day. I rode in a taxi with Linda and Matt to pick up our Paralympics tickets and to visit an outdoor antique market. We browsed through an amazing array of goods, from figurines to statues and wood boxes to furniture. We squeezed through narrow aisles as sellers yelled out prices to us. The numbers lowered as we walked by.

Matt explained that you never paid full price in Beijing and needed to bargain. The vendors knew how to say numbers in English but no other words. My deal of the day cost the equivalent of three U.S. dollars for a box of white metal doves made with an ancient cloisonné technique using enamel paste fired in a kiln. Intricate and lovely. I wish I'd bought many more. For me, the surprisingly low prices in China compensated for the harassment of shopping. I loved a good bargain.

Beijing sprawled on a grand scale. Colorful banners hung down whole sides of tall buildings, showing Chinese Paralympians playing their sport. Every element of Beijing contrasted to other big cities I'd seen. The highways with at least six lanes clogged with bumper-to-bumper traffic. The hundreds of bicycles in sight at any one time packed together right next to vehicles. The traffic typically was much heavier because they had banned most cars and trucks from the city during the Paralympics. Impossible to imagine.

The Opening Ceremony of the 2008 Paralympics overwhelmed many spectators, including me. The incredible details pushed normal parameters of life. The mammoth size of the stadium, track, and stage matched the hordes of humanity filling every seat in the endless stands. On my seat, a large fabric tote bag held a cloth-bound program and several nice gifts. The audience would use some to participate in the ceremony at specific times, like the flashlight and a bright scarf.

The performance left me in awe and a little uncomfortable with the massive scope. Legions of people executed perfectly synchronized movements on the immense stage. Besides the precise orchestration of thousands, each imaginative segment focused on positive portrayals of different disabilities. Deaf students executed a choreographed dance in a set of creative waves. In the sunbird segment, acrobatic aerialists performed above us while a blind woman sang. The dances showcased fanciful, elaborate costumes and complicated, mechanized sets throughout. The crystal clear sounds of synchronized music enhanced the artistry of a magnificent opening ceremony.

The climax of the evening featured one Chinese athlete. He moved out of his wheelchair into one with an impressive pulley system. A lighted torch attached to the back of the chair. He pulled himself up to the open section on the dome of the tall stadium and kept climbing higher to light the Olympic torch over the top.

The athlete procession followed. Team USA wore flashy Ralph Lauren suits with red, white, and blue silk scarves. On the taper phase of her training cycle, Beth let Peggy push her wheelchair on the track in the midst of about two hundred USA athletes plus staff. I found her, but she couldn't see me.

"You're surrounded by Team USA and you go down the ramp to the floor of the National Stadium which has 91,000 screaming fans," Beth said. "It was a pretty surreal experience."

Swim competitions began the day after Opening Ceremony. I had tickets for prelims and finals on the two days Beth would race, plus finals for the other seven days. She had several days off before her first event. To prepare for her races, she rode the bus to the Water Cube twice a day to work out in the warm up pool and watch the races in the competition pool. U.S. swimmers could leave their restricted area of the Water Cube to visit family and friends in a designated area. I talked to her in an upper hallway between the two pools each day.

The exterior of the Water Cube fascinated me with enchanting lights flowing in the imaginative water-like façade. Colorful water fountains burst from the concrete in the central section of the Olympic Green, built on the same invisible vertical line connecting the Forbidden City and the Temple of Heaven. Immense, majestic spaces. Each day, I learned more about the importance of tradition in China.

I sat with Matt and Linda one evening at finals after visiting the Forbidden City. The crowd buzzed when a group of men and women entered the stands in the athlete section. Matt pointed out Hu Jintao, the President of China, before the announcer introduced him. The President watched the competition without any apparent security. Matt said some of the people with the President would be guards. However, only police possessed guns in China, so public appearances held less threat for the President than in the United States.

Capacity crowds of 17,000 packed the dazzling Water Cube for each session.

Finals at big swim meets, always exciting, notched up in Beijing with the addition of an amazingly responsive crowd and the fanfare of the Paralympics. I followed every race closely, cheering for Beth's friends and teammates. Many swimmers from other countries also had become familiar to me after six years of national and international meets.

Team USA battled to win the gold count. After a medal ceremony, U.S. families and friends cheered as Linda's daughter Elizabeth tossed her flower bouquet to her mom up in the stands.

After finals, Matt shared the best dumpling shop. From the dark street in his neighborhood, it didn't look like a business of any kind. We sat at one of a few old wood tables in a cluttered little space. A cook stood at a small flour-dusted table in the same room to make the dumplings and carried them to a back room to be cooked. Matt practiced his Mandarin language skills with the cooks who brought us several round wooden bowls of delicious dumplings. They were the best I ever had, served with an unusual and wonderful dipping sauce. The entire meal for all three of us cost the U.S. equivalent of $2, including three water bottles.

Walking back to Matt's apartment, we passed a building with a big rectangular window frame with no glass or screen. Inside, two men cooked little pieces of meat on a flat grill and speared the meat on sticks. We bought three beef sticks, one for each of us. Exotic spices complimented the meat. Linda and I shared a nervous laugh, wondering if the beef was really beef. Would we get sick from undercooked meat or something else? We didn't. We also made sure to use only bottled water to drink and to brush our teeth.

On September 10th, Matt showed us his favorite places in Beijing. The one far off the tourist path had curious boutiques and restaurants in a "hutong," an old narrow alleyway. Matt worked at an Internet café while Linda and I browsed the shops. Exploring was fun. We paid $4 each for elaborate foot massages at a small salon and soaked our feet in wood buckets filled with flower petals and water. We experienced "cupping" for the first time. A young girl sat by my feet next to clear rounded cups with a wide opening. She lit matches at the opening of the glass cups, one at a time, and suctioned it to the bottom of my foot to draw out toxins. When she removed the cups, they left round bruises.

We also visited my new favorite place in Beijing, the Temple of Heaven. First constructed in 1420, the circular temples on different levels incorporated exquisite detail. We walked through the Temple of Heaven Park under a canopy of ancient trees. I asked Matt about the groups of residents everywhere. Some played badminton or string instruments while others sang or danced and more. Did they gather specifically for tourists brought by the Paralympics? Matt said no. Residents met friends there throughout the year.

Most of them lived in very small apartments, so they socialized in public places like the park.

I followed a formal procedure and security checks to visit Beth at the Athlete Village. I couldn't wait to have more time with her than a few minutes at the Water Cube. She greeted me with a radiant smile and a big hug. Her hand patted my back, with fingernails sporting new red, white, and blue polish, almost professional-looking despite the fact she painted them by herself. Animated, Beth talked about new acquaintances from other countries and fun times with her teammates. I loved how easily she laughed. We strolled through elaborate gardens between the buildings where the athletes stayed. We sat in the midst of the lavish flowers and ponds. I told her I was proud of her. Unconditionally.

The best-case scenario for Beth's two races: making finals or beating her best times or setting a new American Record. The odds of rising from 10th and 11th place to the top three for a medal? Slim to none. She also might go home with no best times *and* not make the top eight in the morning sessions to earn a place in finals. Whatever happened would be more than okay. I remembered the uncertainty after the accident when we had no way of knowing what the future would hold or if she even had a future. I considered every moment since her injury a gift.

My first week in China passed quickly. Before Linda and I checked into the Continental Grand hotel, we rode in a taxi to Matt's favorite Peking Duck restaurant. The popular dish arrived unassembled at our table with duck pieces, artistic condiments, and very thin pancakes.

Matt showed us how to combine the duck and condiments on the pancake before folding it over to blend the different textures. We ordered traditional moon cake for dessert. It was a delicious meal, but I preferred the dumplings from Matt's neighborhood hole in the wall. He suggested leaving some food on our plates to avoid being rude, contrary to our American instincts. After dinner, Linda and I said our thanks and goodbyes to Matt, grateful for his hospitality and insights into Beijing culture.

At the Water Cube, the morning prelims sessions included all the qualified swimmers in a specific event. The top eight of that larger group returned for evening finals. Beth qualified for finals in the 50 back with a top eight time in the morning. Only 13 S3 female swimmers competed in the 2008 Paralympics in one or both S3 events. Higher-numbered classifications filled several prelims races with eight swimmers in a heat—in many different events, some with long distances. Beth had remarkable stamina in the water, rare for an S3. The odds of her medaling in any longer event? Probable to certain. And not an option.

The adorable pink cow mascots in Beijing entertained the crowds before finals. Unusual plastic costumes inflated around and above the wearer, extending to about seven feet tall.

"Before every finals," she wrote in her blog, "three of these blow-up cows jumped around on deck and occasionally fell down . . . and couldn't get back up!"

In the finals for the 50 back, Beth finished eighth in the world, quite close to her personal best time of 1:16.13 for the stroke she learned first. Her smooth forward freestyle beat her backstroke times.

The morning of September 13th, I watched in dismay as another swimmer in Beth's heat moved too soon. The false start sent all eight of them back to begin again. An unfortunate and rare occurrence for arguably the most important race in Beth's swimming career. It could be difficult to mentally refocus. She placed sixth in the race following the false start, an outstanding swim that qualified her for the 50 free finals.

That evening, the antics of big pink cows attempted to diffuse the tension of finals. Exuberant spectators packed the stands. In the ready room before her most-anticipated race, Beth listened to the Van Halen song "Jump" on her iPod, smiling at the "Right Now!" refrain. After 50 months of continuous year-round workouts, this was it!

"I felt prepared going in from all my amazing training at Harvard behind me," Beth wrote, "and I was able to enjoy the moment as my heat was paraded out onto the deck and behind the blocks."

With music and fanfare, the announcer introduced the eight S3 competitors for the 50 free from Australia, Germany, Great Britain, China, Singapore, Mexico, and South Africa. Plus, the USA! Peggy pushed Beth's chair up the ramp to her lane. I watched a competitor jump on one leg to the starting blocks. Two others walked. They climbed onto the blocks to jump off while the other five started the race in the water.

For maybe the hundredth time, Peggy lay flat on her stomach with her body on the deck and her shoulders and head over the pool. She grabbed my daughter's ankles to hold her feet on the starting wall. Beth floated parallel to the lane lines, then turned on her left side with her right arm straight and pointing the way. She held still until the buzzer sounded, and the event began.

Eight women left the starting wall, most swimming the backstroke. Beth's forward freestyle looked effortless and beautiful. An extraordinary work of art. I stood with her friend Brittany in the USA section. We yelled as loud as we could though with most of the crowd cheering for the Chinese swimmer, Beth heard only an enthusiastic din. She could see other competitors, and she gave it her all.

"I swam a 1:10.55, a best time and a new American Record, which places me fifth in the world," Beth said. "What a great race!"

She dropped three seconds off her previous best time in the event, even faster than I had hoped. For the 50 free finals, the top S3 women in the world clocked in from 0:57 to 1:18. At this elite level of competition, the broad variation of 21 seconds seemed to reflect differences in physical function and starkly contrasted to other finals races at the Paralympics.

"I was so psyched to see Beth at this level of competition," Brittany said. "I knew how seriously she took swimming, but I didn't have a sense of the enormity of her accomplishment until I was in the Water Cube, donning my handmade 'Go Beth' T-shirt, screaming as she tore down the lane. Watching her swim, I was so proud of her, thinking about how insane it was that one of my best friends is fifth in the world in swimming!"

Happy with her ultimate American Record and her jump in the rankings from 10th to fifth, Beth celebrated with Peggy. Their post-meet ice cream tradition carried on with the soft serve at McDonalds in the Athlete Village. U.S. Paralympics Swimming won the official gold medal count, with lifetime bests in over 90 percent of their swims despite tough competition from China, Great Britain, and Australia.

When the sessions at the Water Cube ended, USA swimmers had two days for sightseeing in Beijing, a sprawling city of over 6,000 square miles. On September 16th, I picked up Peggy and Beth at the Athlete Village in a taxi to visit the Silk Market and the hutong Matt showed me. At my request, Brittany had called ahead to make afternoon pedicure appointments for Beth and Peggy at the same salon Linda and I enjoyed. At a hutong teashop with glass jars of loose tea, Beth bought jasmine blossoms that bloomed in hot water. I found inexpensive silk flowers, intricately sewn by hand.

When we entered the salon for the pedicures, the sky suddenly dropped hard driving rain. Peggy and Beth decided to cancel the appointments and return to the Athlete Village instead.

The day turned tense as taxis full of passengers passed us by. A few available ones refused to take us. A helpful shopkeeper translated for us with one of the taxi drivers. He said the Athlete Village was too far away. We learned that taxis stay in one area of the gigantic city. The shopkeeper called security.

After a long wait, a police car pulled up along with a taxi to take us back. We thought our troubles ended, but the taxi driver couldn't find the Athlete Village despite our Beijing maps and written directions in Mandarin provided by U.S. Paralympics. In pouring rain, the taxi dodged a multitude of bicycles, most with more than one rider on seemingly endless flower-lined streets. We finally arrived at the Athlete Village, soaked and cold. From there, I relied on my sense of direction to help the frustrated taxi driver find my hotel. I left him a big tip and hoped he found his way home.

The following day, I picked up Beth and Peggy again in a taxi. We met Brittany at Wangfuying, Beijing's most famous shopping area. We stopped first for Starbucks coffee and tea. In the open-air market, we dared each other to eat roasted scorpions and seahorses. No one accepted the challenge.

Next, we made our way to my favorite place in Beijing. Near a magnificent temple, Brittany filmed a video of Beth navigating a ridiculously steep ramp with help. Brittany also practiced her Mandarin with friendly locals at the Temple of Heaven and answered their questions about her friend's injury and swimming. It made me happy that Beth loved the serene park as much as I did.

Under the shade of gorgeous old trees, I drew Beth into a hug and smiled as she patted my back. A perfect moment. Finally free, guilt no longer clouded my view. With eyes wide open, a breathtakingly beautiful world surrounded me—not in spite of Beth's injury but because of it.

Life wasn't just good, it was better than before the accident. Among the lucky ones, we gained a deeper appreciation of the connections that made our lives meaningful. I shared her smile as we left the canopy of ancient trees and moved into the sunshine.

"I could have spent all day exploring there," Beth wrote, "but we left for lunch at a Peking Duck restaurant where I was peer-pressured into eating duck brain. It tastes like chicken, but I almost gagged from the texture."

The most honored guests traditionally received the brain of the duck, a delicacy. When pickled sea cucumbers followed, marine animals known for their leathery skin, Beth declined. Brittany filmed another video at the restaurant of a quad learning to use chopsticks. With no storm and no taxi problems, the day passed too quickly. Time for the Closing Ceremony.

On September 17th, Team USA paraded into the Bird's Nest. After all the countries assembled, we watched more stunning performances that created magnificent scenes with thousands of performers, young and old. As the ceremony ended, athletes danced with performers on the stadium floor, and Beth found herself blue eyes to bellybuttons with pink cows. The cow costumes caused visual problems for the wearers.

"After Closing Ceremonies," Beth wrote, "at least a hundred of these cows stormed the floor of the stadium. They kept running into us and running away. They would also begin to deflate, so volunteers would run up and herd them off the track to get blown back up. My teammates and I were literally crying we were laughing so hard."

Back home, the U.S. Paralympics team joined Michael Phelps and the other Olympians to meet President George W. Bush at the White House. Beth shook the President's hand and smiled for the pictures. Later, athletes congregated at the hotel lounge. Flirting with Olympians on the men's swim team marked the official end of Beth's four-year plan and the Beijing experience. Real world adventures in her future would be equally exciting.

❧ Chapter 23 ❧
FREESTYLING

Beth: *I need to figure out what I want to do with my life because anything is possible.*

FOR THE FIRST TIME since the car accident, months stretched ahead with nothing but time. Abruptly back in Massachusetts, Beth planned to get a job with almost a year until law school. John and I lived far from public transportation and with independence a top priority, she decided to rent her first apartment and assumed she would find a full-time job to pay for it. A leap of faith.

Separate plans converged in serendipity. Calling from Tiffin, Lizzy asked to stay with us for a while to look for an apartment. She decided to relocate to the Boston area to find a teaching job. Beth and Lizzy made an easy decision to be roommates. They invited Ellen to join them. She declined, never a fan of big cities.

They applied for jobs in Cambridge and looked at more affordable apartments farther away. I drove them to tour a nice complex in Malden. When Beth asked for my opinion, I pointed out the considerable distance to Cambridge. Nevertheless, they signed a year lease for an apartment near the Malden T stop before either of them had a job.

Lizzy's parents arrived from Ohio to help with the move. I set up a single mattress on a metal frame for Beth and a small computer table from IKEA. She borrowed a shelving unit and a lamp from John and me. Beth's Stanford Law dorm would be fully furnished, and it didn't make sense to buy more. Her sparse bedroom contrasted with her overflowing clothes closet.

Within a week of signing the lease, Beth accepted a full-time job as a research assistant for the Harvard Dept. of Health Policy. Maria recommended Lizzy for a job in the Cambridge schools which turned into a successful interview where she procured the job. Beth and Lizzy each had a 30-minute commute from Malden to Cambridge on the T red line. Twice a day.

In the Malden apartment late one night, Beth transferred from the wheelchair to her bed, and a wheel lock didn't hold. She tumbled to the floor. Lizzy slept nearby in the next room. Beth's deep aversion to asking for help resulted in close to an hour's struggle to get back into bed. And, raw rug burns on her knees. She accomplished the feat only after creating a series of higher levels with pillows and anything else she could reach. If it had been me, I'd have asked for assistance right away. Beth considered the solo achievement a victory. John called it unnecessary stubbornness. I nagged her about taking care of the rug burns to avoid infection.

Meanwhile, Maria taught her second school year as a lead teacher while Ben attended graduate school at Brandeis. I started a new nonprofit job in Wellesley, running programs for residents in need. John settled in at Waltham's MacArthur School. He soon made many close friendships with the exceptional staff.

Some weekends, I met Beth and Maria for lunch or clothes shopping. Maria often sat on the floor with her preschoolers and dressed casually for work, like me. Beth established her preferred style, dresses (or tops with skirts), and boots. The wheels of her chair ruined light colors despite side guards. She avoided white clothing but not buttons and zippers. She threw away the elastic strap I sewed for her to keep her knees together under a dress. Instead, she crossed one leg over the other, alternating them when she felt uncomfortable sensations in one or the other.

Mint Julep in Harvard Square remained Beth's best source for dresses though a few she bought weren't appropriate for work. She saved those for dancing in Boston clubs. Wearing two small white pearls from China in each earlobe, she had blond highlights in her brown hair from the Judy Jetson salon in Cambridge. She replaced the Harvard Swimming backpack with a leather messenger bag that hung from the unused push handles of her wheelchair. We ordered a set of Spinergy wheels with black spokes instead of yellow, to look more professional.

Beth's job focused on international health systems and extensive research for a $7,000,000 grant proposal. Meeting new people in and out of her office, she never hesitated to extend her bent hand with the HOPE ring. After a workday in Harvard Square, Beth occasionally wheeled over the Charles River to swim laps at Blodgett pool and say hello to the coaches though she welcomed the break from swim training.

John and I hosted cookouts for the five of us in our immediate family and a boyfriend or girlfriend. Scrabble games sometimes followed that Ben almost always won. We teased Beth about choosing a law school in California as far across the country as she could get from us! Especially since she influenced most of our migrations from Ohio to the Boston area. Beth reassured us, laughing, that she'd be back on the East Coast after Stanford.

I cooked my first big turkey dinner after 50 years of traveling to Thanksgiving feasts in Ohio. My mom and grandma had cooked for crowds and timed everything perfectly, with the turkey carved and the potatoes mashed just minutes before we ate. I had roasted a turkey before but not with all the extra side dishes. My first attempt resulted in dry turkey and lumpy gravy. The pumpkin pies I made from my great-grandma's recipe didn't last long.

In December, Beth's boss asked her to attend Harvard's Health System Research Agenda Workshop with him in Cambridge. Late in the evening of the third, Beth sent me an email.

"OMG. Bill Gates was at my meeting. Then at dinner, I sat by a lovely French man who is the head of the World Economic Fund. He asked ME about my research and said I was helpful! So I'm having an existential night, and I need to figure out what I want to do with my life because anything is possible. Love from your daughter, who has a big head tonight and danced alone on the T with her iPod."

The inauguration of President Barack Obama began the New Year. Beth and I flew to California for the first time, taking the BART train from the San Francisco airport and the Caltrain to Palo Alto and Stanford. We stayed in a hotel near the Caltrain station and walked to campus. Beth met with staff at the Diversity and Access Office and the law school. A large area under construction near Stanford Law would be the new graduate dorms where she'd live. Much closer to classes than when she lived in Harvard's Quad, with the added advantage of no snow and ice. We walked under the canopy of trees on Palm Drive to downtown Palo Alto. She reconnected with two Harvard friends who worked for Facebook.

At one of Stanford's heated outdoor pools, I watched Beth while I returned work-related calls. She put her hair in a ponytail, stretched on a swim cap, and swam freestyle, backstroke, and butterfly laps. Each movement was the result of years of practice. After, she lifted herself out of the pool at the corner to sit on the deck. Shining in the sun, she looked up at me with clear blue eyes and an easy dimpled smile. I wish I could have glimpsed that moment after her injury.

Beth couldn't move at all in intensive care almost 10 years earlier, a time when no one imagined her swimming laps in January under California's winter sun. She'd also come a long way from floating free in the rehab pool in Green Springs, Ohio.

Beth's right elbow swelled to the size of a baseball, an occasional recurrence aggravated by any kind of physical stress. Extra wheeling or swimming or maybe getting bumped the wrong way. On our flight back to Boston, I suggested a power wheelchair to use only part of the time. She wouldn't discuss it.

Brittany visited Beth in Cambridge, and they undoubtedly talked about boys they dated. It didn't surprise me that Beth's confidence outshined her disability.

Beth and Lizzy alternated between domestic weekends and party weekends. The first involved cooking an elaborate brunch or hosting a four-course dinner party. Beth's specialty: our family recipe for Hungarian chicken paprikash. Party weekends translated to dancing with friends into the early morning hours. She also prioritized reading more classics as well as must-see Harry Potter movies like *The Half-Blood Prince*.

The three best friends from high school reunited when Ellen visited. They waited in line for brunch at The Friendly Toast in Cambridge and rode the elevator to the top of the Prudential Center in Boston.

Peggy and her daughter arrived for the Boston Marathon in April. Jess qualified for the marathon, a runner in addition to a swimmer. Beth and I arranged for a day off from work. We left Jess in Hopkinton to start the race, and I drove Beth and Peggy to Wellesley. We watched the runners and athletes in wheelchairs go by the main drag on Washington Street. Next, we drove into Copley Square where the sculptures of the tortoise and the hare celebrated the marathon since 1897.

The crowds and traffic in Boston swelled to even more intense levels with the event. Runners finished the 26 hilly miles proudly—and in pain. I struggled to understand but then again, I've never been an athlete. The numbers for the 2009 event topped 20,000 athletes and 500,000 spectators.

A pro at long plane travel, Beth flew to Manchester in May for her fourth and last trip to England's Paralympic World Cup. She earned a final bronze medal in the 50 back, a nice surprise since she hadn't been training. The IPC approved an official reclassification request for Beth from U.S. Paralympics, and she would schedule a classification appointment at the CAN-AM meet in San Antonio.

The Boston area never bored me. I attended a yoga class with my girls where Maria helped Beth into some of the positions. On the weekends, John and I discovered interesting places in our big backyard, including Plymouth Rock, Arnold Arboretum, Thoreau's Walden Pond, President John Adams' residence in Quincy, and the John F. Kennedy Museum.

John and I traveled to Cape Cod for an extraordinary trip with our friends, Rich and Deb. They had picked up Maria from the hospital the night of the accident. Rich and John had taught together in Tiffin, and I valued my growing friendship with Deb. From Sandwich to Provincetown, we viewed swimming seals and beautiful beaches. The first of many fun trips. Deb and I also started a tradition of beach walks, shelling, and long conversations. I finally learned to make time for good friends.

Ben graduated with his master's degree from Brandeis and applied for jobs in the area, accepting one in the office of Harvard's Registrar. He avoided driving in the crowded streets of Cambridge and preferred to take a bus to work instead. Ben made plans to apply to graduate schools for a doctorate in literature. Maria taught through the summer again, working in the same Cambridge Public School program for preschoolers with disabilities. I continued to help with field trips, proud of how Maria connected with her students. All of them learned how to communicate more effectively, including the children who didn't speak.

In August, Beth took her place in the Stanford Law Class of 2012. I accompanied her on the flight to California to help her move in. The routine of boarding a plane had changed a bit. Beth transferred from the airline's aisle chair to get to her assigned row in the airplane, then scooted herself over to the window. She reserved the window seat so no one would need to climb over her.

I rented a car at the San Francisco airport to transport the extra luggage we carried. The brand new Munger dorm gleamed with a baby grand piano in the lobby and colorful paintings on the walls. Beth and her three roommates shared a beautiful apartment with a large furnished living room and a huge kitchen with two full-size refrigerators. They each had a separate bedroom with a full-size bed, desk, dresser, and a private bathroom. There was a fifth bathroom for guests off the living room. Tall palm trees and green grass (realistic-looking artificial turf) replaced the dirt between the fancy dorms.

As a "1L," a first-year law student, Beth dove into her studies. She spent extra time preparing for classes with professors who asked questions of random students without warning, cold calling. Some tests required long essays in a short time, and Beth reluctantly asked for additional time to compensate for her ability to type with only three fingers. She volunteered for the law school's pro bono Social Security

Disability Project to help homeless people at a shelter obtain monthly payments.

"They appreciate that there is someone who is helping them who understands what it's like to be disabled," she said in the *National Law Journal*. "Anytime anyone has an interesting life experience or has overcome obstacles in the past, they have a different take on things. It's made me more interested in the client perspective."

Beth spent extra time on the project as co-case manager, supervising other law students. She ran for and was elected to Stanford's Student Law Association (SLA).

"I was extremely nerdy at Harvard compared to Stanford," Beth said. "Nerdy isn't the right word though, because I'm still nerdy—I love to read—but I'm not as introverted and shy."

Loving everything Stanford, Beth worked on the SLA social committee and planned party breaks on Thursday nights at local bars, facetiously called "bar review." Her Facebook friends topped one thousand. Brittany visited and joined Beth and her friends for bar review. Brittany also recorded more videos to post online of Beth putting her hair up in a ponytail and inserting her contact lenses.

In her kitchen, Beth burned her right thigh with hot chili, not as severe as her earlier coffee burn. She treated it promptly this time, thankful her tattoo escaped damage. Even so, she acquired another scar.

Over Christmas break at our Waltham apartment, Beth told me about a boy she met, a fellow Stanford Law student who baked the best chocolate chip cookies and made her laugh. They had graduated from Harvard in the same class.

Beth hesitated to start a relationship. I offered my two cents worth and encouraged her to take the risk. She would never know unless she tried. I shared my favorite corny quote from the movie *Meet Joe Black*. "Love is passion, obsession, someone you can't live without. I say, fall head over heels. Find someone you can love like crazy and who will love you the same way back. How do you find him? Well, you forget your head and you listen to your heart."

However, it helped to have the right guy first. I had the right guy. I didn't take John for granted. He loved me unconditionally even when I didn't feel lovable for a long time after Beth's injury. My best friend, he knew me like no other. And loved me anyway.

As 2010 began, Beth emailed my parents. "I'm winding down on my winter quarter classes. I've loved Constitutional Law and the Regulation of Political Process, but I found Property to be a little boring. This semester we also took a writing and oral argument class where we get a fake case and actually go through bringing it to court. I've found that I really enjoy the oral arguments! Next quarter, I'll be taking Constitutional Law 2, Evidence, Intellectual Property and the writing class. It should be fun!" I know that wouldn't have been fun for me.

John, a sports fan, teased Beth about being a lucky charm. Her first autumn in Cambridge, she watched the revelry in Harvard Yard when the Boston Red Sox won the World Series for the first time in 86 years. A few months later, the New England Patriots earned the Super Bowl XXXIX title. Later when Beth started at Stanford, the San Francisco Giants won the World Series for the first time.

I called Beth on the morning of Super Bowl Sunday as she fried pounds of bacon to make bourbon bacon popcorn for a big party. Most Sundays, she wheeled a mile and a half to the local farmer's market with friends. The unused push handles on the back of her wheelchair made handy holders for bags of fruit, vegetables, bread, and cheese. She also liked the market at San Francisco's Ferry Building. Vendors offered enough free samples to make up a meal.

On a weekend trip with her roommates, Beth held a parrot on the San Diego boardwalk. She toured Wine Country in the rolling countryside north of San Francisco. When Maria visited over spring break, Beth read from a thick law book while they sunned on the beaches at Santa Cruz and Half Moon Bay.

Beth received an email from one of her mentees, an undergraduate at Stanford, about a scholarship fund for physically challenged athletes. Thankful for the referral, Beth filled out an application and received help with tuition from the generous Swim with Mike Foundation. At their annual fundraiser at Stanford, she swam a smooth freestyle with friends. Beth loved swimming in heated outdoor pools year-round.

One night, she fell to the floor when a chair brake didn't hold as she transferred into bed. The bed she had eventually climbed into in Malden had been lower. She attempted to get off the floor on her own for only a short time before texting her three roommates to ask for help. One of them saved the day (night). Beth's aversion to asking for help evolved to a reluctant acceptance and the realization that it wasn't a weakness. All of us need help sometimes.

"I totally loved law school—and I recognize that's rare!" Beth said in an interview. "Stanford was a sunny, social place where everyone was brilliant and interesting. I was very involved in the school, eventually becoming class president, and made friendships that are still some of my closest friendships today."

In March, Beth flew to San Antonio with her boyfriend for her spring reclassification appointment and her first swim meet since Beijing. I encouraged her to sign up for long races; with her unusually high stamina, she easily could rack up several more American Records in addition to the 14 she held. She chose not to since the number of records never mattered to her.

The international experts at the Texas meet assigned her the same exact classification despite the wide range of physical function among her competitors. Unless a mass retesting of S3 women resulted in classification changes—not at all likely—Beth's odds of medaling at the next Paralympics remained low. Reconnecting with Peggy and other friends at the meet balanced the disappointing news.

Beth's swim times in San Antonio earned her a spot on Team USA for the World Championships in the Netherlands despite not training for the meet and enjoying the River Walk each evening. She declined the Netherlands trip since it interfered with her upcoming summer internship. After her last race in Texas, Beth hugged Peggy goodbye to return to law school, fondly remembering their seven years of swimming quests. She retired from competitive swimming with 14 S3 American Records, seven short course and seven long course.

Beth worked on the national conference for the National Association of Law Students with Disabilities (NALSWD). Elected Vice President at the conference, she bought her first smart phone to check her email more often. She learned to write emails and texts quickly with her left index finger, relying heavily on spell check. Voice recognition software had improved, but she still preferred to type everything herself. Beth regularly fielded questions from other students around the country.

"At first, it was outside my comfort zone. But I enjoyed giving back and being part of organizations that can improve life for students with disabilities. A lot of it is about bar accommodations, and also LSAT. If someone isn't receiving extra time, and they think they need it, or they're not getting large-print materials in time. Some of it is aimed at the fact that their disability is not being kept a secret.

Disability rights in general is becoming a bigger issue. It's filtering into the law school environment. More students with disabilities are going to law school which is incredibly encouraging."

As Beth's 1L year ended, she finalized her 2L schedule, adding Stanford's Youth and Education Law Project (YELP) to fight for school services for children with a disability. I helped her clear out of her dorm and move stuff into storage. I flew with her to Washington, DC. She shared an apartment for the summer with her boyfriend, each with an internship at different law firms. She immersed herself in research for her first law job and enjoyed time on Capitol Hill with a legal team who lobbied for disability issues. At my request, she carried something to her summer office on a high floor: an extra vinyl sheet, the same kind they used at the high school for emergency drills. Never used, left behind, and never replaced.

The 10th anniversary of Beth's injury came and went without notice, except for my new compulsion to write about it. When my job at the nonprofit ended, I began my writing project by researching events and gathering media quotes. The actual writing part was daunting. I wasn't sure I could do our story justice, but I had to try.

Propelled by millions of small choices, time converged—and converges—into infinitely improbable moments.

࿓ Chapter 24 ࿓
RIPPLING

Beth: *It's incredible to be a part of this community where we have a shared experience. It's given me a more interesting life, a new perspective, and experiences that I wouldn't otherwise have had.*

July 26, 2010

ON A GORGEOUS summer day, an excited law student wearing a new red dress hurries down Pennsylvania Avenue. It isn't her first trip to the White House. At the gate, security checks her name off the list, and she proceeds to the lawn. Her smile dims momentarily when she can't see the podium over the packed rows of chairs.

Pushing her manual wheelchair through the grass with effort, she aims to the right of the chairs, parking at the end of the front row where she won't block anyone's view. Event staff approach to ask her to move. They retreat as the ceremony starts to mark the 20th Anniversary of the Americans with Disabilities Act. She discovers only dignitaries in the first row but stays put rather than risk looking disrespectful with the ceremony underway.

I watch on TV, and I can't see Beth. I listen to Nathaniel Ayers, a gifted musician battling mental illness, give a moving performance on the trumpet after struggling to tune his bass. President Barack Obama talks about the ADA as a touchstone for additional progress. He energizes the crowd with, "Yes, we can!" After the ceremony concludes, the President walks toward one end of the front row and shakes the bent hand of the beaming young lady in a red dress. He probably wonders, "Who is this girl?"

Beth laughs when she tells me how she shook his hand, flustered, and said thank you more than once! That evening, in a fancy ballroom at the ADA Gala, she dances in a one-shouldered black satin dress. And shines.

November 24, 2011

It's Thanksgiving Day in Vermilion, Ohio. Maria and her fiancé, Ryder, greet us at the farmhouse door and bump Beth up the porch steps. I'm drawn to more warm hugs waiting in the chaos of the kitchen. Photos and crayon pictures cover the refrigerator as always. Nostalgia takes tangible form in the pumpkin and pecan pies.

My Grandma Henning's dressing recipe with apples and ground meat had been tweaked with love by my talented sister-in-law, Dar, a recent victim of cancer. I carry a steaming bowl of dressing to the antique dinner table. My mom's prayer before the meal honors Dar's memory and our loss.

The long table of solid maple remains a rare constant through my years though the people around it have changed. Thanksgiving has been observed at the Henning homestead for 126 years.

When we have no room for one more bite, we clear the table for a serious game of bridge, with lottery tickets for the winners. Not for me. I make my way to the front parlor where Dar's daughter Meghan entertains her two sons. Dar's three-year-old grandson is on a mission to complete the puzzle on a card table while her three-month-old grandson squirms in Maria's lap. My dad questions Beth about law school in California. Doesn't she know it's a crazy state? We laugh, but he means it. He is genuinely relieved to hear that his youngest granddaughter will return to the East Coast after graduation.

John's side gathers in Lorain at his mom's home. His dad passed away three years ago. Special locks on the doors prevent Jean from wandering away in the confusion of Alzheimer's. When John teases Jean about dishrags for a present, she finds a moment of clarity to respond with an emphatic no!

At the Cleveland airport, I love Beth's lingering goodbye hug with soft pats on my back. I develop snapshots of my kids in front of the Christmas tree, and more. The farmhouse with snow-dusted trees. My dad laughing at a long-forgotten quip. John's mom smiling in front of stacks of poker chips and a small pile of dollar bills, the Texas Hold'em winner. Beth and Maria taking turns to hold Meghan's baby.

Spring, 2012

Beth shows me an email from one of her mentees. The subject line reads, "A random but necessary thank you," followed by, "I cannot thank you enough for all the love and support. I have endless gratitude and deep, deep appreciation for you, and I wish there was a less cliché way to say how lucky I am! Love, V."

Beth's law school days are a whirlwind of activity. I don't know how she manages it all. She works at a homeless shelter and appears in court with a penniless client who sobs when the judge approves her Social Security Disability application. She attends classes and completes assignments. Plans the annual NALSWD conference in Washington, DC. Hands over the Presidency to another at the conference. Begins a term on the American Bar Association's Commission on Disability Rights. Answers questions in a video about disability at Stanford. Supports the Swim with Mike scholarship fund by recruiting friends to swim with her at a fundraiser. Speaks to a Stanford class about sports opportunities for those with a disability. Meets with a mentee, a quad, who asks questions about dating and intimacy. Answers emails from law students with a disability. And works on her YELP cases through Stanford's Mills Legal Clinic.

A *Law Crossing* article explains one of Beth's cases:

"She worked with another YELP student to file a 'Williams' complaint for a second grader who relies on a power wheelchair, a ventilator, and a feeding tube. Kolbe met with school representatives to discuss the needs of this child, addressing issues including exposure to sewage in the bathroom, mold in the classroom, and feces from a student in a neighboring classroom. Beyond these immediate health concerns, Kolbe also requested an assessment for occupational and physical therapy, as well as an assistive technology assessment on behalf on the student's family. The child's speech and language and adaptive physical education services were also adjusted as a result of Kolbe's work."

Beth accepted a dinner invitation at the child's home. The mom thanked Beth for being a positive role model for her bright little girl.

June 16, 2012

Beth sits in the front row, her head tipping toward the sun. Graduation day at Stanford Law School. John and I watch from farther back as she adjusts her cap, re-tucks the extra folds of the gown under her thighs, and uses her forearms to switch which leg is crossed over the other. She wheels up a ramp to the raised stage and parks next to the podium for the next presentation.

Beth's roommate, Christy, introduces her as the winner of the Dean's Award for Excellence in Service. John and I smile for slightly different reasons. Pride, yes, though it also amuses me to hear Christy describe my daughter's passion for volunteering. It is accurate, of course, but incomplete and minimized since Beth provided the details. Typical.

A reception follows the ceremony, and many approach to congratulate her. Would they be more impressed if they understood the extent of her disability? I admire how Beth thanks them gracefully with radiant smiles and hugs.

For many graduates, the celebration is short-lived. Beth stays in the dorm for a few more stressful weeks to study for the difficult California bar exam. She experiences panic attacks for the first time. We talk on the phone about coping strategies. She doesn't see a counselor or try the meditation I suggest but with the support of good friends and deep breathing techniques, she carries on. She plans a "bar trip," a much needed vacation after the exam in July. A last hurrah of sorts before signing over her weekdays, evenings, and weekends to a big law firm in the fall.

I renew my passport before Beth packs for a three-week trip with her boyfriend to Spain, France, Germany, Belgium, and the Netherlands. I have no travel plans, but I need to know I can fly to Europe if she needs me there. She doesn't.

One day, Beth prepares to board a fast train, not remotely accessible. At the station, her boyfriend carries her on the train and drops her in a seat before running back for the wheelchair. He barely makes it onboard before the doors close, and the train rushes forward.

Beth's favorite destination is the boardwalk in Barcelona where she orders cava and paella for dinner before dancing at a club on a moonlit beach.

August 17, 2012

Beth removes a purple satin bow and opens a box. Wrapped with love in fancy tissue, a canvas shows two preschool sisters, adorable even with mullet haircuts. They peek out from under a bed, side by side, in identical poses. Heads tilted and resting a cheek on a hand. Snow White and Cinderella.

Beth wipes her eyes as Maria hugs her maid of honor.

September, 2012

Beth and I prepare for what might be our last road trip. This one will carry us from Boston to Washington, DC. After numerous moves in the previous decade, she plans to stay in her favorite city indefinitely. All of her belongings fit in my car.

Years before, Beth discarded Honeybee Bear. He's mine now, still smiling with hope from a time when I had none. Hope with surprises.

Beth and I arrive at her new M Street apartment, and it is empty except for a recently delivered box that holds a new mattress. We unload the packed car. She secures a pile on her lap with her chin as she wheels forward.

Beth will be living alone, a first. She's not concerned even though she is vertically challenged, and the apartment is not accessible. Things that don't matter until they do: high clothes rods under a higher shelf in the closet, a dryer stacked on top of a washer, deep cupboards below the kitchen counter, and a cedar chest too heavy for Beth to move. Not a problem until a cat she babysits gets stuck behind the chest. She needs to ask a neighbor to move the chest. I add shelves in the pantry and a rod extension in the closet. She uses a clothes hanger to empty the dryer. The low kitchen cupboards are practical only for the space in front she can reach from her chair.

Taking a break from unpacking, Beth asks me to record a video on her iPhone. Brittany requested a demonstration for her website about how to put on boots and shoes. I hold the phone steady as Beth ties shoestrings by slowly setting the laces in place and tightening the bow — without using her teeth. An empty room is in the background. A new bed frame and a table will be delivered soon.

The next day, we shop for a pair of dress shoes with low heels, closed toes, and a strap across the back. Suit shopping also is problematic. Most jackets bunch up on the wheelchair seat, so we search for short ones. Beth also needs skirts and dresses to replace ones not long enough for her brand new job at a law firm on K Street.

May 19, 2014

I land at Reagan airport after a short flight from Boston. From the airport, I take the underground Metro to the Mt. Vernon Square station and roll my suitcase the remaining blocks to Beth's apartment. She works late at the law firm, and a key waits for me at the front desk. On her refrigerator, a magnet holds a picture of her and a friend with the President and Mrs. Obama at last December's White House Holiday Press Reception. Between Beth's black lace dress and dress shoes, bare legs show.

On cold weekends, she usually wears thin leggings with short skirts and dresses. For work in the winter, she often pairs a longer dress with sheer black tights, difficult to put on by herself initially. The reason for tights? Not to hide the coloring in useless legs from poor circulation. Not for the tiny bit of warmth since she can't feel temperature in her legs, and her time outdoors in frigid weather is limited. The only reason? To simply prevent the otherwise frequent question, "Aren't you cold?"

We catch up over a late dinner at one of our 14th Street favorites. Beth orders a margherita pizza with fresh mozzarella, and I indulge in fancy pasta. She drapes her suit jacket on the back of a chair, pulls hand sanitizer out of a bag, and presses the bottle between her hand and chin to squeeze out drops onto her other palm. I reach out my hand for some.

"How do you think I can do that?" she asks, laughing.

"Because you can do anything," I tease.

I take the sanitizer bottle from her and squeeze it between my thumb and index finger, one small skill of many that most take for granted. It's easy to forget she's a quad.

Animated when she talks, Beth gestures for emphasis. She's loved her job ever since the first months when she stressed about billable hours and whether or not she passed the bar exam. (She did.) She extracts intricate information from government documents, like needles in a haystack, and enjoys more and more contact with clients. When I ask a specific question about work, she says with a smile, "If I tell you, I'd have to kill you."

Beth takes on pro bono cases continuously, all related to disability. Avoiding confidential topics like corporate mergers and health care compliance, we talk instead about family, friends, and finding time for dates. She's glad she waited until later in college to date and until graduate school to have a boyfriend.

I don't always get the full scoop and not only about Beth's job. When she ended the relationship with her first boyfriend after four years, I didn't find out until later how rough the breakup had been. I consoled myself with the fact that she has wonderful friends. She didn't want me to worry. I never wanted her to worry about me, either.

Comfortable in her skin 14 years after her injury, Beth's disability and wheelchair create no impediment to dating in her mind. Her friend, Catherine, is also dating and between themselves, they assign potential boyfriends a nickname: sleeper cell, world bank, secret agent, ground hog, Maine boy, the reporter, future president. "Onward and upward" is the phrase they use if it doesn't work out.

May 29, 2014

Closed sinus passages opening. Sharp, stabbing pain. I tell myself it won't get worse. It does. I alert the doctor that my forehead hurts. He responds, "Yes, that's where I'm working."

With my eyes shut, I see a red light within. My teeth clench, and I wish for it to be over. The relief is palpable when the tube is pulled out of my nose.

A new soreness settles just under the surface of my face. My off and on neck pain is on. The circle of aching around my head weighs in as always. But something is different. My head feels lighter, with less pressure.

At the follow-up with the doctor, I am ecstatic. For the first time in two decades, no pain or pressure fills the deep recess behind my eyes. Half of the headache is gone. A victory. I wonder about the old saying, "Is happiness merely the remission of pain?"

A month later, John retires after 37 years of teaching, and we move from expensive Boston to Summerville near the coast of South Carolina. Low cost of living, less crime, perfect weather, proximity to an airport, and the hope our family and friends will visit more often because of nearby beaches and the attractions of Charleston. (They do.) No matter where we live, it's home if John is there with me.

My new doctor says my daily dose of Celebrex is too high—toxic. I gradually reduce and eliminate it, exposing the full impact of my remaining head pain, advanced arthritis, and fibromyalgia. I know why exactly why my body hurts which makes it somewhat irrelevant, a nuisance. A side note, not personal. My headache is different and tests me every day. Despite my daily meditation, it remains embedded in my self-concept and point of view. However, I also have learned a few things from Beth.

Perceptions matter. When I think of the pain as better than before, it doesn't trigger as much frustration. Not a miracle, but I appreciate having one less dependency without Celebrex and a duck or two towing the line. I'll never get all those ducks in a row, and that's okay.

My new mantra comes from my daily Jon Kabat-Zinn meditation. Finding peace by living in "a realm of wellbeing in which your limitations are not confining." What a gift, to be free. Like Beth.

Some of us are paralyzed metaphorically by grief or pain, by conditions or circumstances. And then there is Beth, literally paralyzed, and not feeling limited. So much so, she considers her injury a fortunate accident. One that sparked waves of serendipity.

Beth embraces life enthusiastically. Unconditionally. Joyfully. Loving life requires more effort for me. I look for reasons to be grateful, from working legs to the sun in the sky. From family and friends to the extraordinary disability community. But. It's not an easy world for most of us, including Beth. She somehow filters challenges and limits through an amazingly forgiving lens.

In frustrating situations, I always ask myself, "What is the worst-case scenario?" I compare the answer to the night of the accident, and problems pale in comparison. When I overreact to anything that startles me in the car, the panic it triggers is fleeting. My depression is managed most of the time now and less of an issue than chronic pain. Headaches are a common symptom of depression. When the headache beats along with my heart, I know it could be worse. I walk a different kind of tightrope these days, one that is thick and woven and wide. It takes a strong wind to knock me off.

Everything really *is* okay. What a relief to finally believe what Beth knew all along.

February 28, 2015

I land at Reagan airport after a short flight from Charleston, South Carolina. From the airport, I again take the Metro to the Mt. Vernon Square station and roll my suitcase the remaining blocks to my daughter's apartment.

Beth shows me her new manual wheelchair. Her first chairs sported bright colors, then later ones toned down to the professional-looking black. Her newest chair? Black with pink accents. She loves it.

I bring her the latest update of my family phone number list. It's a carryover from 9/11 but with no emergency meeting place because of the distances between us. My suitcase also holds a new toaster to stop Beth from broiling bread on an oven shelf. To stop her from using her bare left hand to put two slices of bread on the metal shelf, flip them over later, and take them out. I also bring a new quad-friendly garlic press since I had a nightmare after watching her dice a clove of garlic with a regular knife.

An earlier visit, I packed an electric coffee bean grinder to replace the hand grinder Beth had used with difficulty. Part of her pour-over coffee process along with an electric water pot set to the perfect temperature. I also bought her the Brella Bag, an adjustable tote bag to hold an open umbrella, hands free. If she wanted to, she could master it in minutes, but it has never been used. When it rains, she wears a raincoat, puts up the hood, and wheels like crazy. I have hopes she might use an umbrella one day.

On a Saturday, we walk to a spa with an infinity pool. Beth likes the idea of it, a narrow lane with wave motion all to herself. An alternative to the crowded lap lanes at the YMCA pool. She called ahead to reserve a time for the infinity pool and to check on access. No problem.

At the front desk, a girl shows us the elevator and directs us to the second floor. The spa has unusual split-levels and we can't find the pool. Someone tells us to go to another floor. No pool there either. I find it between two floors with a flight of steps to reach it.

We go back in the elevator to the locker room to change before I bump her down the steps to the pool level. More small steps ascend to the ledge of the pool. With no space for a wheelchair at the top, I ask a worker to help me balance.

Beth falls into the pool and treads water while we figure out the two controls. At one setting, the wave pulse is surprisingly forceful. She tries different starting positions. Each attempt pushes her roughly to the back wall of the pool. The second pulse setting is even more powerful. A reality check. A reminder she is a quad.

If asked, Beth will say she has "full" arms. Through rose-colored glasses, this means she can use her arms to do most everything she wants to do—though definitely not full muscle function or sensation. Being independent keeps her arm strength maximized. She moves in and out of her chair on her own to a variety of surfaces and heights, including cars and shower benches. She wheels long distances often. If she tells you a place is not far to walk, don't believe her.

Instead of laps at the infinity pool, Beth suggests a mimosa brunch followed by a trek to the local farmer's market. The back of her wheelchair holds tomatoes, greens, cheese, fresh pasta, and sausage. When her boyfriend, Dan, arrives, Beth makes us a perfect spaghetti dinner with meat sauce from scratch.

June 7, 2015

Brittany invites Beth to be a bridesmaid in her wedding. And to serve on the Board of Directors for her new international nonprofit, AbleThrive.

"When I was injured," Beth told a reporter. "I had no one with a similar injury to learn from. AbleThrive provides tips on how to become independent more quickly."

The weekend of the wedding, Brittany asks her bridesmaids to prepare a speech about their connection to her. Beth takes the assignment seriously.

Through college, they volunteered once a week at a Boston school for kids with a disability. As their senior year started, Brittany convinced Beth to venture out beyond her usual bubble of swimming, classes, assignments, and volunteering. Brittany played rugby so when a party in one of the houses on the river had no elevator? No problem. She carried Beth up and down stairs. A broken elevator at the Harvard T stop? No problem. They didn't change their plans to go clubbing in Boston. When an ancient sanctuary on the other side of the world wasn't accessible? No problem. Brittany helped Beth to a front row view on the marble steps of Beijing's Temple of Heaven.

When we lived in Ohio, stairs and access disappointed us. Beth wrote off many places as ones she didn't need—or want—to enter. That continued until her senior year of college.

The bridesmaids gather, and Beth starts her speech with how they met on move-in day for freshmen. She ends in tears with what she's learned from Brittany. With the help of a friend, the world is wide open and welcoming, even with a wheelchair.

"Strong friends are worth their weight in gold," Beth wrote after the wedding. *AbleThrive* published her article about being a bridesmaid with a disability.

Late June, 2015

On a warm summer day, Beth calls an Uber to get to the airport. She uses taxis and Uber independently with the exception of high vehicles like SUVs and vans. Taxi drivers rarely stop for a young woman in a wheelchair, and Uber is the dependable alternative. She pushes the car door open as much as possible, wheels into the corner, and locks the chair. She lifts her body with one hand (and a straight arm) pushing down on a locked wheel while the other hand is on the back seat. Bridging the gap and landing precariously on the very edge of the seat, she leans back and shifts her arms to scoot back into a safer position. Next, she sits up to tell the driver how to remove the big wheels of her chair to fit in the trunk. When she picks up her legs under her knees to draw them inside, her shoes scuff on the bottom of the car door and sometimes fall off. She thanks the Uber driver for picking up a shoe. Her favorite pairs no longer last forever.

Waiting for her flight at the Newark airport, Beth opens her laptop on the long skirt of her suit and makes additional notes on the meeting with a client. She hears her name and turns to see coaches and swimmers, part of the U.S. Paralympics Swimming National Team on their way to the IPC World Championships in Scotland.

The reunion makes her day. Just another fortunate accident.

July, 2015

In a large room filled to capacity, a senior partner opens an event with a detailed introduction of a young associate in the same Washington, DC, law firm. Beth sits on the side in a stylish blue suit, embarrassed by the unexpected attention. She organized the Diversity Dialogue event to commemorate the 25th Anniversary of the ADA.

Government and private sector leaders discuss issues relating to inclusion, support, and access.

A few weeks later, Beth flies to San Francisco. She interviews Stanford Law students for her firm and extends the time on the West Coast for a perfect vacation with Dan. She includes reconnecting with old friends as always. And swimming in a roof top pool.

August 13, 2015

At a wedding celebration, I squeeze the hand of my best friend as we smile for photographs with Maria, Beth, Ben, and his new bride Cathy. Others join us for more pictures: Maria's husband, Ryder, and Beth's boyfriend, Dan. Dan's dating nickname? "Future president." All of us are lucky to be in love.

John makes a toast at an elegant dinner, and we raise our glasses high. To happy-ever-after.

November 15, 2015

I scan Facebook and find a photo of a gold medal with a post from Laura, one of Beth's friends.

"Every day when I hop in the Harvard pool to train, I am encouraged when I walk by this. I feel fortunate to have had awesome people pave the way for other swimmers like myself. Hopefully Blodgett pool will have more great para swimmers in the pool soon. Thanks for your legacy Beth!! Let's swim together soon."

February, 2016

Beth ends up in the emergency room with Dan one night, sick and in pain. She returns home with antibiotics. An ultrasound the next day reveals bladder stones. I offer to travel to DC. She asks me to wait until her surgery and stay the week after, a longer visit than usual. I tease that she should have surgery more often, so I can spend extra time with her.

Since Beth graduated from high school, I had reminded her once a year to schedule an ultrasound to check for stones since her Toledo urologist recommended it. Usually feeling good, she thought it would be a waste of time.

Surgery day. I meet Beth's doctor for the first time just before her hospital bed is wheeled away down the hall. My wait is easy compared to her earlier surgeries. I work on a chapter until my name is called. The doctor tells me all is well. He made a small incision on her abdomen and pulled out the stones. "Boulders," he says, smiling. Bigger than the ones he usually sees.

The days after the surgery, I enjoy the rare opportunity to do things for my independent daughter. I make her old favorites on different days. Noodle soup, chicken and rice, lentils and carrots, and paprikash. I organize her closet. I bank extra hugs and snuggles. Before my visit ends, she feels better than she has in months. She returns to working her usual long days with another new man in her life: a good doctor to call for an ultrasound once a year.

March, 2016

When I was a little girl, I wanted to save the world. She's still part of me and in my empty nest, I realize I have more to give. I sign up to be a peer mentor for the Reeve Foundation and connect with moms dealing with their child's spinal injury. I volunteer for disability organizations. I start writing and submitting articles related to disability, but I'm not comfortable writing about mental illness. Yet.

My book manuscript begins to take shape though the perfect words escape me. Like my favorite song in the *Rent* musical, I think of my memoir as my one song—minus the glory part. I need it to be my one pure and true thing. My small contribution to the world.

It's time to move to the next level. I take a deep breath and plunge into a new website and blog. I make plans for a Facebook page and sign up for Twitter and Instagram. If I need to be more visible to see my book in print, so be it. I focus on sharing words of hope.

January, 2017

Two steps forward, one step back. I reluctantly tell my doctor about a swallowing change, different for months. I hate medical tests. My swallowing scan shows two bumps pressing into my esophagus from two neck vertebrae. Osteophytes caused by advanced arthritis grow on the vertebrae. If it gets worse, a risky surgery could remove the growths and fuse the vertebrae with a titanium plate.

Another round of physical therapy for neck and head pain ends with new symptoms. Uncomfortable sensations concentrate on my left side, face to feet. Neuropathy. A neurologist orders more tests and refers me to a neurosurgeon. My neck MRI shows advanced arthritis, rotated joints, mild compression, and one vertebra slipped forward on the one below.

At my appointment with the neurosurgeon, he walks in, looks briefly at the MRI, and says, "The pain has to be a lot worse before I recommend surgery."

I didn't want immediate surgery. Still, he irks me. "What a convenient superpower," I think, "to know the amount of pain someone else experiences."

What I labeled as low pain tolerance years ago proves to be the opposite. I try different drugs for nerve pain, but I can't tolerate any of them. The initial flare of neuropathy gradually fades from constant to random. No such luck with the headache, with a base level of pain that slowly elevated through the years. The neurologist recommends going back on the anti-inflammatory, Celebrex, the only thing that helped with my head and neck pain in the past. The low dose doesn't make a dent. I resign myself to taking the high dose and accept the health risks.

The neurologist hands me another new diagnosis: trigeminal neuralgia, a chronic pain condition affecting the trigeminal nerve in the face. Burning the nerves is an effective treatment and I talk to a different neurosurgeon who does that procedure. His testing reveals numbness on my face, and he won't do it. He says that burning the nerves causes numbness, too, and I could lose muscle function in my face. I tell him I'll take that risk, but he says no. Instead, he recommends extensive neck surgery to address the rest of my head and neck pain. It seems to be my best option even though one of the risks is cutting the spinal cord and causing paralysis. I'll put off neck surgery as long as I can.

May 20, 2017

Before 2016 ends, I find two handicapped-accessible tickets for *Hamilton* after a late night computer search. Beth plans to go with her boyfriend. She calls me a few weeks before the play about a memorial service Dan will attend which means he can't use his ticket.

"How about a weekend in New York City?" she asks.

"Yes!" I exclaim. No hesitation. We make plans to meet there on a Saturday later in May.

"Do you know what day that is?"

"No."

"The anniversary. It's been 17 years. I think we should go out to a nice restaurant that night and talk about it."

I agree. My memories of the accident remain sharp and clear. Even so, guilt no longer defines me. Other labels define me now, ones I gladly wear. Mom, wife, daughter, friend, and mentor. Over many years, I pieced my identity together bit by bit. Cemented by the love of family and friends. Healed by countless dimpled smiles and hugs with soft pats on my back. By sunsets, Life is Good shirts, and felt peace doves. And travels with Beth, always an adventure.

On the evening of the anniversary, she guides me through teeming city sidewalks and construction cones to a restaurant. We sit at a table beside the prep area for fancy appetizers. Near wheels of cheese, two small wooden mice watch us from a ledge as a manager in a suit brings an empty wine goblet for Beth and a glass for me, tall and narrow with a lime wedge and a steel straw. Our server pours a small carafe of wine into her glass and a bottle of ginger beer into mine. A far cry from our Taco Bell days in Tiffin, Ohio.

I listen to a confident young woman with expressive gestures. How she knew everything would be okay the night of the accident. And after.

"If only I had believed her from the start," I say to myself.

As a teenager, she wondered if health risks like blood clots and pressure sores would plague her future. The first 17 years? No.

"Who would I be without my injury? I can't imagine." She pauses, her beautiful bent hands resting on the table. I reach over to cover hers with my own.

"I wouldn't change a thing. I love my life!"

My Cinderella found more than a happy ending. She created a happy-ever-after life.

June 3, 2017

Years before at law school, Beth lost the HOPE ring she wore every day after her injury. No longer needed?

My phone chimes with a FaceTime request. Beth with a dazzling smile. She shows me the ring finger on her right hand. A diamond nests on curving gold bands with tiny leaves.

A new story begins.

February, 2018

John and I drive to Reagan Airport, about an hour's drive from our new house in the Shenandoah Valley. We moved back north from South Carolina to see our kids more often. They live in Baltimore, Boston, and Washington, DC.

We fly to Orlando and meet Beth and Dan at Universal Studios. I board the Hogwarts train at The Wizarding World of Harry Potter with Beth, Dan, and John. It's a first for all of us. Beth and I fondly recall her days in rehab reading Harry Potter. We had no clue what might be ahead, things like sharing butterbeer at the Leaky Cauldron in a perfect replica of Diagon Alley.

March, 2018

My memoir manuscript is better than it's ever been. Query letters lead to more interest from literary agents, so I decide to up my visibility. I book interviews on radio shows and podcasts. I add to my previous total of 40 published articles since March of 2016. I build my Twitter following to 18,000 and read a tweet about auditions in Washington, DC. The nonprofit This Is My Brave is on a mission to end the stigma of mental illness through live shows in big cities.

On an impulse, I book an audition. Dismay and anxiety quickly follow. What am I thinking?

It's way out of my comfort zone. I know my shortcomings, and they include speech writing, public speaking, and talking about my chronic health issues. Only a few people know I have a long history of depression. Do I really want to share that story?

June 8, 2018

Celebrity suicides are in the news: Kate Spade, Anthony Bourdain, and more. My friends and family talk about it, puzzled about the suicides of successful people who smile in public. I find myself speaking up and trying to explain.

Once upon a time, I felt like a bad mom unworthy of help because I hurt my child. My friend Susan said it perfectly. "As parents, our biggest fear is the damage we might accidentally do to our children, but we need to know that we only can do our best to love and support them. Love is messy and imperfect and even painful, but it's life."

I understand that now. I didn't after Beth's injury when no light appeared at the end of the tunnel. No hope and way too much pain and fear. If Beth or Maria had died in the accident, I would have ended my life. The lies of depression say that loved ones would be better off without us. It's not true but since we feel worthless, we believe it.

I'm here because Beth needed me after her injury.

This is hard for John to hear, the same way it bothered him when he first learned about the depths of my guilt and depression. I explain again that he didn't know because I didn't want him to know. I worked hard to keep him safely away from the darkness.

My guy gets it now. He gets *me*. I'm one of the lucky ones.

July 28, 2018

Summer in Ohio. The day of Beth's wedding shower is a rare combination of cool breezes and bright sun. It's also rare because my kids and their significant others are in the same place at the same time. Rarer still, extended family and old friends I haven't seen in years.

Maria hosts the party at the Henning homestead. Her pretty signs and special touches add to the charm of the family farm. She stands next to her sister and quizzes the crowd about Beth and Dan. Some of the answers surprise the guests. Who is the best cook? Beth. Which one is a lawyer? Both. Who is the best dancer? Beth. It's no surprise to me, with fun road trip memories of CDs blaring, and Beth feeling the beat in the passenger seat of her little blue car.

Under a white canopy, Beth and Dan open fancy packages in a smooth dance of partnership and familiarity. When Dan tells a joke, Beth's head tilts back a little as she laughs, followed by a few small claps of joy. Modified, of course, with contracted fingers meeting instead of palms.

Next, Dan hands her a sealed envelope. She smiles up at him, perhaps appreciating that he doesn't cater to her disability. She holds the envelope between both fisted hands and doesn't find an opening for the one finger she can move a bit. She uses her teeth, but the paper is thick. In any other situation, she would keep trying until it opens, sometimes tearing the contents. But today, with more gifts to open in front of a crowd, she gives the envelope back to Dan. Without a word, he opens it quickly, hands her the card inside, and returns Beth's smile.

Maybe fairy tales aren't all fantasy.

November 8, 2018

I wait behind the curtain with 10 storytellers as the audience arrives. Center stage, a banner on the podium says,

"This Is My Brave." Empty chairs form a semicircle behind the podium, one for each cast member. The show is about to begin.

I walk out with the others and take my seat. The stage sparkles with hanging lights and decorations for a future Cinderella play. It's perfect. Beth—my Cinderella—watches from the audience with her fiancé and her dad.

A new friend introduces me, and suddenly I'm at the podium. "Have you ever seen a movie where someone falls asleep and wakes up to a completely different life? That happened to me. But I didn't snuggle under my covers and wake up with Tom Hanks." My opening lines get a laugh.

I am surprisingly calm. John and Dan smile at me with Beth adding a little wave and a nod. Like her, I keep moving forward.

My story weaves with Beth's. I no longer feel the need to minimize challenges, hers or mine. I'm certain now that our challenges will never define us.

I tell the audience about my new book contract with a publisher who received my 58th query letter in the past three years. The ending of my speech sums it up.

"After the car accident, I followed the lead of a brave teenage girl. Today, I'm brave enough to share with you what I learned along the way." Pausing, I feel the love and support around me.

"Hope is an incredibly powerful thing. And if you never give up? Hope wins."

✢ ACKNOWLEDGMENTS ✣

IN MY FAIRY TALE childhood, I dreamed of writing books. My first story told the tale of Fala and Nala, princesses who lived in a magical castle. I grew up to be a mom raising two princesses and a prince but with better names. Our own wondrous tale found a home in this book, with a little help along the way.

Susan Ranes: "Maybe fairy tales aren't all fantasy." Susan, thank you for allowing me to use this line from your critique. You are a phenomenal editor with the gift of seeing the big picture and posing clear questions to prompt quality writing. Every aspect of my story is better because of you. (The less-than-perfect parts are all mine.) Can't wait to read *your* book!

Sarah Fader, Mariah Ashlyn Elkes, and the other extraordinary folks at Eliezer Tristan Publishing: I love your passion for sharing stories that matter.

Paula Morrow, Trish Reeb, and Michael Miller: Thank you for sharing your writing expertise with me.

Jan Cheripko: Four years ago, your valuable advice helped me find my authentic writing voice and shifted this book to the right track.

Dr. Ariana Vora: The Foreword you wrote is perfect! Beth and I appreciate your exceptional skills as a caring physician as well as your support of *Struggling with Serendipity*.

Sandy Asher: You are truly a wonderful mentor and teacher. I'm grateful we met at the Highlights Workshop in 2011.

John Kolbe: I love our story. Thank you for reading and re-reading my manuscript and caring about my words.

Debra Gardner: You always believed in me and in this book. It evolved over walks and talks including many on our favorite beach. Thanks for being a good listener, a devoted cheerleader, and the best kind of friend.

Ben, Maria, Beth, and my parents, Richard and Helen Barnes: I love you always. You are the priceless part of my story.

Cindy Kolbe
Shenandoah Valley
November 22, 2018

&ORIGIN; BETH'S LETTER TO READERS &ORIGIN;

Dear Readers,

Thank you for reading our story! While parts of the book are difficult to read, I hope you finished with a greater understanding of mental health and spinal cord injuries, and perhaps a greater sense of what is possible. All too often, society puts limits on what people with disabilities can accomplish, and I hope this book can be at least a part of countering those limits.

However, there are many stories of people with disabilities achieving great success. I think our story, told from the perspective of a mom who is struggling with guilt and depression while being the primary caretaker, is a new spin that I hope is helpful to anyone dealing with challenges. It is important to note that my success is not one of only internal strength, but also of access to resources and an incredible support system of family, friends, physical therapists, surgeons, teachers, coaches, and more. We should do better to ensure that all people with disabilities have access to resources that help them thrive.

Reading this book feels familiar, but I also learned so much about what our story looked and felt like to my mom. I have a new appreciation for what my parents, and particularly my mom, went through. At the time of the accident and in the years that followed, I had no idea of my mom's mental health struggles. To me, she was always a loving presence of encouragement and was up for whatever I asked of her—helping me with daily tasks when I was still recovering, driving to physical therapy three times a week, traveling cross country to swim meets, or encouraging me to apply to Harvard. Looking back, I wish I had been more aware and supportive of her. I can chalk up my lack of awareness to typical teenage self-centeredness, but none of us could have known what she was dealing with. She hid it well. I am glad she is now sharing her story. It has made us closer than ever.

The car accident feels like a lifetime ago. I have been in a wheelchair for over 18 years, and it is fully incorporated into my life and my identity. Today, I truly feel like I didn't lose anything in that accident. I am proud to be part of the extraordinary disability community and am passionate about giving back to that community. I cannot imagine what my life would be if I had not been injured, and honestly, I would not go back and change it if I could.

Much love,
Beth Kolbe
Washington, DC
December 10, 2018

❧ SPINAL CORD INJURY 101 ❧

STRUGGLING WITH SERENDIPITY focuses on "person-first" language to refer to disability. This is the generally accepted, politically correct wording to emphasize that everyone with a disability is a unique individual—one who might happen to also have a disability. Instead of saying someone *is* disabled, the person-first alternative is someone *with* a disability.

Language changes as communities evolve. For example, in the 1970s, my high school friends and I advocated for person-first language through the youth wing of the Ohio Association for Retarded Citizens. Now it is The Arc of Ohio, without the derogatory "R" word. The word "handicapped" is also outdated unless you're referring to parking. However, the language someone chooses to embody their identity is a very personal one.

My daughter Beth and others with a disability choose specific labels to identify themselves. When a spinal cord injury in the back damages two limbs (the legs), the result is paraplegia. People with paraplegia often refer to themselves as a "para." When a spinal cord injury in the neck damages all four limbs, the result is quadriplegia. (In Europe, the term tetraplegia is popular which means the same thing.) Many with quadriplegia/tetraplegia refer to themselves as a "quad" or "tetra."

Identifying as a quad reflects Beth's disability pride and connects her to a larger community; the use of the word quad in this book reflects her choice. Others consider even the word disability to be negative, leading to labels like differently-abled, mobility challenged, or neurodiverse. Also, there is no perfect way to describe the degree of disability. "More (or less) severe" can be interpreted in different ways. In this book, the phrase refers to physical function, and no judgment is intended.

Spinal cord injury changes the body and causes a physical disability, not a cognitive one. When you have a spinal cord injury, there is damage to the cord. The spinal cord extends from the base of the spine, the sacrum, up to the neck where it connects to the brain stem. Spinal injuries are categorized according to the location of the damage. For example, the damage to Beth's spinal cord occurred at the sixth and seventh cervical vertebrae in the neck, and she was diagnosed with a C6-7 injury.

Human vertebral column

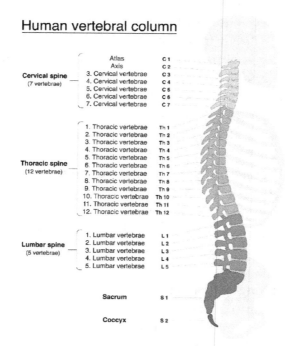

©Peter Hermes Furian #59485353 Dreamstime.com

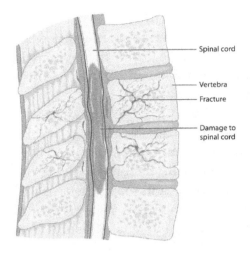

Spinal cord

Vertebra

Fracture

Damage to spinal cord

©Legger #60816860 Dreamstime.com

It is impossible to make assumptions about any individual with any kind of disability. There are endless causes, kinds, and manifestations. "Complete" spinal cord injuries indicate a cord that is cut through, making the right and left sides of the body equally impaired with no sensation and no voluntary movement below the level of injury. In contrast, a person with an "incomplete" injury may be able to move one arm more than the other or feel parts of the body that cannot be moved. Incomplete describes a cord that is partially cut, bruised, or damaged in another way. Initially, doctors diagnosed Beth's injury as complete. Weeks after the accident, limited sensation returned to her legs and trunk, proving that a strand of her spinal cord was intact and redefining her injury as incomplete.

Spinal injuries near the bottom of the backbone cause the least harm, and those with this diagnosis may be able to walk. Injuries to the cord in the neck cause the most damage.

For example, someone with a complete C3 spinal cord injury (cut through at the third cervical vertebrae) will most likely need help to breathe and be unable to move any limbs. These quads can control computers and other electronic devices with remarkable technology.

People with quadriplegia are successful programmers, teachers, artists, parents, public speakers, lawyers, composers, writers, politicians, and much more. In the words of Harriet McBryde Johnson, a famous disability advocate: "We take constraints that no one would choose and build rich and satisfying lives within them. We enjoy pleasures other people enjoy and pleasures peculiarly our own. We have something the world needs."

❧ DISABILITY RESOURCES ❧

AbleThrive
"AbleThrive is a one-stop platform for people with paralysis and their families that shares customized information and resources to adapt and thrive."
ablethrive.com
Beth serves on the Board of Directors for this nonprofit, founded by her passionate friend, Brittany Déjean. "Quality connections and relevant information" drive this growing venture because "everyone deserves a chance to thrive!"

Adaptive Sports USA (formerly Wheelchair and Ambulatory Sports, USA)
"To engage, evolve, and empower individuals with a disability to be involved in adaptive sport through education, coaching and advocacy."
adaptivesportsusa.org
Junior Nationals is the oldest continuously held competitive sports event for young athletes with physical disabilities and/or visual impairment in North America. Beth competed at the 2003 Junior Nationals in Connecticut.

Adversity 2 Advocacy Alliance
"Promoting and fostering the power of turning personal challenges into service to others with similar challenges."
a2aalliance.org
Jeff Bell, founder, hosts a radio show and podcast. Jeff interviewed me for his A2A Spotlight Podcast in August of 2018. The A2A site also includes mental health resources. "We help ourselves by helping others."

American Association of People with Disabilities (AAPD)

"A convener, connector, and catalyst for change, increasing the political and economic power of people with disabilities."
aapd.com

The summer of 2006, Beth was one of six Congressional Grant Interns sponsored by AAPD and the Mitsubishi Electric America Foundation. She worked for then-Senator John Kerry and joined him on the Senate floor for the stem cell debate. In 2017 and 2018, she revisited the same summer program as a mentor for Grant Interns.

American Chronic Pain Association (ACPA)

"To facilitate peer support and education for individuals with chronic pain and their families so that these individuals may live more fully in spite of their pain."
theacpa.org

I joined a support group in Tiffin, Ohio, in the 1990s with a constant low-level headache. One of the ACPA steps recommended accepting the pain. I resisted that good advice until many years later in Boston.

Americans with Disabilities Act (ADA)

"Information and Technical Assistance on the ADA."
ada.gov

This resource includes wheelchair ramp specifications that we used for our Tiffin home as well as a wide range of facts. At national conferences, Beth learned the history of the ADA from those who led the fight. She attended the 20th anniversary celebration of the ADA at the White House in 2010. For the 25th anniversary, she planned a successful diversity event for her law firm.

The Arc
"Is the largest national community-based organization advocating for and serving people with intellectual and developmental disabilities and their families."
thearc.org
I volunteered in The Arc's youth wing in the 1970s at the county and state level before I managed group homes in Ohio. The Arc website shares resources as well as contact information for local chapters.

Association of University Centers on Disabilities (AUCD)
"Is a membership organization that supports and promotes a national network of university-based interdisciplinary programs."
aucd.org
Beth volunteers for this active organization which supports numerous programs that provide needed services. The website includes a Diversity and Inclusion Toolkit and the location of AUCD centers.

Challenged Athletes Foundation (CAF)
"Opportunities and support to people with physical disabilities, so they can pursue active lifestyles through physical fitness and competitive athletics."
challengedathletes.org
Through CAF's Access for Athletes grants, Beth appreciated travel funds for one swim meet a year. "CAF believes that involvement in sports at any level increases self-esteem, encourages independence and enhances quality of life."

Christopher and Dana Reeve Foundation
"Is dedicated to curing spinal cord injury by funding innovative research, and improving the quality of life for

people living with paralysis through grants, information and advocacy."

christopherreeve.org

Call a Reeve Information Specialist to ask questions, request a peer mentor, or to receive their free Paralysis Resource Guide. I'm a guest blogger, peer mentor, and regional champion for the foundation. The late Christopher Reeve directed the 2004 movie, "The Brooke Ellison Story." Ellison was featured in 2002 billboards that said, "Quadriplegia at Harvard: A+." Billboards that planted the seed of Harvard in Beth's mind.

Determined2Heal

"Helps simplify the transition into life with paralysis."
determined2heal.org

Beth met founder Josh Basile when he co-founded SPINALpedia. Determined2Heal provides "information and advice for people with spinal cord injuries, their families and friends, as well as rehabilitative adventures."

Facing Disability

"Created to connect families who suddenly have to deal with a spinal cord injury to people like them who have already been there."
facingdisability.com

My guest blogs are included on Facing Disability, created by Thea Flaum of the Hill Foundation. They also produce professional videos. "Designed to help families cope effectively, resiliently and creatively with the changing realities of all their lives."

Fishing Has No Boundaries

"Provides recreational fishing opportunities for all anglers with disabilities regardless of their age, race, gender, or disability."

fhnbinc.org

Fishing Has No Boundaries supports chapters across the country. My family looked forward to the annual event in Sandusky, Ohio, for three years in a row, with our friends in the Northwest Ohio spinal cord injury group. Firemen volunteered to lift participants with manual and power wheelchairs in and out of the boats.

Giving Voice to Depression

"To start healthy, healing conversations that reduce stigma, and promote understanding."

givingvoicetodepression.com

Two sisters founded this nonprofit and host in-depth podcasts. The site includes the podcast about my story, "Guilt and Depression: Cindy Kolbe."

International Paralympic Committee (IPC) Swimming

"Athletes can have a physical, visual or intellectual impairment. Both male and female competitors, who are classified on their functional ability to perform each stroke, test their skills in freestyle, backstroke, butterfly, breaststroke and medley events."

paralympic.org/swimming

Official website of World Para Swimming. At the 2008 Paralympics in Beijing, 547 athletes from 62 countries competed in 141 medal events. World Rankings between 2002 – 2010 include Beth's swim times as high as third place in the S3 women's classification.

Mitsubishi Electric America Foundation (MEAF)
"Investing in innovative strategies to empower youth with disabilities to lead productive lives."
meaf.org
Co-sponsor of Beth's 2006 Congressional Intern Grant with the American Association of People with Disabilities. MEAF supports youth with disabilities through Leadership Development, Employment Preparation, and Ability Awareness.

mobileWOMEN
"Our mission is to bring together current and accurate information on issues of interest to our community."
mobilewomen.org
My guest blogs have been published on this site. MobileWOMEN "believe that women with disabilities steer their own lives."

National Association of Youth Leadership Forums
"To improve employment and independent living outcomes of youth with disabilities transitioning from high school."
nationalaylf.org
This site includes contact information for all of the chapters across the country for students with a disability. Beth credits the Youth Leadership Forum in Ohio (ohioylf.com) for introducing her to disability rights and connecting her to a dynamic community.

National Collegiate Athletic Association (NCAA)
"Dedicated to the well-being and lifelong success of college athletes."
ncaa.org
A 2008 article in the NCAA Champion magazine publicized a hopeful trend for swimmers with a disability. It featured

four U.S. Paralympics National Team swimmers who also competed on varsity college teams, including Beth. She was a member of the Harvard Women's Swimming and Diving team.

Option B
"Helps people build resilience and find meaning in the face of adversity."
optionb.org
Sheryl Sandberg's nonprofit shares resources in the following categories: grief & loss; incarceration; health, illness & injury; raising resilient kids; abuse & sexual assault; resilience; and divorce & family challenges. In April of 2018, Option B published my first story.

Quad Foundation
"Assisting and supporting survivors of spinal cord injury resulting in quadriplegic paralysis."
quadfoundation.org
The Quad Foundation raises funds for activity-based therapy. The foundation also hosted the first Warrior Momz Summit/Walk & Roll on DC in March of 2018 to coincide with the end of Kay Ledson's cross-country Warrior Momz Walk.

Rehabilitation Services Administration (RSA)
"To provide leadership and resources to assist state and other agencies in providing vocational rehabilitation (VR) and other services to individuals with disabilities."
rsa.ed.gov
An Ohio RSA counselor helped Beth with driver's training and the modified equipment to drive her car. Counselors also provide job training opportunities. Attending college out of state made Beth ineligible for RSA tuition assistance.

Shriners Hospitals for Children®

"Provide the highest quality care to children with neuromusculoskeletal conditions, burn injuries and other special healthcare needs within a compassionate, family-centered and collaborative care environment."

shrinershospitalsforchildren.org

Beth and I loved the Chicago hospital where we met with a large interdisciplinary team in the spinal cord injury program. We returned for follow-up visits over four years and highly recommend the Shriners Hospitals for outpatient or inpatient care.

Spaulding Rehabilitation Network

"Delivering compassionate care across the healthcare continuum to improve quality of life for persons recovering from, or learning to live fully with, illness, injury and disability."

spauldingrehab.org

Spaulding achieved a "Best Hospitals" rank of #2 in the 2018 US News and World Report. Beth sailed in the Boston harbor through Spaulding's popular adapted sports and recreation program, and a wonderful Spaulding physiatrist, Dr. Ariana Vora, treated her elbow bursitis before the Beijing Paralympics.

SPINALpedia

"A social mentoring network and video archive that allows the spinal cord injury community to motivate each other with the knowledge and triumphs gained from our individual experiences."

spinalpedia.org

Brittany Déjean recruited Beth in 2006 to help develop the concept. Brittany co-founded SPINALpedia in 2007 with Josh Basile. When Brittany traveled to the 2008 Beijing

Paralympics, she made video clips of Beth eating with chopsticks, swimming the backstroke, and getting help on a crazy ramp at the Temple of Heaven.

Stigma Fighters
"A mental health nonprofit dedicated to helping real people living with mental illness."
stigmafighters.com
Sarah Fader and Allie Burke founded Stigma Fighters in 2014 to fight the stigma of mental illness, one story at a time. In 2018, Sarah Fader also launched Eliezer Tristan Publishing with co-founder Sarah Comerford. They publish books with a focus on survival, including this memoir.

Struggling with Serendipity
"A mom on a mission to offer hope to those in crisis."
strugglingwithserendipity.com
My website includes a printable PDF of this resource list, my weekly blog, book news, photo gallery, resource newsletter, and more!

Swim With Mike
"To provide financial resources for advanced education that pave the way for physically challenged athletes to overcome their tragedies and realize their full potential."
swimwithmike.org
Mike Nyeholt is Chairman of the Board. We learned about his scholarship fund through a mentee. Beth participated in their annual swim-a-thon at Stanford, grateful for help with her law school tuition from the Swim With Mike community.

This Is My Brave

"To end the stigma surrounding mental health issues by sharing personal stories of individuals living successful, full lives despite mental illness."

thisismybrave.org

This Is My Brave hosts live shows across the country. Cast members share their stories on stage in front of a live audience through poetry, essay, and original music. Videos of the shows may be found on YouTube. I participated in the Washington, DC, This Is My Brave Show in November of 2018.

United Spinal Association

"Dedicated to enhancing the quality of life of people living with spinal cord injuries and disorders (SCI/D)."

unitedspinal.org

Thank you, Northwest Ohio chapter, for the warm welcome after Beth's injury. Membership in United Spinal is free and the national website offers a wide variety of resources.

U.S. Paralympics

"Promoting excellence in the lives of people with Paralympic-eligible impairments, including physical disabilities and visual impairments."

teamusa.org/US-Paralympics

U.S. Paralympics includes more than two-dozen sports, with elite, military, and community programs. For five years, Beth enjoyed the camaraderie of her talented teammates on the U.S. Paralympics Swimming National Team as she set 14 Paralympic American Records. A decade after retiring in 2008, nine remained.

USA Swimming

"Promotes the culture of swimming by creating

opportunities for swimmers and coaches of all backgrounds to participate and advance in the sport through teams, events and education."

usaswimming.org

Local USA Swimming coaches are valuable swimming resources for children and adults with a disability. Our hometown coach dedicated countless hours to help Beth move more effectively in the water. I supported swimmers with a disability as Adapted Chairperson for Ohio Swimming. State websites offer additional information.

Wounded Warrior Project (WWP)

"To honor and empower Wounded Warriors."

woundedwarriorproject.org

Beth's roommate at the Beijing Paralympics was a young woman injured in the Iraq War who led the U.S. Paralympics team into the Bird's Nest for Closing Ceremonies. Check out the WWP website to support wounded veterans.

YouTube Channel, Struggling with Serendipity

bit.ly/VideoSerendipity

My Struggling with Serendipity channel shares my video about dealing with a new spinal injury plus my podcasts. I also gathered Beth's how-to videos in a playlist on this channel; this includes putting her hair up in a ponytail, inserting contact lenses, opening a wine bottle, tying shoes, eating with chopsticks, and swimming.

❧ BOOK CLUB DISCUSSION GUIDE ❧

Would you like to connect with Cindy Kolbe through a live video chat with your book club about *Struggling with Serendipity*? If you email her, she'll do her best to make it happen: cindy@strugglingwithserendipity.com.

1. Did you wonder about the quote that opens the first chapter? "The most defining—and, in many ways, positive—moment of my life might also be considered the most tragic by those who do not know me?" Have you experienced a defining moment?

2. In the first section, *The Deep End*, Cindy waits for Beth's optimism to crash. What were your expectations at that point in the story? Why did Cindy hide her emotions?

3. Could you relate to Beth's challenges? To Cindy's? Does adversity give rise to strength?

4. The second section, *Staying Afloat*, shifts to a new normal. Do you agree with Cindy's decision to let Beth lead the way? How would you describe the ideal role for a parent when a child has a physical disability? Other disabilities?

5. When a goal seems impossible, do you tend to cast it aside or go for it? How can we nurture perseverance in children?

6. In the third section, *Breathing Lessons*, how does pain impact Cindy's identity? Is there a connection between

physical and mental pain? Why do some of us find mental illness so difficult to admit and talk about?

7. The concept of resilience is a recurring theme. Do you think we are born with a capacity for resilience or is it something we learn?

8. What surprised you the most in the book? What incident best represents Beth's character? Cindy's?

9. The last section, *Racing Forward*, includes happy accidents. Are they really accidents? Is serendipity simply the result of fate? Or is it a matter of perspective?

10. What is your favorite quote in the book?

11. How does the story challenge negative stereotypes of disability and mental illness? Did you learn anything? Is it true that adversity often leads an individual to advocacy?

12. What is the main takeaway of *Struggling with Serendipity*?

❧ QUOTES AND CITATIONS ❧

Chapters also include quotes from memory.

Chapter 1. CRASHING
"The most defining—and, in many ways, positive—moment of my life might also be considered the most tragic by those who do not know me." ~ *Beth, graduate school admission essay*

———————

Chapter 2. SHATTERING
"When I was injured, I really had no idea what was in store for me." ~ *Beth, Waltham Daily News Tribune (MA): 8-20-08*

"I was, strangely, very calm. A nurse told me I was in shock. The doctors stuck many needles in me during the helicopter flight that seemed to last only a minute. I found out later these were high doses of medicine that slows the chain reaction of nerve damage. I landed at St. Vincent hospital in Toledo. I was taken to an exam room, and they cut off my clothes. They jokingly asked me if those were my favorite jeans and of course, they were. I had tests taken while I was trying to get some sleep. Through a speaker on the wall, they were yelling at me to stay awake. When I was taken to a room in intensive care, my dad asked me if I wanted to know what the doctors had just told him minutes before. I was paralyzed from the chest down. I believed it, but it did not scare me." ~ *Beth, ninth grade English essay*

"My room was constantly full of people moving busily around. I didn't realize until a few days later how large and pretty the room was, because all I saw then were the white ceiling tiles since I had to lay flat and wear a rigid neck brace." ~ *Beth, 10th grade English essay*

"I remember my family always being there, and I remember not being afraid or worried." ~ *Beth, Sports 'N Spokes Interview: May 2017*

"At one point they were amazed because I was still conscious even though my blood pressure took an unexpected plunge. They jokingly said I should become a fighter pilot but who knows, it could be a fun job. I thought it was funny at the time, but I also was on morphine." ~ *Beth, 10th grade English essay*

Chapter 3. HOPING

"Accepting my new disability never was a real issue for me. The issue was what needed to be done next." ~ *Beth, 11th grade criteria statement*

"Instead of fixing it, she wanted to see if the other nurses were paying attention. She took off the wire connected to my heart monitor and tapped the wire so it looked like a heart attack. A few other nurses poked their heads in the door but when they saw us laughing they got the picture." ~ *Beth, 10th grade English essay*

Chapter 4. HEALING

"I had to relearn how to do everything." ~ *Beth, 11th grade criteria statement*

"I learned how some people, given the same situations, react in opposite ways. I have seen how people take so much for granted." ~ *Beth, ninth grade "Learning" essay*

"Some people had a tendency to stop. They wouldn't try to be independent. That's always been a goal of mine, to be independent." ~ *Beth, Boston Herald (MA): 11-15-05*

"I call on Beth to talk to newly-injured spinal cord patients. Her attitude is positive and motivating." ~ *Laraine Bauer, reference letter: 1-6-04*

"At the rehab hospital, the simplest tasks of putting my shoes on or sitting up by myself were the hardest challenges of the day. Transferring from place to place was impossible for me to do on my own. Wheeling myself any distance was difficult. My life consisted of two long physical therapy sessions a day, where my therapists had no concept of being tired. They pushed me to exhaustion but I knew how much they were helping, and I appreciated it."

"I've regained only partial feeling in my trunk and legs but still no movement. I can move one finger on my left hand, and my handgrip is still weak." ~ *Beth, 11th grade criteria statement*

Chapter 5. REBELLING

Pressed if she has ever asked, "Why me?" Kolbe said, "No, I never did. I never did the whole grieving process thing. I was too busy during rehab. I had great physical therapists." ~ *Bucyrus Telegraph Forum (OH): 3-24-04*

"The director told me I should never get in a pool because my body would go into autonomic dysreflexia. My blood pressure would shoot up, my temperature would rise, and I could have a stroke. Luckily, my physical therapists disagreed with the doctor, but I had to wait until I was an outpatient to try their heated therapy pool." ~ *Beth, 12th grade essay*

"Her counselor seemed a little distressed because she didn't go through the text book stages of depression, anger, and denial. Beth's attitude has been positive from day one. I tell people that she is the one who carried me emotionally." ~ *John Kolbe, Healthy Living News (Toledo, OH): May 2003*

"You don't really have time to cope with things. You just kind of get thrown back into the world." ~ *Beth, The Advertiser-Tribune (Tiffin, OH): 5-21-02*

"I always knew I was just going to get stronger and get back to my life as soon as possible." ~ *Beth, Diversity & The Bar: Sept. Oct. 2016*

"Life is about making choices. At this point, some people may have taken a year off of school to rest and build their strength at home. I wanted to start at Tiffin Columbian High School with the rest of my freshman class." ~ *Beth, speech transcript: June 2004*

"Beth worked long hours in rehab, learning to feed and dress, move about in her wheelchair and moving from place to place from her chair. To do these tasks, innervated muscles need to be very strong and much of her day was spent weightlifting and exercising." ~ *Laraine Bauer, reference letter: 1-6-04*

"Rehab was a great experience. I was too busy to think about what had happened to me or to become depressed. Every new thing that I accomplished, like eating independently or lifting an extra five pounds during physical therapy, became a celebration. I was in another world. My family was always there. My best friends visited me often and even moved a birthday party to the rehab center so I could be there. The therapists and nurses became a second family to me." ~ *Beth, 11th grade criteria statement*

"Everyone was so nice. My night nurses would always come in and talk to me." ~ *Beth, The Advertiser-Tribune (Tiffin, OH): 9-26-2000*

"I first knew Beth Kolbe after the car accident when she was in the same rehabilitation center as my father. Beth was so pleasant that I stopped in to see her every time I visited my father." ~ *Betty Kizer, Tiffin Columbian High School, reference letter: 12-19-03*

"It felt like the entire town rallied around us. At the Tiffin Center where my mom worked, people donated months of their vacation time for her so she could stay with me, and my dad had meals cooked for him while we were at the hospital. We even had people come over and build a ramp at our house. Everyone kind of just pitched in." ~ *Beth, Diversity & The Bar: Sept. Oct. 2016*

———————

Chapter 6. PUSHING

"I had a small group of very close friends who helped me in many ways." ~ *Beth, speech transcript: June 2004*

"Some people assume I'm not intelligent because I am in a wheelchair. They talk loud and slow when they first see me. When I do normal things such as moving around or crossing a threshold, some people will tell me 'good job' like it is the most amazing thing." ~ *Beth, ninth grade "Learning" essay*

"My friends have been very positive and treated me just like everyone else." ~ *Beth, speech transcript: 6-2004*

"Kids stared a lot at first. They wanted to get my attention, to talk to me, to see how I had changed. I was already used to being stared at." ~ *Beth, interview: 4-11-11*

"They thought they would offend me by confirming that I use a wheelchair as if I didn't know." ~ *Beth, college scholarship application*

"Most of my classsmates only knew me as the shy volleyball player that I was before my car accident, but everyone was welcoming and supportive." ~ *Beth, 11th grade criteria statement*

Chapter 7. EXHAUSTING

"I began high school as a different person than I was in junior high." ~ *Beth, 12th grade personal statement*

"She has a great future ahead of her. We're feeling like things are going to be okay." ~ *Cindy, The Advertiser-Tribune (Tiffin, OH): 9-26-2000*

"The first time I took the girls to the mall (after the accident), Beth's wheel fell off her chair, and we had to use one of the mall's wheelchairs which was awful. I was a wreck and all the girls could do was laugh!" ~ *Deb V., Facebook comment: 8-23-17*

"My choir teacher pretty much freaked out at first and he got me back into my chair really fast. It was funny!" ~ *Beth, "Kids on Wheels" p. 113, book by New Mobility magazine: 2004*

"Wheelchairs were the most common sights, everyone was completely accepting, and nothing about my injury seemed out of the ordinary. High school was different." ~ *Beth, 11th grade criteria statement*

Chapter 8. FLOATING

"I immediately loved the water and the freedom I had in it." ~ *Beth, The Harvard Gazette (Cambridge, MA): June 5–11, 2008*

"Once she entered the water, wow. It was awesome!" ~ *Jill Hire, interview: 3-15-13*

"I discovered I had good water technique and was able to keep myself afloat pretty well. Not at the beginning. It obviously took me awhile to learn how to swim." ~ *Beth, The Harvard Gazette (Cambridge, MA): June 5–11, 2008*

"With the vinyl sheet on the floor next to my chair, two teachers lower me onto it, careful to keep my neck supported as I lay down. They really don't need to be so careful. After my car accident, doctors reinforced my neck bones using titanium plates and screws. Four teachers lift the vinyl sheet using four sets of handles, two on each side, and down the stairs we go. Behind us, another teacher carries my chair." ~ *Beth, "This Way Out" essay, winner of National Chemistry Council contest*

"It took awhile for them to realize I don't break." ~ *Beth, "Kids on Wheels" p. 113, book by New Mobility magazine: 2004*

Chapter 9. BREATHING

"When I began water therapy as part of my physical therapy, no one expected me, a quadriplegic, to ever move in the water without someone holding me up." ~ *Beth, 11th grade personal narrative*

"I was one of a few panelists who shared our experiences and answered many questions. I also participated in the hands on part with Laraine showing specific techniques. Then the seminar participants tried the exercises with me while we talked. I hope it helped them understand a patient's perspective a little better and also to see that a quadriplegic can do more than is usually expected." ~ *Beth, 12th grade essay*

"Beth's insights and down-to-earth presentations enlighten students and motivate them to challenge the spinal cord injury patients in their care." ~ *Laraine Bauer, reference letter: 1-6-04*

"I realized that my biggest challenge would be to insist on doing things myself and to become independent again. At the risk of sounding corny, people are generally kind, so it was my responsibility to speak up for myself." ~ *Beth, college scholarship application*

"Auditions for the show required all performers to act, sing, and dance, but we were going to waive the dance for Beth. She informed us that she wanted to take part in all of the audition, including the dance, and with her wheelchair and use of arm movements, it was obvious that she was going to fit right in with our concept of the show." ~ *James G. Koehl, Ritz Theatre, reference letter: 1-5-03*

I have been in other plays, but this was the first since my injury. Most everything about my play experience was the same, everything that is, except the dancing. The wooden set they built was difficult to move on since everything was on a slant, but I stayed on the flat part of the stage. The theater was recently renovated to include an accessible backstage, so it was easy to get around, apart from the time when the elevator was broken, and I had to be bumped down the steps in my wheelchair." ~ *Beth, Shriners SCI Informer: September 2001*

"I slowly progressed to swimming laps at the YMCA." ~ *Beth, 11th grade criteria statement*

Chapter 10. SHIFTING

"Early on, I decided that I was going to become completely independent no matter how long it took." ~ *Beth, 11th grade criteria statement*

"I really liked my little spot." ~ *Beth, interview: 4-11-11*

"Everyone I know with an injury who is doing well has a sense of humor about it. You need that." ~ *Beth, ninth grade "Advice" essay*

"My small group of really close friends in high school helped me in many ways, including breaking my leg spasms and carrying my book bag. By the second year, I had those things under control, but a friend continued to sit by me in class only because it was more fun that way." ~ *Beth, "Kids on Wheels" p. 113, book by New Mobility magazine: 2004*

"I have always wanted to do something important with my life. After my injury, this goal became more focused. I want to make a difference from the start of my career." ~ *Beth, applicant essay: 1-8-04*

"I think it would be fun to work on stem cell research. Finding new or better medications would also be something I might do after college. Science has always been my favorite subject." ~ *Beth, 10th grade statement*

"My newest challenges are learning how to drive a car with adapted hand controls and how to transfer in and out of the driver's seat independently." ~ *Beth, 11th grade criteria statement*

"At my first swim meet, I met Cheryl, a Paralympic swimmer, and her husband Shawn, a Paralympic coach. They encouraged me to compete nationally." ~ *Beth, Diversity & The Bar: Sept. Oct. 2016*

Chapter 11. VISUALIZING

"I really didn't expect to ever be able to compete so that surprised me." ~ *Beth, The Advertiser-Tribune (Tiffin, OH): 12-1-03*

"I wish you could really see how Beth has dealt with her disability. In so many ways, she is more able than most of us. She accepted her paralysis before she understood it. She never cried in intensive care. Beth focuses on what needs to be done next and works incredibly hard to be less dependent. And in her view, there's no reason to not enjoy the moments along the way. You look at her and assume that not walking is the worst thing. You have no idea how much more she's lost, but you won't hear her complain or ask for pity. She feels genuinely grateful for the arm movement the injury left her with, for friends and family, and for the amazing people she's met since the accident." ~ *Cindy Kolbe, letter: May 2002*

"I advanced from being held up or sinking to basically falling in and swimming laps." ~ *Beth, 10th grade statement*

"I saw a billboard with a girl in a power chair and a Harvard graduation cap on." ~ *Beth, The Advertiser-Tribune (Tiffin, OH): 5-3-04*

"There were about two hundred athletes from eight different countries. The entire Australian and Mexican National Teams were there." ~ *Beth, The Tiffinian (Tiffin, OH): Fall, 2002*

"The trip was truly amazing. Seattle was beautiful. My mom and I were able to tour the city in the afternoons and evenings after I swam." ~ *Beth, 11th grade personal narrative*

"I was hooked. I knew it wasn't going to be my last national meet." ~ *Beth, 12th grade essay*

"For the first time, I began training with swim coaches. I am one of two swimmers with a disability on GTAC (Greater Toledo Aquatic Club)." ~ *Beth, 11th grade personal narrative*

"After attending the orientation, I volunteered in the outpatient physical therapy department for one afternoon a week. This was a particularly interesting assignment for me since I was still going to outpatient physical therapy as a patient at a different hospital closer to my home. I liked being busy with bed-making and clerical work, and it was easy to relate to the staff and patients."

"Laraine said that when therapy gets in the way of life, then it is time to move on."

"I continued physical therapy as an outpatient for two years. Three times a week at first, then going twice and then once a week, we drove to St. Francis after school to workout for about two hours. I recently graduated from physical therapy since I get plenty of exercise on my own now, and I am always extremely busy." ~ *Beth, 11th grade criteria statement*

"Beth still faces many new challenges. I know she is up to the task." ~ *Laraine Bauer, reference letter: 1-6-04*

"My next goal is to make the U.S. National Team that will attend the 2004 Paralympics in Athens, Greece." ~ *Beth, 11th grade personal narrative*

―――――――――

Chapter 12. TESTING

"I started doing the backstroke. Then, learning to swim on my stomach and still breathe was a big challenge initially." ~ *Beth, Bucyrus Telegraph Forum (OH): 3-24-04*

"Beth is one of the best-natured individuals I have ever known. I forget many times she is rolling along beside me, rather than walking." ~ *Betty Kizer, Tiffin Columbian High School, reference letter: 12-19-03*

"When I first swam the breaststroke, I went backward." ~ *Beth, speech transcript: 6-2004*

"Coach Ewald was excited to work with me from the first time I met her." ~ *Beth, The Advertiser-Tribune (Tiffin, OH): 12-1-03*

"It was a new adventure for me." ~ *Peggy Ewald, The Harvard Crimson (Cambridge, MA): 9-20-07*

"I was in the water with anatomy books on the deck, and I would ask her to move certain parts of her body and then I'd try to trace where the nerve ending connected to the muscle. The light bulb went off then because I understood that she didn't have the necessary nerves firing to do a particular movement. So we'd try a different movement to attempt the same goal. It took a lot of trial and error, but she was very willing." ~ *Peggy Ewald, "London Calling" article on Ohio Northern University website: 4-19-12*

"from what she didn't have to what she did have access to." ~ *Peggy Ewald, The Harvard Crimson (Cambridge, MA): 9-20-07*

"I often swim with non-disabled swimmers at 'regular' swim meets. Many people are surprised that I compete in swimming since I use a wheelchair, and it has been fun for me to show how people with disabilities can be competitive in sports just as much as others. A swimmer who uses a wheelchair is still an unusual sight at most swim meets." ~ *Beth, 11th grade personal narrative*

Chapter 13. RACING

"I basically swim with my upper body and pull my entire body with my arms. Since my hands can't cup the water, my arms do all the work. It would be something like an able-bodied swimmer with their legs tied together and their hands in fists." ~ *Beth, Waltham Daily News Tribune (MA): 8-20-08 (slight modification for clarity)*

"The travel I did with swimming opened up the world to me."
"Once I realized I was good in the water, I trained really hard and put a lot of focus and effort into it because it was this new avenue for me. I hadn't thought I could be an athlete anymore." ~ *Beth, Diversity & The Bar: Sept. Oct. 2016*

"Harvard first got my attention because of the national billboard campaign which suggested an appreciation of the contributions that students with disabilities can make." ~ *Beth, college scholarship essay*

"The staff was great, and there were a number of outstanding speakers. The event had a big impact on my life my first year as a delegate." ~ *Beth, NewsNet, Ohio Rehabilitation Services Commission: May/June 2006*

"The Ohio forum proved to me that the disability community is widely diverse and vitally important." ~ *Beth, graduate school admission essay*

"Peggy has helped me make all my strokes better." ~ *Beth, The Advertiser-Tribune (Tiffin, OH): 12-1-03*

"I think walking is over-rated." ~ *Beth, The Harvard Gazette (MA): June 5–11, 2008*

"I toured the Harvard campus and just fell in love with it." ~ *Beth, The Advertiser-Tribune (Tiffin, OH): 5-3-04*

Chapter 14. SURGING

"I don't think it really hit me until I told my friends, and I saw how excited they were for me." ~ *Beth, The Advertiser-Tribune (Tiffin, OH): 5-3-04*

> "I didn't tell everyone since I didn't think I would get in."
> "I didn't want both, so I gave the rich title away."
> "I was shy in high school. I had more fun than most, but I wasn't a cool kid."
> "I wheeled myself everywhere, but my escort wanted to push my chair across the field. But, I kept my hands on the wheels and pushed myself at the same time!" ~ *Beth, interview: 4-11-11*

"I volunteer for many projects, including the National Honor Society's annual food drive. I go to an elementary school once a week as an athlete mentor." ~ *Beth, applicant essay: 1-8-04*

"I love mentoring!" ~ *Beth, Diversity & The Bar: Sept. Oct. 2016*

"Walls are bad for me." ~ *Beth, journal: Summer 2004*

"It pushes her to train with us, and it pushes the other kids because it's taught them that all things are possible." ~ *Peggy Ewald, The Advertiser-Tribune (Tiffin, OH): 12-1-03*

"Three years ago, the only way I could swim was with two physical therapists holding me in the water. Since then, swimming (on my own) has become a significant part of my life." *Beth, 11th grade personal narrative*

"My favorite event is the freestyle, but fewer people who have (severe) disabilities can do the butterfly and breaststroke, so I'm grateful I can." ~ *Beth, The Advertiser-Tribune (Tiffin, OH): 12-1-03*

"I was able to score quite a few points in high school. My coach put me in the harder events that nobody wanted to do, like the butterfly. Since the top three swimmers scored, as long as I finished I would score points." ~ *Beth, Waltham Daily News Tribune (MA): 8-20-08*

"Beth just keeps improving with every meet. It's awesome to watch her strokes and racing ability move forward." ~ *Peggy Ewald, The Advertiser-Tribune (Tiffin, OH): 12-28-03*

"It's fun climbing out of the pool and hearing people clapping for you. It gives you a little boost of confidence." ~ *Bucyrus Telegraph Forum 3-24-2004*

Chapter 15. CHOOSING

"I had to pick Harvard starting on time or Athens," said Kolbe. Athens loss was Harvard's gain. ~ *Boston Herald (MA): 11-15-05*

The first page listed her top three goals for Greece: 1. swim my best and feel good about races, 2. swim in finals one night, 3. have fun with the U.S. team. Then she added three more summer goals: 1. stay healthy and fit, 2. improve strength, endurance, and stroke to drop time, 3. have fun with SAK and enjoy the process. ~ *Beth, journal: Summer 2004*

"The mild-mannered, quiet, bright little girl we met as an incoming freshman has grown into an assertive yet humble young woman. Beth is in a wheelchair but is by no means wheelchair bound." ~ *Nancy Roberts, Tiffin Columbian High School, reference letter: 1-28-04*

"I've already decided to postpone grad school for a year. Nothing's going to stop me this time. I want to medal in China." ~ *Beth, The Advertiser-Tribune (Tiffin, OH): 6-30-05*

"It was my first independent flight. I'm not sure why, probably just something new and being nervous, but I got teary when Mom left me at security." ~ *Beth, journal: Summer 2004*

"When I represented Ohio at the national conference, I came to understand that the ADA and the work of the early pioneers in disability rights was far from over." ~ *Beth, graduate school admission essay*

"My generation has grown up since the ADA, so it's easy to take it for granted because we didn't have to fight for it. Learning from the people who *did* have to fight and listening to their stories was empowering." ~ *Beth, Disability Issues, vol. 28, No. 2, University of Massachusetts Medical School: Summer 2008*

"I needed a pool to swim." ~ *Beth, Boston Herald (MA): 11-15-05*

Chapter 16. STRUGGLING

"College is a time of growth for everyone but for me, it was also a time of learning to be truly independent in a world far away from my Ohio hometown." ~ *Beth, interview: 4-11-11*

"My dad, a quadriplegic like Beth, met her before I did. He came wheeling up to me saying, 'Britt! You'll never believe it! There's another C6-7 quad in your dorm!' He was absolutely impressed." ~ *Brittany Martin, email: 1-19-12*

"I tried to see how far I could go, and I continually tried to do more on my own. It took a little over four years. The doctors told me they had never seen anyone with my type of injury become completely independent." ~ *Beth, Diversity & The Bar: Sept. Oct. 2016*

Chapter 17. STORMING

"It changes everything but then again, I don't think it really does change much." ~ *Beth, Boston Herald (MA): 11-15-05*

"As a swimmer with a disability going into a Division 1 school, I didn't know how I would be welcomed onto the team because I am not going to be able to score points." ~ *Beth, The Harvard Crimson (Cambridge, MA): 9-20-07*

"We were not sure how it was going to work."
"Everyone is absolutely impressed by her." ~ *Stephanie Wriede Morawski, National Collegiate Athletic Association Champion: Summer 2008*

"I had no idea Harvard would accept someone with a fairly severe physical disability on the team." ~ *Beth, Waltham Daily News Tribune (MA): 8-20-08*

"I heard stories from the other swimmers, but I don't have any regrets. I knew I'd have more chances." ~ *Beth, The Harvard Crimson (Cambridge, MA): 9-20-07*

"It's quite an accomplishment to see Beth take her swimming to such a high level in such a short period of time and know that she is still improving. This was the first international meet for Beth to swim in a whole heat of like disability classifications from all over the world. To place third and earn a Bronze medal is just incredible. There is a big horizon ahead for Beth." ~ *Peggy Ewald, press release: May 2005*

Chapter 18. BELONGING
"I couldn't imagine a better college experience, and a large part of that was being a member of the Harvard Women's Swimming and Diving team." ~ *Beth, Swim With Mike scholarship application*

"Peggy is immensely caring, very driven, and she thrived on the challenge of coaching me in a new way." ~ *Beth, interview: 1-15-12*

"I'm definitely not going to miss out on China, and have put myself on a three-year training schedule to qualify." ~ *Beth, The Oregonian: 7-18-05*

"I directed a volunteer program that mentored students in special education classrooms in Boston Public. We visited classrooms every Friday and took the students on field trips." "I made amazing friendships." ~ *Beth, Swim With Mike scholarship application*

"She's probably one of the easiest people to coach in the sense that she always has a smile on her face, she's got a great positive attitude, and she's willing to try anything. And she just kept getting faster and faster." ~ *Stephanie Wriede Morawski, The Harvard Gazette (MA): June 5 – 11, 2008*

"For her to make that commitment to coach me and this year I'm on the roster, is really important. It's been great. I've loved it." Edited to, "I love it." ~ *Beth, Boston Herald (MA): 11-15-05*

"Coach Peggy has helped me get better with almost every meet. She's been with me every step of the way." ~ *Beth, The Advertiser-Tribune (Tiffin, OH): 5-3-04*

Chapter 19. CONNECTING

"I spent my summer in DC where I fell in love with the excitement on the Hill and the chance to make policy that makes a difference." ~ *Beth, Disability Issues, Vol. 28, No. 2, University of Massachusetts Medical School: Summer 2008*

"I think that limits are self-imposed. I don't believe there are limits." ~ *Beth, NewsNet, Ohio Rehabilitation Services Commission: May/June 2006*

"I was accepted into Senator John Kerry's office first, so I jumped on that." "I was so excited because I respect him." ~ *Beth, Disability Issues, vol. 28, No. 2, University of Massachusetts Medical School: Summer 2008*

"It was a life-changing experience. The disability community is so active in DC." ~ *Beth, Diversity & The Bar: Sept. Oct. 2016*

"We had installed handicapped door openers, and she never used them. She has an unbelievable attitude and is sweet as can be. Nothing will stop her." ~ *Mary T., StrugglingwithSerendipity.com #10 Blog, Comment: 6-26-16*

"I asked him if I could be on the (Senate) floor with him. I hope that as the Senators are voting, they can see a face that reminds them of what they're actually voting for." ~ *Beth, The Boston Globe (MA): 7-18-06*

"As a person in the disability community, I've met so many people whose main goal is just to get better, and stem cell research is their one opportunity to find a cure." ~ *Beth, The Advertiser-Tribune (Tiffin, OH): 7-19-06*

"If you ever need to be reminded of why it's morally right to lift the ban on stem cell research, just listen to Beth." "She's more eloquent on this subject than any lobbyist or member of Congress." ~ *Senator John Kerry, The Boston Globe (MA): 7-18-06*

(Beth serves as a) "silent, powerful reminder of what is at stake here." ~ *Senator John Kerry's stem cell speech, The Advertiser-Tribune (Tiffin, OH): 7-19-06*

"As her Dad, I'm just intensely proud of her. She's a courageous young lady. How many 20-year-olds spent the day on the floor of the U.S. Senate tracking an issue that's so important to them?" ~ *John Kolbe, The Toledo Blade: 7-19-06*

"She's not someone who is focused on the cure. She's very much living her life today. We're all hoping that stem cell research will offer her more options in the future but in the meantime, she's making the most of everything she has." ~ *Cindy Kolbe, The Boston Globe (MA): 7-18-06*

"I really fell in love with the policy side of things." ~ *Beth, National Law Journal: 10-11-10*

"After the (summer) internship, there was an opening in Senator Kerry's Boston office to work specifically on disability issues with one of his staffers. They invited me to do that. So throughout my entire school year, I worked in his Boston office. It's completely different because it's much more focused on his constituents. But I really loved that because you get to talk to people on an individual basis." ~ *Beth, Disability Issues, Vol. 28, No. 2, University of Massachusetts Medical School: Summer 2008*

"When I answered phone calls, I recognized a desperation in their voices as they reached out to their Senator who was all too often their last hope in solving their issues. It was rewarding to resolve specific disability-related complaints, but some we could not help." "I explored health care policy and disability issues with courses at Harvard's Kennedy School and Law School." ~ *Beth, graduate school admission essay*

"My undergrad was devoted to swimming and health policy. It was a struggle sometimes to be independent and keep up with the work, but I grew a lot during that time. I learned how to make new friends, to manage my disability, and to advocate for myself, not to mention becoming a much stronger swimmer with HWSD. I like to joke that ~~I was in the pool more than the classroom~~." ~ *Beth, Sports 'N Spokes Interview: May, 2017*

"I spend more time in the pool than I do in class. I love this pool!" ~ *Beth, Boston Herald (MA): 11-15-05*

"The trips sounded exciting but staying back gave me more time for school work and volunteer activities." ~ *Beth, email: 2-9-16*

Chapter 20. LEADING
"Rio was an absolutely amazing experience." ~ *Beth, The Advertiser-Tribune (Tiffin, OH): 8-25-08*

"I have met many people with disabilities who are limited by inadequate health services. This stark reality has shifted my focus from a childhood desire to be a doctor to fighting for disability rights." ~ *Beth, graduate school admission essay*

"Beth just has a great personality. She's dedicated, intelligent. She's got all these pieces, and she's one of the athletes we look to for leadership." ~ *Julie O'Neill, The Advertiser-Tribune (Tiffin, OH): 8-5-07*

"She's an incredibly positive person, and it rubs off on people she comes in contact with." ~ *Peggy Ewald, The Advertiser-Tribune (Tiffin, OH): 12-1-03*

"I am really excited about being here, and I am very honored to serve as the captain for the women's team. It is a great learning experience for all of us." ~ *Beth, USA DAILY (U.S. Parapan American Team): 8-12-07*

"Hearing our national anthem while on the podium is something I will never forget." ~ *Beth, Swim with Mike scholarship application*

"It made it extra special to be the one to win the 54th medal (the team's goal)." ~ *Beth, The Harvard Crimson (MA): 9-20-07 from U.S. Paralympics Press Release*

"Totally felt like rock stars. Everyone wanted our autographs and pictures. We got mobbed by young children. It was wonderful." ~ *Beth, The Harvard Gazette (MA): June 5 – 11, 2008*

———————

Chapter 21. REACHING
"Becoming independent. That is my greatest achievement." ~ *Beth, AbleThrive article: 8-23-15*

"Brittany got me out of my shell during my senior year. Before then, I hardly ever went out socially." ~ *Beth, interview: 1-15-12*

"I carried her into a few restaurants and bars. We refused to let inaccessibility stop us. Inadvertently, we ended up getting a lot of people talking about why accessibility isn't more consistent and reliable." ~ *Brittany Martin, email: 1-19-12*

"I never heard her complain." ~ *Becca Agoglia, The Harvard Crimson (MA): 9-26-08*

"added another level of excitement to home crowds at Blodgett Pool, especially when records were at stake." ~ *NCAA Champion magazine: Summer 2008*

"No matter what team we raced against, people always came up to me and congratulated me. It was kind of strange sometimes, but I guess it's great for them to see someone with a disability compete on a college varsity team." ~ *Beth, Waltham Daily News Tribune (MA): 8-20-08*

"She's an inspiration to many." ~ *Stephanie Wriede Morawski, NCAA Champion magazine: Summer 2008*

"The most amazing thing about Beth is though we classify her as someone who's disabled, she's just someone who shows the people around her how able she is." ~ *Becca Agoglia, The Harvard Crimson (MA): 9-26-08*

"Beth's talents lie in her ability to set goals, both short and long term, overcome obstacles, and accomplish those goals while consistently maintaining a positive and fun attitude." ~ *Peggy Ewald, reference letter: 11-10-05*

"My goal was to create a support resource that uses the power of people's experiences to motivate people with new injuries to adapt their lives." ~ *Brittany Martin, The Harvard Crimson (MA): 4-25-08*

"As a musician, I love stories that are real, and there's nothing more real than someone sitting in a wheelchair, saying that there's always hope." ~ *Brad Corrigan, The Harvard Crimson (MA): 4-25-08*

———

Chapter 22. COMPETING

"Thanks to four years of HWSD training, I know I am ready to take on my international competition in Beijing!" "It truly is an honor to represent the United States at the Paralympics and to be part of such an incredible team. Go USA!" ~ *Beth, Poolside: Official Newsletter for the Friends of Harvard Swimming and Diving, Sept. 2008*

"Watching the amazing Olympic swimmers shatter record after record in The Cube has been incredibly exciting, especially knowing that I'll be there soon!" ~ *Beth's blog (www.bethkolbe.blogspot.com): 8-18-08*

"I'm excited to race in The Cube. I feel faster than I ever have before." ~ *Beth, The Advertiser-Tribune (Tiffin, OH): 8-25-08*

"You're surrounded by Team USA and you go down the ramp to the floor of the National Stadium which has 91,000 screaming fans. It was a pretty surreal experience." ~ *Beth, The Harvard Crimson (MA): 9-26-08*

"Before every finals, three of these blow up cows jumped around on deck and occasionally fell down and couldn't get back up!" ~ *Beth's blog (www.bethkolbe.blogspot.com): 9-22-08*

"I felt prepared going in from all my amazing training at Harvard behind me and I was able to enjoy the moment as my heat was paraded out onto the deck and behind the blocks." "I swam a 1:10.55, a best time and a new American Record, which places me fifth in the world." "What a great race!" ~ *Beth's blog (www.bethkolbe.blogspot.com): 9-13-08*

"I was so psyched to see Beth at this level of competition. I knew how seriously she took swimming, but I didn't have a sense of the enormity of her accomplishment until I was in the Water Cube, donning my handmade 'Go Beth' T-shirt, screaming as she tore down the lane. Watching her swim, I was so proud of her, thinking about how insane it was that one of my best friends is fifth in the world in swimming!" ~ *Brittany Martin, email: 1-19-12*

"I could have spent all day exploring there, but we left for lunch at a Peking Duck restaurant where I was peer pressured into eating duck brain. It tastes like chicken, but I almost gagged from the texture." ~ *Beth's blog (www.bethkolbe.blogspot.com): 9-17-08*
"After Closing Ceremonies, at least a hundred of these cows stormed the floor of the stadium. They kept running into us and running away. They would also begin to deflate so volunteers would run up and herd them off the track to get blown back up. My teammates and I were literally crying we were laughing so hard." ~ *Beth's blog (www.bethkolbe.blogspot.com): 9-22-08*

———————————

Chapter 23. FREESTYLING

"I need to figure out what I want to do with my life because anything is possible." ~ *Beth, printed copy of 12-3-08 email*

"OMG. Bill Gates was at my meeting. Then at dinner, I sat by a lovely French man who is the head of the World Economic Fund. He asked ME about my research and said I was helpful! So I'm having an existential night and I need to figure out what I want to do with my life because anything is possible." "Love from your daughter, who has a big head tonight and danced alone on the T with her iPod." ~ *Beth, email to her mom: 12-3-08*

"They appreciate that there is someone who is helping them who understands what it's like to be disabled. Anytime anyone has an interesting life experience or has overcome obstacles in the past, they have a different take on things. It's made me more interested in the client perspective." ~ *Beth, National Law Journal: 10-11-10*

"I was extremely nerdy at Harvard compared to Stanford. Nerdy isn't the right word though, because I'm still nerdy—I love to read—but I'm not as introverted and shy." ~ *Beth, interview: 1-15-12*

"I'm winding down on my winter quarter classes. I've loved Constitutional Law and the Regulation of Political Process, but I found Property to be a little boring. This semester we also took a writing and oral argument class where we get a fake case and actually go through bringing it to court. I've found that I really enjoy the oral arguments! Next quarter, I'll be taking Constitutional Law 2, Evidence, Intellectual Property and the writing class. It should be fun!" ~ *Beth, email to grandparents: Feb. 2005*

"I totally loved law school—and I recognize that's rare! Stanford was a sunny, social place where everyone was brilliant and interesting. I was very involved in the school, eventually becoming class president, and made friendships that are still some of my closest friendships today." ~ *Beth, Sports 'N Spokes Interview: May 2017*

"At first, it was outside my comfort zone. But I enjoyed giving back and being part of organizations that can improve life for students with disabilities." ~ *Beth, Diversity & The Bar: Sept. Oct. 2016*

"A lot of it is about bar accommodations, and also LSAT. If someone isn't receiving extra time, and they think they need it, or they're not getting large-print materials in time. Some of it is aimed at the fact that their disability is not being kept a secret."
"Disability rights in general is becoming a bigger issue. It's filtering into the law school environment. More students with disabilities are going to law school which is incredibly encouraging." ~ *Beth, Student Lawyer: April 2012*

Chapter 24. RIPPLING

"It is incredible to be a part of this community where we all have a shared experience." "It's given me a more interesting life, a new perspective, and experiences that I wouldn't otherwise have had."
~ *Beth, Diversity & The Bar: Sept. Oct. 2016*

"She worked with another YELP student to file a "Williams" complaint for a second grader who relies on a power wheelchair, a ventilator, and a feeding tube. Kolbe met with school representatives to discuss the needs of this child, addressing issues including exposure to sewage in the bathroom, mold in the classroom, and feces from a student in a neighboring classroom. Beyond these immediate health concerns, Kolbe also requested an assessment for occupational and physical therapy, as well an assistive technology assessment on behalf on the student's family. The child's speech and language and adaptive physical education services were also adjusted as a result of Kolbe's work." ~ *LawCrossing.com: 2011/2012*

"When I was injured, I had no one with a similar injury to learn from. We provide tips on how to become independent more quickly." ~ *Beth, Diversity & The Bar: Sept. Oct. 2016*

"Strong friends are worth their weight in gold." ~ *Beth, AbleThrive, "6 Tips for Bridesmaids on Wheels": Summer 2016*

"Every day when I hop in the Harvard pool to train, I am encouraged when I walk by this. I feel fortunate to have had awesome people pave the way for other swimmers like myself. Hopefully Blodgett pool will have more great para swimmers in the pool soon. Thanks for your legacy Beth!! Let's swim together soon." ~ *Laura D., Facebook post on Elizabeth Kolbe's wall: 11-15-15*

❧ SERENDIPITY ❧

SERENDIPITY was coined by Horace Walpole in 1754. In a letter he wrote to a friend, Walpole explained an unexpected discovery he had made by reference to a Persian fairy tale, *The Three Princes of Serendip*. The princes, he told his correspondent, were "always making discoveries, by accidents and sagacity, of things which they were not in quest of." – Wikipedia

CPSIA information can be obtained
at www.ICGtesting.com
Printed in the USA
LVHW101536230419
615241LV00007B/265/P